Clem Cattini

MY LIFE, THROUGH THE EYE OF A TORNADO

Written by
Clive Smith and Bip Wetherell

Foreword by
Jimmy Tarbuck MBE

Mango Books

First edition published 2019

The right of Clive Smith and Bip Wetherell to be identified
as the authors of this work has been asserted in accordance
with the Copyright, Designs & Patents Act 1988.

ISBN: 978-1-911273-74-5 (softcover)
ISBN: 978-1-911273-73-8 (ebook)

All images are from the authors' collection unless otherwise stated.

www.ClemCattiniBook.com

Published by Mango Books

18 Soho Square
London W1D 3QL
www.MangoBooks.co.uk

MY LIFE,
THROUGH THE EYE
OF A TORNADO

Dedication

I would like to dedicate this book to my wife Anna and daughters Giulia, Daniella and Victoria, my grandchilden Tomas, Louis, Freddie and Isobel, and to the memory of my brothers Laurie and Terry.

I would like to thank all the great musicians I have had the pleasure of working with that made my career more than I deserved.

Thanks also to Clive and Bip for all the hard work you did in bringing the book to fruition.

Clem

Through the Eye of a Tornado

Session Man by The Kinks

Session Man by The Kinks

From *Face To Face*, 1966

He never will forget at all
The day he played at the Albert Hall.
A million sessions ago it seems.
He is a session man,
A chord progression,
A top musician.

Rock 'n' roll or vocal star
A philharmonic orchestra,
Everything comes the same to him.
He is a session man,
A chord progression,
A top musician.

He's not paid to think, just play,
A session man
A session man
A session man
Playing at a different studio every day.

He reads the dots and plays each line,
And always finishes on time.
No overtime nor favours done.
He is a session man,
A chord progression,
A top musician.

He's not paid to think, just play,
A session man
A session man
A session man

Writer: Ray Davies
Publisher: Warner/Chappell Music, Inc.

Foreword

by Jimmy Tarbuck MBE

Clem Cattini is an Arsenal fanatic - he loves his club.

Oh yes, he plays the drums as well!

He is, as they say in showbiz terms, a Great Driver of the Band... and what bands! They include Johnny Kidd (*Shakin' All Over* - one of the best British rock songs), Tornados, Billy Fury, Cliff, Marty, Gene Vincent. The word was, "Need a drummer? Get Clem!"

The Guvnor.

More important than his prowess on the drums, Clem Cattini is a nice man, great company, good cook and one of the lads.

I always enjoy his company, the laughter and his love of life and 'The Arsenal'. I'm always pleased to say he's a friend of mine - so is Big Elsie from Bradford.

Read and enjoy this book about one of the *true* rockers. In the words of John Lennon, Rock & Roll should be called Chuck Berry.

Rock on.

JIMMY TARBUCK

Introduction

by Clive Smith and Bip Wetherell

It was 2016 when I received a text message off my old friend Bip Wetherell, asking if I'd be interested in helping to write a biography of one of the world's most famous drummers. Bip and I have been friends since we were in the 3rd Corby Cubs, our paths crossing many times since those days back in the late 1950s. Growing up in the same area, playing football, chatting the same women up, working together.

I remember Bip playing with his first group The Pacifics when we were 15; the start of a career in the music business, singing in numerous bands, a disc jockey in venues all round Northamptonshire, radio presenter, night club owner, hotelier, during the 1980s and '90s, keyboard player with The Tornados, which is where his friendship with Clem Cattini began.

I was in America when I received the text off Bip, touring Memphis and New Orleans on the trail of the famous music venues and studios: Sun, Stax, Beale Street, Bourbon Street.

I wasn't sure how serious Bip was about the project until I got home and bumped into him in his hotel, The Raven, when buying tickets for a forthcoming blues gig.

Writing has been a hobby for a number of years. Three books on the local music scene covering the 1950s through to the 70s have been published: *It's Steel Rock and Roll To Me*, *Alive In The Dead Of Night* and *No Occupation Road*, all reflecting the social side and the steady demise of the steel industry in the town. I've also been a feature writer for local magazine *The Pilot*, wrote features for a Royal Mail monthly magazine, wrote a feature for the Rod Stewart Fan Club magazine and been programme editor for the local football team, Corby Town, when Bip happened to be the Chairman in the early 90s.

Sitting down in The Raven, we discussed how we could go about researching and writing Clem's biography; what was occurring, the worldwide events, during the various aspects of his career. Everyone knows about '*Telstar*', and '*Shakin' All Over*', two massive number one hits in the early 60s which had Clem's stamp all over them. It would be fun finding out more about these two great seminal records, but what about the rest of Clem's story?

Thus began a trail, another one, of studying and researching Clem's career. From working in his dad's restaurant on leaving school to the beginnings of his musical career in Soho, playing initially the washboard with Terry Kennedy's Rock 'n' Rollers; the start of a journey that would lead Clem to play drums with Terry Dene's Dene Aces and Johnny Kidd and The Pirates during the British rock and roll era. The Joe Meek, Tornados and Billy Fury years. The Merseybeat years, working and becoming friends with The Beatles, The Kinks, The Hollies and all the other great names of the time. The 1960s and 70s session man period, racking up over 40 number hit records to his name. The Top Of The Pops Orchestra decade backing hundreds of top line artists, including American icons Stevie Wonder, The Jacksons and Gladys Knight, and some not so top line... who we won't mention here! Sessions with a plethora of 1970s Progressive Rock outfits, requests to play on albums by Lou Reed, Ralph McTell, Ike and Tina Turner, head-hunted to join the emerging Led Zeppelin and Paul McCartney's Wings. Tours with The Kids From Fame and *The Rocky Horror Show* in the 90s. So much more... a daunting but exciting prospect for us, it seemed.

Tracking down and meeting many of Clem's contemporaries and hearing their memories and anecdotes, their obvious pleasure and pride to be associated with him, has been an amazing and wonderful experience. And much fun.

When I mentioned to Fairport Convention and former Joe Cocker, Cat Stevens and Jethro Tull drummer Gerry Conway after a recent Fairport gig that Clem had told me a story about him for the book, his eyes lit up. 'How do you know Clem?' he asked. Caught him by surprise, I admit; we were washing our hands after shaking hands with the vicar, but the instant recognition and esteem he held for Clem was clear.

Throughout the process, Clem has remained unpretentious and humble. Meetings with Clem and his lovely wife Anna, going to lunch at the local 'Tali', going over different tales, reminding him he once played with The Yardbirds, for instance: 'Did I? Oh yeah... forgot about that!'

I tell folk that meeting Clem is like talking to somebody who plays dominoes in the pub! Remarkable. This guy is a much-revered and absolute legend! A word much overused nowadays, but not in this case. Clem would baulk at being called a celebrity.

I just hope that between us, Bip and I have done his story justice. A fascinating and amazing story it has been.

CLIVE SMITH

*

The first time I met Clem Cattini was at his home in North London. Thinking about it, I could have said 'house', but the minute his lovely wife Anna opened the door you had a welcoming feeling from her lovely smile and a nice warm reception from Clem.

As I write my contribution to Clem's life story, I always appreciated that, although Clem was held in awe within the Sixties musicians' circle, he was never 'up his own rear end', as were, unfortunately, many of the stars I would meet, and work with, over a period of nearly thirty years.

I suppose I better give you some of my background as to how I became a musician and, more importantly to me, a performer.

Hailing from a working class family in the steel town of Corby in Northamptonshire, I started piano lessons at an early age and soon became adequately proficient (a polite way of saying I would never be playing Chopin at the Royal Albert Hall). This was despite the unusual habit of my elderly piano teacher, Miss Riddle, who had an off-putting habit of standing in front of her open fire, lifting up her skirt, and letting rip with the most impressive farts. Being a young innocent lad I was mortified.

Years later, whilst working with Georgie Fame and the Blue Flames at the Alconbury American Airbase, I was told by Georgie's roadie that the guitar player had a real special talent of being able to pass wind at any time of asking. I thought of Miss Riddle. The guitarist would drop his trousers, take out his cigarette lighter, and ignite the gas emitting from his posterior, making a nice little 'blue flame'. Hence the name 'Georgie Fame and the Blue Flames' was born.

Throughout the book I recount many such stories of the Sixties, and I have a feeling that, occasionally, some of them might be true!

My first attempt at singing in public was at a Corby Grammar School singing competition where, at the age of 11, I completely froze and had my first experience of stage fright, something I still struggle with because of a deep feeling that I'm not good enough to be up there on a stage. Walking off that day, to the sound of my own footsteps, in front of the whole school, is something I will never forget and something I thought about years later when I walked onto the stage of the London Palladium to fulfil a lifetime's dream of performing at one of the world's most famous venues as a featured artist with my name in lights outside the theatre. A quantum leap from playing pubs and clubs where my name would be outside written in chalk!

I had always had the same dream of performing. I can faintly recollect myself playing my Dad's tennis racket as a guitar and singing Tommy Steele's *'Singing the Blues'* in the shed attached to my house in Corby.

I found that singing lifted my spirits. (Obviously lifting future audiences' spirits would be a different challenge.)

I always tried to connect with the audience. Although it would be impossible on a Saturday night at the local Labour Club, where the band coming on stage, after the Bingo, seemed to be a signal for the fighting to start!

I was lucky enough to have Clem introduce me to The Shadows at the Circus Tavern, Luton, one of the top cabaret venues of the 80s and 90s. In conversation with Hank Marvin, I asked him why he used a foot volume peddle to play *'Cavatina'* (the theme from *The Deer Hunter*), whereas a guitarist friend of mine from Corby, John Grimley, could produce the same rising and falling of volume effect using his little finger on the volume pod of his Fender Stratocaster. I was stunned to learn from Hank that this was a technique he hadn't mastered. Hank told me he was always amazed that he was talked about in the same breath as Jimi Hendrix as one of the world's greatest guitar players when, similar to me, he had to practice for hours to become note perfect.

'Think about it Bip,' said Hank, 'I've got to do the 'Shadows Dance', play the instrumentals, and, at the same time, smile at the audience to try and make that connection that is so vital when you are trying to be an entertainer.' He continued, 'I try not to look down at my fretboard whilst I'm playing as I know, if I do, I'm likely to make a mistake.'

I have seen Cliff and The Shads numerous times 'live' and I have yet to see Hank make a mistake.

So I made it my mission to spend the necessary long hours practising *'Telstar'* and the other Tornados instrumentals so I didn't have to look at my keyboard. I could concentrate on projecting myself to the audience to become a part of that mysterious situation all performers get a kick from. Trying to create an atmosphere within the venue. When you achieve this, the feeling you get when the audience applauds, to show its appreciation, it's like having a lovely warm shower. You feel it all over your body. There is no other feeling quite like it.

The highlight of my time with Hank was when he let me 'have a shot' on his very valuable Fender Stratocaster. Whilst I was playing it I thought to myself, 'This is a lot better than my Dad's tennis racquet.'

I have sung with bands since the age of 15, with my first public performance at the local school disco. *Nellie's Bin* started with '*You Really Got Me*' by The Kinks, a song I am still singing nearly 50 years later. Who would have thought!

Elaine and I have been together now since getting hitched in 1972. We share four wonderful children, Tamla, Glen, Steve and Louise. We currently have four grandchildren: Harvey, Holly, Kai and baby Tabatha. I never would have thought having grandkids would be so much fun. They are brilliant! Harvey is now a real cool teenager; Holly, at the age of 9, is standing for school council and announced today, quite proudly, that she voted for herself. My 8-year-old grandson Kai recently won a school talent competition singing '*Bohemian Rhapsody*'. What's that about? He was word-perfect and didn't freeze on stage unlike his grandfather all those years ago. When we look after Tabby my heart just melts. She is as bright as a button.

I seemed to have made a career of singing for name bands when they have reformed!! In 1976 I was asked to sing for a reformed St. Cecilia, and spent many memorable gigs driving up and down the country singing '*Leap Up and Down (Wave your Knickers in the Air)*' – not exactly an all time classic, but still, it gave me a chance to play at some top venues with some stars of the day. I can still recall a really terrible Norman Vaughan spending nearly an hour just repeating his catchphrases 'Swinging' and 'Dodgy'! His material was rubbish compared to the genius comedians of today, of which Peter Kay is my favourite.

I was asked to do a summer season with The New Dreamers, playing at caravan parks that all seemed to blend in with one another. I didn't mind singing Freddie's hits, but I drew a line at doing his silly dance moves. Dancing is not one of my strong points and I must be one of the few who don't watch *Strictly Come Dancing*.

I spent two years singing for White Plains, including the hit '*Julie, Julie, Julie, Do You Love Me?*', where I distinctly remembering crossing my legs to get to the high notes!

A very enjoyable part of my varied career was being asked to organise backing musicians and backing vocalists for an Elvis tour. After six weeks of intense rehearsals we set off to tour a lot of the major theatres in England. I was the featured artist. I basically used White Plains as the backing band, and Tony Hoffman, a businessman from Nottingham behind the project, supplied the girl singers.

But obviously the main part of my career is the 20-odd years I spent with Clem and The Tornados. We still perform occasionally, mostly at my fundraising concerts where, after being diagnosed with prostate cancer, I raise cash for a local prostate cancer support charity, PROSTaid.

It was whilst I was playing with a fake Tornados band that I got the idea of contacting Clem to reform the band using an original member. The local band, who are still performing using their original name The Valentines, asked me to join them, playing keyboards, as they were getting work as 'The Tornados'. How this came about was they were called The Valentines as they used to back Ricky Valance, hence the name 'Ricky Valance and the Valentines'. They also did some work with Heinz Burt, and the show was called Heinz and The Tornados. So their agent was now getting them work solely as The Tornados.

Today there are numerous tribute bands calling themselves The Strolling Bones, The Cavern Beatles, Kast Off Kinks and many, many more, but back in the 80s there weren't any as it was frowned upon if there was no original member in the band. So, at one of our band meetings, I suggested contacting an original Tornado to play with us and give the band some authenticity. I contacted directory enquiries and asked for the London number of Clem Cattini. I was put straight through!

Clem invited us down to his home so we could meet up and discuss the possibility of him joining the band to give the act more credence. I played him an instrumental I had written called *Satellite* and he complimented me on the 'Tornados' sound. (I was later to record this with Hal Lindes of Dire Straits as a 'B' side to a re-release recording of 'Telstar').

The 'fake' Tornados were booked to play at a Sixties weekend in Ayr, Scotland, and I suggested Clem came along to perform with us. He brought his good friend Lynn Alice with him, who would later on become the female vocalist of The New Tornados. We played our set with two drummers and it went down well. I remember Sixties artists Brian Poole and Tony Crane of The Merseybeats coming up to Clem that weekend and saying how great it was to see him back gigging.

It was the summer of 1988, and Clem, Lynn and Dave Harvey (later on to be the bass player of The New Tornados) had a summer season in Exeter. I had recently passed my helicopter flying test so I flew down to meet up for a chat.

It soon became obvious that Clem didn't like the idea of joining the existing band. He wanted him and me to form The New Tornados. Clem's golf mate Davy Graham was brought on board to play lead guitar and the line up was complete:

Clem Cattini – Drums
Bip Wetherell – Keyboards and Vocals
Dave Harvey – Bass
Davy Graham – Vocals and Guitar
Lynn Alice – Vocals

This was to be the line up for the next ten years.

The band started rehearsals in London. After a couple of months we had a polished act, with all The Tornados' instrumental hits plus some covers. The vocal side of the band was superb, with really strong three-part harmonies. As Clem had backed Billy Fury in the Sixties we performed a Tribute to Billy Fury set, and we also did a tribute to Clem as we played a medley of some of the best No. 1s that he had played on, my favourite being 'Everlasting Love'.

So we had a band, but no gigs! I decided then to promote the 'Telstar' tour. I booked several theatres and based the show on the old Sixties package shows. The acts I booked were The Honeycombs featuring Honey Lantree on drums, Cliff Bennett and the Rebel Rousers, John

Leyton, and The Four Pennies, with The Tornados topping the bill. The shows went down brilliantly, and word got round the agents that we were back and the work just started to pour in.

BIP WETHERELL

1937

The Spanish Civil War, the precursor to World War Two, was at its height. Thousands were killed when German bombers destroyed the Basque town of Guernica at the behest of General Franco. Volunteers from around the globe joined the so-called International Brigade to fight against Franco's fascist regime.

In the Spanish-controlled Mediterranean Sea, the British liner *Llandovery Castle* was holed by a mine, though all 100 passengers survived and were taken off and transferred to Marseille where they would continue their journey on other liners to South Africa. Japanese bombers battered Shanghai as Japan reignited the conflict with China. Meantime, Britain prepared for conflict, with the RAF training 2,500 pilots and constructing fifty new airbases. Shipyards worked to full capacity building warships. The £3 million aircraft carrier *Ark Royal* was launched at Birkenhead as spending on the defence programme reached its highest level since the Great War of 1914-18.

Into all this turmoil Clemente Anselmo Agostino 'Clem' Cattini was born on 20th August 1937 to Italian parents living in Stoke Newington, North London, England.

How the Cattinis and thousands of other Italian families came to uproot and settle in England during the 1930s, you have to understand the circumstances occurring in their homeland.

Italy in the 1930s was under the control of the National Fascist Party leader, Benito Mussolini who had come to prominence following the First World War. Italy had emerged from the conflict poor and weakened. Post-war saw inflation, massive debts and an extended depression. By 1920 there was mass unemployment, food shortages and strikes. Mussolini criticised the Italian government and organised right wing groups into a single force. Capitalising on public discontent, Mussolini's para-military unit known as the 'Blackshirts' terrorised political opponents and helped increase Fascist influence. By 1922, Italy had slipped into political chaos. Mussolini declared that only he could restore order and gradually dismantled all democratic institutions. By 1925 he had made himself dictator, taking the title 'Il Duce' ('the Leader').

The worldwide depression of the early 1930s hit Italy hard. Industries came close to failure and were bought out by banks in a largely illusionary bail-out, leading to a financial crisis in 1932.

In 1935, determined to show the strength of his regime, Benito Mussolini invaded Ethiopia. The Ethiopians were no match, and the capital Addis Ababa was quickly captured and Ethiopia was incorporated into the new Italian Empire. In 1939, Mussolini sent support to Fascists in Spain, even though the Italian economy was too under-developed to sustain the demands of a militaristic regime. A third of government expenditure being directed towards the Italian armed services left the country 'spectacularly weak'.

To this background, many families like the Cattinis decided to get out. Many went to America, many came to Britain.

It Takes a Worried Man

Sunday September 3rd 1939, 11.15am. Prime Minister Neville Chamberlain is at 10 Downing Street, ready to broadcast a speech on the BBC Home Service that will send tremors through the hearts of the nation.

Poland had been invaded by Germany and, having promised to support the Poles if such an occurrence arose, Britain's ambassador to Berlin, Sir Nevile Henderson, was dispatched to inform the German government that unless they withdrew their troops by 11.00am, a state of war would exist between the two countries.

Chamberlain was sombre; 'I have to tell you that no such undertaking has been received... and consequently this country is now at war with Germany.'

How the ordinary men and women of the country felt about the proclamation, those who would be 'called up' to do the fighting, one can only imagine. Apprehension, despair, panic... Life would never be the same.

Twelve months earlier, in September 1938, Neville Chamberlain had met Adolf Hitler in Munich to talk about a crisis involving Czechoslovakia where three million Germans had suddenly found themselves living after the map of Europe was redrawn and new countries were formed following the Great War of 1914-18. Europe was on the brink of catastrophe again as Adolf vowed to get his exiled countrymen back, but he assured Chamberlain there was nothing to worry about. The two leaders signed the Munich Agreement, which stated that Britain and Germany would never go to war again.

Chamberlain returned home with a bounce in his step. Waving a sheet of paper as he stepped off the British Lockheed airplane at Heston Airport, Hounslow, he declared triumphantly; 'I believe it is peace for our time.'

The document wasn't worth the paper it was written on. In March 1939 Germany invaded Czechoslovakia.

Just a month later, Hitler's ally Benito Mussolini ordered his Italian troops to invade Albania and the Second World War was one step closer. Britain responded to these acts of aggression by introducing conscription, by the end of the year over a million men were 'called up' to serve in the armed forces.

Unabashed, Hitler continued his march through Europe. Following Czechoslovakia and Poland, Denmark, Norway, the Netherlands and France capitulated in the Spring of 1940. Suffering from stress and ill-health, Chamberlain resigned in May and Winston Churchill was asked by King George VI to take his place. Chamberlain was diagnosed with bowel cancer and died five months later, on November 9th. Meantime, Italy, declared war on Britain.

During these dark days the *Daily Mirror* made a clumsy attempt to cheer people up and boost morale by issuing advice to its readers under the headline 'Don't Lose Your Head':

> In other words – keep smiling. There's nothing to be gained by going about with the corners of your mouth turned down, and it has a bad effect on people whose nerves are not so good as yours. So even if a bomb falls in your street – which is unlikely – Keep Smiling.

So full marks to the *Mirror* for trying to defuse the fears but its hard to imagine people would be blasé if they saw a bomb blow up their street.

Stoicism is a British trait though, which basically is what the *Mirror* was trying to say. Chin up, remember us Brits are made of sterner stuff! Laugh in the face of adversity. As emphasised by Bud Flanagan and his Crazy Gang, one of the most popular music hall acts of the time, as emphasised by the World War II song 'Hitler Has Only Got

One Ball', which mocked the Nazi leaders.

At the outbreak of war there was estimated to be around 19,000 Italians living in Britain. Paranoia was rife: would they poison the pizzas? As a precaution, Churchill ordered them to be rounded up – the Italians, not the pizzas. The Cattinis, residing in Stoke Newington, were just one family awaiting their fate, and it wasn't long before Plod came knocking at their door. Clem Cattini Senior had come over to England with his brother from Tuscany in the mid-1920s and opened a cafe in Princes Street, Oxford Circus. It was where he met his wife Lena, whose parents were also Italian. They settled in North West London and had four children including Clemente Anselmo Cattini, who was aged just two when the police arrived on that fateful day. He has no recall of the event but was assured in later life by his mum that he wasn't happy. 'She always told me I gave the police dog's abuse when they took my dad away. One of the coppers asked her; 'Who's the little Mussolini then?' Dad was taken to Goode Street Police Station before being sent to a camp on the Isle of Man. If Mum wanted to visit him she had to report to the police station to log in, and report back to log out when she returned.'

The Isle of Man was the primary site for the internment of civilian 'enemy aliens' during the war. They were divided into three categories:

- Class A (high security risk)
- Class B (doubtful cases)
- Class C (no risk)

Life for Class C 'aliens' was fairly comfortable. Encamped in hotels and boarding houses, they were allowed to work on farms, go for walks and swim in the sea. Those in Class 'A' were regarded as bad eggs and held in camps with barbed wire fences and guarded over by the military.

Clem Senior was in Class C and found himself in the company of a Scottish gent, also of Italian origin, Charles Forte. Charles was a fellow caterer who later founded the hotels conglomerate which became the Forte Group. A tangential connection with the Cattini family comes to light, as he was involved in the conversion and relaunching of the Hippodrome Theatre in the West End into The Talk of The Town during 1958. Clem Junior would play the theatre many times as a member of the orchestra backing Roy Orbison, Tom Jones, Shirley Bassey and other stars during the 1960s and 70s.

Back on the Isle of Man, Clem Senior worked as a chef before being relocated to a village near Evesham in Worcestershire, not far from a place where a chap who would later play a predominant part in Clem Junior's life came from – Joe Meek.

During this time, the Cattini children, like thousands of others in London, were evacuated to more peaceful areas around the country to escape the bombings from the Luftwaffe.

Clem's memory remains vivid:

> The war had a traumatic effect on my family. I was evacuated along with my brother Laurence and cousin Rini to St. Albans, then Watford before we ended up on a farm in Hereford. It was horrible. The people who owned the farm didn't really want us there. It was probably a familiar story for everyone during these times, but there we were. We had our meals in a separate room which was cold. The meals were basic and miniscule. If it wasn't for mum sending us food parcels, we would have starved to death! It was that bad me and Laurence used to make bows and arrows and shoot Brussel sprouts off their stems in the garden. We were later transferred to a Boarding School in Oxford; right next to the Cowley factory where they were building Spitfires! Which wasn't a great place to be! We were then moved yet again to another Boarding School in a place called Burwash, Sussex, which was right in the middle of the South Coast Defences. We used to play in the fields and watch Messerschmitts and the RAF in dogfights and had no fear at all until a German fighter strafed us as we all ran for cover into the woods! We slept in a shed which was like a makeshift dormitory and I can still remember one battle when tracer bullets went right through the hut. It's amazing really, we weren't that frightened. We were too young to understand. The war? What's that? During school holidays we were allowed to go home and I remember watching from afar as the city of London burned after the bombings. Everything seemed sort of an

adventure, we didn't comprehend that people were dying or had been killed. On reflection it was a major upheaval and I hardly knew my dad because of the war. It wasn't until the end that we were truly reunited as a family when the return of evacuees to London was officially approved by the government in June 1945.

'Somehow,' Clem confessed, 'despite all the moving around with the schools, I did manage to pass the Eleven Plus exam.' Along with his brother Laurence, Clem gained a place at the St. Ignatius Grammar School in Stamford Hill, Tottenham.

'I hated it,' Clem recalled, 'and the Jesuit Priests who ran it weren't too enamoured with me either as it happens. I was useless at everything, and considering how my life panned out, not once in all my time there did I show any inclination towards music. Everyone assumed I was tone deaf. My music lesson was with an old girl we called Mrs Nobbo. Her real name was Mrs Knobbs. All she ever did was put 'The Best of Brahms' or 'Beethoven's Greatest Hits' on a record player and disappear for a cup of tea and a Park Drive cigarette. I didn't get on at all and in the end, I left school when I was 15 after Mum had wrote a letter to the Headmaster to say she thought it would be a good idea as she could see my school career was going nowhere. He wrote back and said he agreed!'

Guitarist Pete Townshend of The Who offered his thoughts on the problems faced with post-war schoolchildren in the film *Lambert & Stamp*:

> The generation above us had real difficulty engaging with us. You had terrible trouble with schoolteachers who just expected you to do what they said and it wasn't necessarily what you wanted to do. It wasn't that you went out of your way to disobey but they would get angry with you and it would end up with a situation where it was outright rebellion.

If youngsters were regarded as a pain in the backside during Pete and Clem's day, it's hard to believe but apparently, back in the 8th century BC, a Greek poet called Hesiod was just as despondent when commenting on the adolescents during his time.

'I see no hope for the future of our people if they are dependant on the frivolous youth of today,' Hesiod groaned, 'for certainly all youth are reckless beyond words. When I was young we were taught to be discreet and respectful of elders, but the present youth are exceedingly disrespectful and impatient of restraint.'

Which begs the question, could this have been the bloodline of the 1950s Teddy Boys then? All the way back to the ancient Greeks of 2,500 years ago? Makes you wonder what they got up to back then! Or is that just a myth?

Clem:

> So that was me, out of school, with the only prospect being of working in my dad's cafe for the rest of my life. By then he had sold up and opened a new one in Borough at the southern end of London Bridge. It was six days a week, egg and bacon, sausage and mash, wiping down those damn tables. I loathed it almost as much as I had school. And my dad was old school – the customer was always right. Not me. If someone complained about the mash being lumpy or the bangers were undercooked I would tell them to go and eat somewhere else! Perhaps I was representative of the youth of that time, but I was not going to take the 'Yes Sir, No Sir' attitude to life. I argued with my dad, and it drove him mad.

Following the war cities took years to recover and rebuild. Housing was in short supply, families were living in slums. Rationing continued until February 1953, leaving the young Pete Townshend distinctly unimpressed, complaining; 'I thought we won the effin' war!'

Food Minister Gwilym Lloyd-George eventually decided there was enough sugar available to allow sweet manufacturers to restart production, and eight years after the end of the war Pete was able to buy Spangles, bubblegum and gobstoppers, which were back on the shelves of the sweet shops. All were snapped up enthusiastically by post-war kids, but the biggest sellers were said to be toffee apples.

Rationing of meat and bacon continued for a further year, until 1954, by which time many families had resorted to breeding rabbits and keeping chickens in their gardens as a source of protein.

Entertainment could also said to be have been rationed as television was yet to make an impact, regarded as a fantasy thing which was beyond the comprehension of those who survived the war. It took the Queen's Coronation in 1953 to cause a ripple of excitement as families around the country congregated around the often one-and-only set in a street. There was always one family more affluent than the rest!

Wireless was the one piece of technology that was commonplace. BBC's Home Service, Light Programme and Third Network kept the nation up to date and amused during these pre-television days. The Light Programme had evolved in 1945 from the General Forces Overseas Network. Presenter Denis Norden describing it; 'Very typical of the BBC to call it Light as we were living in blackouts, rationing, dark days following the war. It was light music, light comedy.'

The weekly schedules included *Music While You Work*, *Workers' Playtime*, *Children's Favourites* on Saturday and Sunday mornings with a chap called Uncle Mac. Drama with *The Archers* and *Mrs. Dale's Diary* and *Journey Into Space,* which followed the adventures of Jet Morgan on his travels to the Moon and beyond. Comedy with *Hancock's Half Hour*, *The Navy Lark* and *The Glums*, a sketch about a long-time engaged couple featuring Jimmy Edwards, June Whitfield and Alma Cogan. *The Goon Show* – Spike Milligan, Peter Sellers, Harry Secombe and Michael Bentine – described as 'anarchic with their disregard for authority'.

Scriptwriters of all these shows had to adhere to a strict BBC policy of 'keeping it clean'. Nicholas Parsons recalled writing a gag which included the line 'The lady stands naked'. Parsons: 'Naked was a taboo word. The producer said to me, 'No, no, can we change that to 'The lady stands there with no clothes on?' I told him it would ruin the joke but I asked him, 'How about 'The lady was starkers?'' He said, 'Ah yes, that'll be fine'.

Educating Archie, a ventriloquist act featuring Peter Brough was another very popular show, even if, as one critic railed, 'He was the worst ventriloquist ever!' A young Petula Clark appeared on the show with Peter and his wooden dummy Archie, and thought the whole concept was bizarre. A ventriloquist on radio! Scriptwriter Barry Cryer saw him at The Hippodrome: 'He was dreadful! Peter's lips were moving all over the place, yet, the audience seemed to accept it! I suppose it helped if you'd had a few beers or glasses of wine!'

Also popular was Wilfred Pickles presenting the forerunner of shows like *Opportunity Knocks* and *X Factor.* Wilfred's effort was called *Have A Go!*, in which members of the public were invited to, well... have a go! Wilfred's wife Mabel sat by a table on the edge of the stage and gave out prizes to the contestants... 2/6d, a bag of nuts... a far cry from the yachts and kitchens that Jim Bowen gave you a chance to win on his 1980s show *Bullseye.*

Two-Way Family Favourites with Cliff Michelmore and Jean Metcalfe was a staple offering every Sunday lunchtime which evokes memories in those of a certain age, which has become something of a cliché, for roast beef and Yorkshire pudding being prepared as records and messages were exchanged between servicemen abroad in Germany and their kinfolk back home. Apparently the most popular record of this programme was Pat Boone's *'I'll Be Home'.*

Sunday night's *Sing Something Simple* with the Cliff Adams Singers signalled the end of the weekend when it came on at 6 o'clock. Comedian Paul O'Grady recalled: 'I hated it! To me it was time to think about getting things ready for school next morning. Doing your homework which you'd put off, it was depressing!'

The BBC controlled everything and dictated what we should be listening to. A documentary on television's History Channel explained:

> The BBC was permeated by the austere prejudices of its founder John Reith and the controller of programmes, Basil Nicholls who shared his conviction that the BBC should be a moral, spiritual and aesthetic guardian of the nation. Basil hated the insincere and over-sentimental performances of women singers like Vera Lynn.

Clearly, Vera's *'We'll Meet Again'* was not Basil's bag then. Similarly, the BBC governors deplored her show:

> Music is an ennobling spiritual force which should influence the life of every listener. It is the BBC policy to exclude crooning, difficult to define but easily recognisable in various forms such as sub-tone, falsetto and other modes of effeminate singing. The jazzing of dance and classical tunes or borrowing or adaption of this is quite unacceptable. Each example must be reviewed and arbitrary decisions taken regarding inclusion or exclusion recognising that there are degrees of adaptation ranging from the innocuous to the obscene.

You can take it that the BBC wasn't particularly impressed when the *New Musical Express* published the first ever Hit Parade, the nation's top selling records, on 14th November 1952, with Basil Nicholl's favourite, Vera Lynn, prominent with three entries:

1 *'Here In My Heart'* – Al Martino
2 *'You Belong To Me'* – Jo Stafford
3 *'Somewhere Along The Way'* – Nat King Cole
4 *'The Isle Of Innisfree'* – Bing Crosby
5 *'Feet Up (Pat Him On The Po-Po)'* – Guy Mitchell
6 *'Half As Much'* – Rosemary Clooney
7 *'High Noon (Do Not Forsake Me)'* – Frankie Laine
8 *'Forget Me Not'* – Vera Lynn
9 *'Sugarbush'* – Doris Day and Frankie Laine
10 *'Blue Tango'* – Ray Martin
11 *'The Homing Waltz'* – Vera Lynn
12 *'Auf Wiederseh'n Sweetheart'* – Vera Lynn
13 *'Cowpuncher's Cantata'* – Max Bygraves
14 *'Because You're Mine'* – Mario Lanza
15 *'Walkin' My Baby Back Home'* – Johnnie Ray

Coinciding with this was the production of the Dansette record player, advertised as 'an artefact of the vibrant, popular youth culture, setting a standard look for all portable record players. The size of a small suitcase with a latched lid on top, a speaker and control knobs on the front, plus a carrying handle.' Retailing at the price of 33 guineas, it was probably a hard sell initially as most households had a radiogram, which was what it said on the tin – a radio and a gram' (short for gramophone) combined into one unit of furniture. The sales pitch was: 'An instrument of entertainment for the house, the radiogram features a record auto changer, which will take six or seven records and play them one after another.' Much the same as the Dansette in fact. Sales of the radiogram in the 1950s, and the popularity of 78rpm and later the 7-inch 45rpm single and LP (Long Playing) records, meant that many manufacturers considered the radiogram to be more important than the television, which in 1952 had just the one BBC channel. The 'gram would eventually be superseded by the Dansette. Between the years 1950-70 over one million were sold.

The advent of the transistor radio was another milestone in the entertainment industry, as record producer Keith Harris remembered:

> Most people had a wireless or radiogram in their sitting room in the 50s which was the parents' territory, but the transistor allowed young people to take their radio into their rooms and listen to what they wanted to.

Which wasn't much as it happened, but the one station that was essential, even if the reception was crap, was Radio Luxembourg, the only music station other than AFN (American Forces Network) that offered alternative music to Victor Silvester and the likes of Vera Lynn.

It's a well-worn story about listening to disc jockeys David Gell, Muriel Young and Pete Murray under the bedclothes and the Top Twenty countdown at 11 o'clock on Sunday nights. The signal ebbing in and out like a tide which was irritating to say the least, but for all that Radio Luxembourg was magical. Even the commercials featuring a bloke in Bristol called Horace Batchelor who claimed to have the key to winning the Pools (football pools which fell by the wayside once the National Lottery started). Horace insisted there were fortunes to be won using this thing he called the Infra Draw Method, which sounded like some sort of sexual experience, but all you had to do was write a letter to Horace and address it to 'K-E-Y-N-S-H-A-M,' spelt out like that in case you were an imbecile. Horace drove you mad, when all you wanted to hear was the pop music! And to this day, have you ever heard of anyone who won anything thanks to Horace?

Clem:

> It was mum who controlled the wireless in our house. She used to listen to the Latin American dance music of Edmundo Ros, which was popular in the 1940s and 1950s. It was the only music I heard. I didn't have any musical education at all, apart from Edmundo and the interludes with Mrs. Knobbs!

On leaving school in the 1950s it was the norm for adolescents to follow in their parents' footsteps. Working mundane jobs, wearing hand-me-downs, settling down and getting married, and the cycle would turn full circle. At the age of eighteen teenage boys were invited to do a stint of National Service and spend two years in the army, navy or RAF, and as an added incentive, if they were lucky, 'to do their bit' in the war zones of Korea, Kenya and Suez.

Childhood and teenage life was passed over rapidly.

Clem missed out on National Service after failing the medical for having flat feet with a rating of 4B, but insisted:

> I wanted to 'join-up' but the recruiting people wouldn't have it. Because of my flat feet I was regarded at best as a malingerer or a liability and they didn't want me. With hindsight I was lucky, I was only seventeen at the time and because of the conscription laws plus the fact that I have flat feet, I didn't have to go to the army while a lot of my friends had to.

Being 'called up' was a terrifying proposition for most 18-year-olds. Bob Knight, pub landlord, disc jockey, and friend of radio DJ

John Peel, recalled in the book *Alive In The Dead Of Night:*

> I was called up for national service in 1951. It was the time of
> what has become known as 'The Forgotten War' – Korea. I
> spent a year there with the Royal Norfolk Regiment. We took
> over from the Glorious Glosters. I'd been transferred from the
> Northamptonshire Regiment and sent to Bury St Edmunds for
> training. They told us we were going to Korea, I didn't have a clue
> where Korea was! I was 18 and being sent to the front line. We
> had no idea what lay in store for us. A vivid memory is on arrival
> at Seoul and being transferred onto a train to take us to our camp
> – and a train pulling into the station as we were about to leave,
> full of injured American servicemen. That was a waking up call
> I can tell you. All these guys lying on stretchers with limbs torn
> apart and blood and guts everywhere. Frightening. Because I was
> a big lad I often got lumbered with humping things around. One
> time I was on a patrol with about a dozen others, making our way
> through a terrain that was mountainous, boggy, because of all
> the bombing that had been going on, and I was carrying this big
> heavy wireless on my back! It was scary and then all of a sudden
> I thought I heard these Chinese voices. I told the sergeant but he
> said 'no, no way, they're nowhere near us'. I was convinced but he
> refused to acknowledge it – until we went over a brow of a hill
> and spotted about four hundred of the Chinese coming towards
> us! We turned and ran like hell, tumbling back down the hillside
> to our jeeps. We'd spend the days and nights camped in the
> trenches, every so often giving the Chinese a burst of about 400
> rounds out of our Vickers machine gun, working it in an arc, back
> and for, firing non-stop. Just to let them know we were still there!

The 1st Battalion Gloucestershire Regiment, the 'Glorious
Glosters', were so-called because of a heroic three-day stand where
they held off a Chinese force ten times its size. Fifty-nine were killed
and 526 captured during the battle for the Imjin River, 22-25 April
1951. Bob: 'It was when we saw a 50th anniversary celebration of
the war on television that I realised that the Glosters had suffered
one of the worst defeats in the war.'

Clem may have missed out on Korea but two fellow musicians who
did make the trip were British blues guitar and harmonica player

John Mayall, who spent three years with The Royal Engineers, and American rock guitarist Link Wray, who unfortunately contracted tuberculosis and lost a lung there. Not literally of course... his lung was knackered.

Life back then may have been grim, but a new wave of optimism was just around the corner... heralded in with an exciting new sound of what an American disc jockey Alan Freed called 'Rock and Roll'.

Things were about to change...

3

Rock around the Clock

In July 1953 a nineteen-year-old truck driver walked into the Sun
Recording Studio on Union Avenue, Memphis and recorded a demo
disc of '*My Happiness*'. His name was Elvis Presley.

The Sun Studio was owned by maverick record producer
Sam Phillips, a guy who distanced himself from the segregation
problems inherent in Memphis and the South and recorded black
artists including Howlin' Wolf, B.B. King, Sleepy John Estes and Little
Junior Parker. Sam also recorded a bunch of convicts in Tennessee
State Penitentiary Nashville, dubbed them the Prisonaires and had
a smash hit with '*Just Walkin' In The Rain*'. Sam Phillips dreamt of
finding a 'white' singer who could sing like a 'black' singer. The
blues. The day Elvis walked in for an audition with the two house
musicians Scotty Moore and Bill Black, and started messing around
singing Arthur 'Big Boy' Crudup's '*That's All Right Mama*', Sam
Phillips knew he had found his man. Over the next twelve months
Elvis would record '*Mystery Train*', '*Good Rockin' Tonight*', '*Milk Cow
Blues Boogie*' and '*Baby Let's Play House*', and tour the southern
states, creating a groundswell that would shake the music industry
to its core.

Britain was oblivious to all this. Crooners Tony Bennett, Eddie
Fisher, Jimmy Young and Dickie Valentine held the fort; the BBC
ruled the airwaves. On the day '*That's All Right Mama*' was released,
July 19th 1954, David Whitfield's '*Cara Mia*' was top of the UK charts.

Clem was earning £1 10d a week at his dads' cafe, but feeling less
than satisfied. There had to be something more fulfilling than serving
up bangers and mash, and it was a similar feeling he had to that of a

troubadour across the 'Great Pond' in America. Robert Zimmerman, better known as Bob Dylan, was also working for his dad. In Martin Scorsese's *No Direction Home*, Dylan bemoaned working at his dad's store as 'Sweeping floors, where you were supposed to learn the discipline of hard work, or something. Or the merits of employment.'

Bob and Clem were clearly on the same wavelength.

Around this time Clem met Anna, 'the girl of my dreams' and future wife, whose surname coincidently was also Cattini. Clem tells us:

We were in our teens. We started going down to the Italian-owned Roma Jazz Club in Clerkenwell, a place frequented by hundreds of Anglo Italians during the early 1950s. The Roma was an escape from the drudgery of the cafe for me. I got to know the drummer of the quartet who played there every Sunday night, Bruno Imarini. One night I said to Anna 'I could do that', and Bruno overheard me. 'Come on, have a go,' he said, and as I went to take up his offer Anna burst out laughing at the thought of me playing the drums. I got the hump. 'You watch,' I said with a flash of my Italian temperament. 'You're laughing but one day I'll be famous!' Which made her laugh even more! I'm not saying for one minute I was a natural. Far from it. But it felt good and it turned out to be a life-changing moment.

The guitarist of the group was a guy called Terry Kennedy and he encouraged me to come down to a hall in Kings Cross on Wednesday afternoons to practice. As luck would have it, that was my half day off so suddenly I had a new interest. A real motivation to better my life and forget about the café. Then one night I went along with Terry and his friend Ray Fernandes, who was a bass player, to see *Blackboard Jungle* at the Trocadero Cinema, Elephant and Castle. At the end of the film '*Rock around the Clock*' by Bill Haley and The Comets was played, and our lives were never the same after that. Rock and Roll had arrived in Britain! We came out of the cinema and Terry said 'Let's form a rock and roll group!' It did seem like pie in the sky stuff at the time, but we were coming into an era where ambition was the keyword. This was post-war Britain and the youth were beginning to rebel. In the 1930s all our parents had it hard. We knew that – and then came the war. But this was a whole new generation. We had a few bob in our pockets and although I showed respect to my parents, teenagers began to resent authority figures. In fact it was during this time that the word 'teenager' entered the everyday language. We felt sort of liberated.

Blackboard Jungle was the latest in a series of American films hitting Britain's cinema screens and causing much consternation. The film portrayed juvenile delinquency and violence in an American inner city school, 'Filled with scenes of unbridled, revolting hooliganism'. Marlon Brando's motorbike gang terrorising American townships in *The Wild One* had already been banned by censors, and James Dean's *Rebel Without A Cause* received an X-rating certificate.

In scenes replicated around the country, as '*Rock Around The Clock*' pounded out at the end of *Blackboard Jungle*, youths attired in Edwardian-style dress and nicknamed 'Teddy Boys' danced with their girls in the aisles. Cinema staff attempted to stop them and riots erupted as the Teds ripped up seats with flick knives and fought with the police. Revolution was in the air. The Teddy Boy is acknowledged as being the first statement of youth fashion in Britain with their 'uniform' of long jackets, drainpipe trousers, beetle-crusher shoes, long sideburns, slick haircuts with quiffs like the guy from Memphis, Elvis Presley. As one Teddy Boy at the Mecca Royal Dance Hall, Tottenham, 1954 put it: 'Our dress is our answer to a dull world.'

The press were quick to report of 'a threat to older nervous folk', prompting Home Secretary David Maxwell Fyfe to respond, 'The problem isn't widespread and in any case, is containable.' Max was probably thinking, 'When we get these louts into the army we will soon get them sorted out.'

Fears of the Teds was aired by the Bishop of Peterborough, who told of a conversation he'd had with a Teddy Boy and concluded; 'There is an increased tendency for young people in this country to act in a group rather than an individual, and I believe the future of our democracy is in grave danger at this point.'

Taking a more pragmatic view was the Rev. John Ashplant of the Methodist Church:

Teddy Boys should not be blamed because they try to attract attention through their dress,' the Rev professed; 'Their clothes are just a symptom of their wish to be thought important. In a world of insecurity they are looking for some sort of stability and outlet for personality. If I were to speak to a Teddy Boy, I wouldn't begin by saying take off those clothes and put on a decent suit. I would ignore the clothes and speak to him as a normal human being – and I should hope to lead him ultimately to Christ.

Clem:

The group I formed with Terry and Ray was called Terry Kennedy's Rock and Rollers. Terry told me I could be the drummer, so I said ok and at the start I played the washboard but progressed from there and eventually started playing the drums. The kit was made up of various different bits which overall cost me about £20. I was 17 and didn't know the difference between a crotchet and a hatchet, so I bought a copy of the Buddy Rich drum tutor book and started practising all the rudiments from there, practising around five to six hours a day.

Ray Fernandes and Clem, still close friends sixty years on, recalled those early days, with great amusement, over a coffee in 2018.

Clem: 'Ray was the bass player in Eddie Calvert's band The C Men. They had been in the charts with *'Oh Mein Papa'* in 1954. The drummer was a guy called Bobby Adrian, whom Ray set me up for some lessons.'

Ray: 'Bobby was a precision drummer. He'd been with Eddie Calvert for nine years, playing swing, big band stuff. He said to me, 'Clem will never make a drummer as long as he's got a hole in his arse!' Ray laughed out loud, 'Shows you what he knew!'

Clem: '...and he was the guy I was supposed to be having lessons off! I only had the one lesson with him! He swung like a big bag of shit in all honesty!'

Ray: 'I had a Gretsch guitar and a Martin acoustic at the time. The Martin was a lovely guitar which I bought for £30 and sold it later for £40. I made a profit of £10. A few years later, when I was working with Roy Castle, you couldn't buy one for under £450! That really peed me off! Terry Kennedy started the Rock and Rollers group but I wasn't really interested. Terry said to me, 'I'm getting gigs booked here, there... pubs and clubs all around the East End.' I said to him, 'I can't do that, playing three-chord rock and roll stuff.' I was playing standards in big bands.'

Clem:

> After Ray left we added a tea chest bass to our band, literally a box with a broom handle and one string, which effectively made us a skiffle group which was all the rage at the time. We played all the usual stuff: '*It Takes A Worried Man*', '*Pick a Bale Of Cotton*' etc. Pubs in South London provided regular lunchtime gigs and we managed to get a regular Sunday afternoon gig at the Adam and Eve pub in Peckham. Terry had been blessed with a shrewd business brain and we left all the organising to him. He struck a deal with the landlord where we would keep all the door money – it was 2/6d to get in – and the landlord settled for the increased takings at the bar. It was a small smoky room, but the crowds soon began to grow. These days you would never get it through the Health and Safety regulations, but at the time nobody bothered us.

> I was also helping out in my Uncle John's Cafe in Dalston, the East End on Saturday mornings, serving up ice cream! One morning, after we had played the Finsbury Park Empire, two girls came in and one of them said, 'Didn't we see you last night at the Empire, playing drums?' Talk about embarrassing! I was feeling really cool till that moment!

Inspired by Elvis, Gene Vincent, Eddie Cochran and Lonnie Donegan, youngsters all around Britain formed skiffle groups, performing songs like the aforementioned '*Pick A Bale of Cotton*', '*Goodnight Irene*', '*Midnight Special*' by Leadbelly and '*Ramblin' On My Mind*' by Robert Johnson, songs which originated from the cotton fields of Mississippi. The records were introduced into Britain primarily by blues enthusiast and bandleader Chris Barber, who brought a number of 'Bluesmen' over from America to guest with his band. Barber's banjo player Lonnie Donegan, likewise a big fan of the music, released his own version of Leadbelly's '*Rock Island Line*' in 1956 which, along with '*Heartbreak Hotel*', were the two records that were the protagonists of the fledgling Rock and Roll scene in Britain.

In America, Rock 'n' Roll was exploding with Elvis, Jerry Lee Lewis, the Everly Brothers, Gene Vincent and company recording what was being labelled 'Devil's music'. An alternative was Pat Boone releasing cover versions of Little Richard and Fats Domino songs. Encouraged by the bosses of 'white' record labels who claimed, 'Rock and Roll is too edgy for Middle America', Boone sanitised numbers which included Richard's '*Tutti Frutti*', stating that some of the lines of the song were too erotic:

> I changed the second part of 'Got a gal named Sue, she knows just what to do' to 'She's the gal for me'. When I covered Fats Domino's '*Ain't That A Shame*' I told the record producer that the title wasn't good English and I sang 'Isn't That A Shame' instead, but on hearing it he said, 'That just doesn't sound right.' I reluctantly had to agree and we re-recorded the song singing 'Ain't'.

It sounds farcical and Little Richard's drummer Charles Connor recalled that every time they heard Pat Boone's versions of their songs they all fell over laughing. 'That man just didn't have the soul of Little Richard. It was so funny.'

Boone was blind to the criticism. 'In America nobody realised I wasn't a black soul singer when they heard my Rock and Roll records.' Which with all due respect, seems a little absurd. Pat remained unabashed and in the 1990s even released an album entitled *In A Metal Mood: No More Mr. Nice Guy*, on which he covered hard rock and heavy metal songs. Metallica's '*Enter Sandman*', Hendrix's '*The Wind Cries Mary*' and Deep Purple's '*Smoke On The Water*' were three that received the Boone treatment.

Pat's incursion into the world of heavy rock received mixed reviews: 'I know this is clearly not an album of heavy metal as most fans are used to,' wrote one commentator, 'but I feel that Pat Boone should be respected for this album. A long time Christian, he decided that he would do an album of metal covers as a lark to sort of poke fun at himself and his music.'

True or not, the album wasn't appreciated by his friends in the Christian community. The week *In A Metal Mood* was released he appeared on the American Music Awards and Tonight Show sporting a leather vest and an earring. It was too much for the Christians and his weekly gospel programme on the biggest Christian television network in the world, Trinity Broadcasting, was subsequently cancelled.

1956 saw Elvis Presley signed up by RCA Victor, who paid Sam Phillips 35,000 dollars for his contract. Steve Sholes, RCA record producer, sent a package of Elvis recordings to Wally Ridley at EMI in London. Included was a message 'You probably won't understand a word and what on earth these records are all about, but you should release them anyway.'

Wally did listen to them. 'Sholes was right, I couldn't understand more than a couple of words but I decided to heed his advice and I put out 'Heartbreak Hotel' on our HMV label – and received the worst press we ever had! They said you couldn't understand a word, the record was disgusting – and on the back of that, we got no broadcasts whatsoever on BBC Radio or Radio Luxembourg. Then nine months later the whole Presley thing broke over here following a double-page spread in the *Daily Mirror*.'

'Heartbreak Hotel' entered the UK charts on May 19th, stunning everyone on first hearing. Presley's second release, 'Hound Dog', was equally stunning, even if, like 'Heartbreak Hotel', it failed to impress the jazz-biased *Melody Maker*, where Steve Race was typically pompous and arrogant with his assessment:

> When this record was released, I sat up and took special notice. Many times have I heard bad records, but for sheer repulsiveness, coupled with the monotony of incoherence, 'Hound Dog' hits a new low in my experience.

Race judged that 'Hound Dog' would see the end of Presley and the British public wouldn't buy it. When 'Hound Dog' entered the charts at number three he obviously couldn't contain himself:

I fear for this country and the future of our music industry which allows itself to cater for one demented age group to the exclusion of the majority, who still want to hear a tuneful song tunefully sung! It ought to have had the good taste and good sense to reject music so decadent.

Bruce Welch of The Shadows recalled Race's contemptuousness:

Steve Race hated pop music; he was always slagging the music, rock and roll, and groups off. I used to say that jazz is three or four guys playing music who don't know the melody, but in fairness jazz musicians are often phenomenal players. Cliff Hall, who played keyboards with The Shadows, for years was a fantastic jazz musician and could play anything.

As Rock and Roll continued in its ascendency there was a rush to find a British answer to Elvis, and at first everyone thought it was Tommy Steele, who had showed up at the 2i's Coffee Bar in Old Compton Street, Soho with his guitar, having just returned from a trip with the merchant navy. Steele, who 'looked the part, sounded good and had a smile and a swagger that couldn't fail', was born Tommy Hicks but took the surname from his Scandinavian grandfather, apparently. You would have thought it would have been more likely Molberg or Larrson or something. Whatever, Tommy was spotted by John Kennedy – no relation to Terry – and would later be managed by Larry Parnes. 'Rock With The Caveman', co-written by Steele, Lionel Bart and Mike Pratt, was the song that launched his career.

Released in October on the Decca label and backed with 'Elevator Rock' on the 'B' side, 'Caveman' went to number one in the British charts in December.

The producer was Hugh Mendl, who had worked on Lonnie Donegan skiffle sessions and was keen to get in on the new craze that was rock and roll, music that was still being derided by the music moguls. The way rock and roll was regarded can be seen by the shambolic way the recording took place, as Hugh recalls:

Unfortunately when we booked Tommy for a recording session,

nobody had bothered to check whether there was a studio or anything like that to record him. We had to take him up to an artists' rest room, and it was in there and backed by a bass player and a drummer he started to sing. *'Rock with the Caveman'* was the very first record he recorded and although I hadn't heard him sing before, I knew nothing about how his voice would record or any of the other so-called technical problems, to me his voice had an absolute fabulous magic. This was a performance. Everybody was being rude about rock and roll but this was a magical performance. He'd only got through one chorus when I said 'Yes, this is it! This is absolutely perfect!'

Over the course of the next couple of years Steele would release cover versions of *'Singing the Blues'* and *'Come On Let's Go'* before changing track in his career and going on to appear in West End musicals, films, and recording novelty records *'What a Picture'* and *'Little White Bull'*. Quite what Steve Race in the *Melody Maker* made of it is anyone's guess.

It's significant to note that all of this coincided with the Suez Canal crisis that Britain was embroiled in and young national serviceman were being expected to lay themselves on the line. Along with the Suez crisis, headlines in 1956 told of Hungarian students rising against the rule of the Soviet Union over their country. Russian tanks had rolled into Budapest to quell the uprising, and thousands were executed while thousands fled. It was a scary time, particularly if you were coming up to the age of eighteen. This blazing new 'thing' that was rock 'n' roll, fuelled the angst that many teenagers were experiencing, at home and abroad.

Following on from the success of *Blackboard Jungle*, American producer Sam Katzman brought out a film based on the Bill Haley record *'Rock Around the Clock'*.

The film was released in Britain in August and almost immediately trouble started. Two cinemas in Woolwich were the scene of riots as Teddy Boys and their girls clashed with ushers trying to maintain a semblance of order. Once more the police were called and several Teds were arrested as fireworks and bottles were thrown.

The Gaiety Theatre, Manchester witnessed fire hoses being ripped off the walls and fired at people in the stalls during *Rock Around the Clock*. The *Daily Mirror reported*: 'Police battled with the mob of around 200 youths causing disturbances in and around the theatre. Traffic was caught up in the melee. The police made 14 arrests as they tried to quell the riot.' In court next day the Magistrate condemned 'these rock and roll rhythms', telling the youths charged with disorderly conduct that 'The police would be better to give your unruly mob something to rock and roll about! It's got to stop!'

It was all too much for some, and on BBC's topical radio show *Any Questions?* panellist Lord Boothby was scathing in his attack on the culture of rock and roll films and the teenage generation:

> Jiving! What a thing to do! The sooner this ridiculous film *Rock Around the Clock* is banned the better it will be for all of us. It's giving no pleasure at all, except to lunatics and causing a lot of trouble. One of the purposes of us old fogies in life is to stop these young people being silly!

And in a reference to the escalating Suez crisis, he added:

> If they want to be Teddy Boys and fight I'd rather they would all go off to Cairo or somewhere and be Teddy Boys there! But in cinemas? No!

Curious about all of this was Her Majesty the Queen, on holiday with her family in Balmoral, Scotland. Obviously keeping an eye on events as towns and cities around her realm started to ban *Rock Around the Clock*, she was intrigued. Settling down with her popcorn to watch Humphrey Bogart in *The Caine Mutiny*, she requested that a copy of *Rock Around the Clock* be dispatched by British Rail from London for her to watch as well. One can only imagine Her Majesty and the Duke jiving in the Palace, but who knows? They might have torn the place up!

Tommy Steele, on the path to 'all-round entertainer', gave his opinions on the teenage disturbances that were becoming rampant:

> A lot of adults get the needle that the teenagers do what they used to do. Once upon a time the teenagers would come home from school and have their tea, listen to the wireless, probably *Variety Bandbox* like I used to. Or a Sunday play following that and then it was off to bed. Parents then had the night to go off and see a play in the West End or go down to the Finsbury Park Empire. Well, now it's completely reversed. The parents are looking at the television and the teenagers are going out to the theatres. And I think when you get a lot of criticism that it's getting out of hand I think it's because the parents are getting a little envious that their sons and daughters are doing what they used to do and what they don't want to do anymore.

The two generations, parents and their teenage children, were becoming strangers to one and other. Everyone over the age of 19 seemed desperate to see the back of rock and roll, but it just kept rolling on... the 'oldies' just couldn't figure out what the lyrics of '*Be-Bop-A-Lula*' or '*Tutti Frutti*' were all about!

The music industry was waiting for the fad to pass. Records were released that attempted to extract the urine, the ludicrous '*Barking Dog Boogie*' by The Singing Dogs received favourable airplay. Stan Freberg did a humorous skit on '*Heartbreak Hotel*' in the States. As Elvis, Little Richard and all the British boys continued to record hit records and make headlines, a magazine aimed at the girls called *Marilyn* was launched. On the cover of the first issue was a photograph of Big Band singer Frankie Vaughan, who was riding high in the charts with '*Green Door*'. Included as a bonus for *Marilyn*'s readers was Frankie's 'Book of Songs for Sweethearts'.

Clem:

> Rock and roll was an escape from reality. Our group was doing well, earning a bit of money and building up a following. Terry Kennedy heard about a coffee bar called the 2i's which had opened in Old Compton Street, Soho and we went along and managed to get a gig. The 2i's name came from the owners Freddie and Sammy Irani, who ran the venue until it was taken over by Ray Hunter and Paul Lincoln, an Australian wrestler known as 'Dr. Death'. Big stars from that time would often come and do shows there.

Myself and Brian Bennett of The Shadows suddenly became the house drummers and I think that's when I really started taking the music seriously. I was still working for my father at the time, but after yet another argument he fired me! It was New Year's Eve and I'd been playing at the 2i's and didn't get home until around three in the morning. I was supposed to be working in the cafe at 6! Dad came in to wake me up, I must have turned over, fell asleep again and he came back in, raging at me and that was that. I was sacked! That's when I decided to become a full-time pro.

Our group were playing twice nightly seven days a week, 7.30 to 9pm and 9.30 to 11pm. The punters paid 2/6d to get in, which also included a coffee or soft drink. And serving the drinks was a wannabe singer called Terry Nelhams. He later formed his own skiffle group The Worried Men, changed his name to Adam Faith and became famous. At the time I was keeping him in cigarettes. He was always skint. He occasionally sang with us, as did Tommy Steele. Others who stepped up with us included Tony Sheridan, who played with The Beatles in their Hamburg days, and another chap called Harry Webb who found fame as Cliff Richard.

There was standing-room only for about twenty people. A door at the back led to a narrow stairway down to the basement which had a small stage made of milk crates with planks on top of them. The cellar was lit by a couple of weak lightbulbs. There was just the one microphone and some speakers up on the wall. Lincoln and Hunter started booking skiffle groups, of which The Vipers were the first. Talent spotters and music promoters Jack Good, Larry Parnes and Don Arden were soon attracted, and The Vipers gained a record contract and had much success over the next couple of years with '*Don't You Rock Me Daddy-O*', '*I Know the Lord Laid His Hands On Me*' and '*Hey Liley, Liley Lo*' making the charts.

The 2i's and Paul Lincoln in particular was remembered by Cliff Bennett of the Rebel Rousers:

I used to go and watch Vince Taylor, Clem and all the artists there but a night I remember most was when the 2i's had a visit from a couple of 'heavies', advising Paul Lincoln that he could do with some protection. These guys were Greeks, Italians or something, trying to run a protection racket. Lincoln looked at them with disdain, picked one of them up, turned him upside down and dropped his head right onto the pavement! The other bloke ran off! We never saw them again. It was so funny, I mean, imagine trying to get protection money off Dr. Death!

Clem:

The 2i's became known as the labour exchange for musicians. There was always somebody forming a group, and many came from all over the country looking for work, Brian Rankin and Bruce Cripps from Newcastle to name but two. Brian, who became Hank Marvin and Bruce, who became Bruce Welch, like many other musicians, were scraping a living and there was a kind of kinship between us all. We were all in the same boat, getting by with what work we could get.

Bruce:

Hank and I were friends at school and in skiffle groups when we were 14. Hank was playing banjo in the Crescent City Skiffle group when I asked him to join my band The Railroaders. This was 1957. Then Chas McDevitt arrived to play a gig in Newcastle. Chas was riding high in the charts with '*Freight Train*' and we had to go and see him and his band. We learned he was going to a well known club afterwards for a drink, a place where all the stars who played the Newcastle Empire went to. We went along and managed to meet and have a chat with Chas, and he told us if we wanted to be in this business we would have to go down to London. 'Nobody gets discovered in Newcastle,' he said. So, aged 16 we left Newcastle to hopefully find our fame and fortune. First, Hank had to ask his parents. I had no problem – I didn't have any parents. My mother had died when I was five; we were living in Bognor where I was born and I was sent up north to relations. I don't know where my dad was, I only saw him half a dozen times in my life. Hank's parents weren't keen. We told them that we had entered a Talent Contest at the ABC Cinema, Edmonton in London. His dad, who bought him a Hofner Congress guitar for his 16th birthday, worked on the railways and got us cheap tickets. We arrived in the 'Smoke' with no money, nowhere to go, nowhere to stay. We came third in the contest behind a trad jazz band and a Malaysian opera singer! The manager of the cinema turned out to be a real nice guy. He asked us where we were staying. We told him we didn't have anywhere and he said he'd sort it. He phoned up a lady he knew, Mrs Bowman, who by chance was also a Geordie and told her he had two Geordie boys with nowhere to go. The other two friends who were with us in the band went home. Mrs Bowman told him to send us round – she lived in Finsbury Park – and we ended up staying there for over nine months! We had a room in her attic. The day after the contest we went looking for this place called the 2i's in Soho, which was a seedy area at the time, all-night clubs, strip clubs, smoking dens, brothels. But it was where Tommy Steele had been discovered, Terry Dene too. This would be April 1958. The 2i's in Old Compton Street was the melting pot for all the wannabes. It was a tiny place, a coffee bar with a jukebox, a frothing expresso coffee machine; we'd never seen anything like it. The stage was about a yard wide, eighteen inches high. Anybody could get up to play, the drums would be at the end, the guitars and singers crammed alongside, with the audience looking up your nose!

Hank and I asked Paul Lincoln if we could play. He told us to bring our guitars along for an audition, and if we were any good we could play for four hours a night and get paid 18/- each for our trouble. We ended up playing there every night for the next five months. We were never out of there, the atmosphere was great. People would turn up to jam. Everybody was looking to get discovered. It was where I first met Clem, Brian Bennett, Licorice Locking, Jet Harris. We were all doing Elvis, Fats Domino, Little Richard covers, rock and roll. Marvin Rainwater had a big hit at the time called 'Whole Lotta Lovin'' which was popular, and that's where Hank got his name from! We were all great mates, Clem used to take me and Hank to his mum's house to feed us sugar sandwiches; 'It'll give you energy,' she said. Apart from the sandwiches we'd also go around the Soho streets nicking apples and whatever off the market stalls.

Vince Taylor was another guy who started in the 2i's. He looked like Ricky Nelson, looked the dog's bollocks and was a great performer, but he couldn't sing, couldn't hold a note. Licorice was in his band The Playboys at the time, playing a big stand-up bass. He used to take it on the tube! Colin Hicks, Tommy Steele's brother, was also there trying to make a name for himself. He thought that because his brother could do it, so could he. But like

Vince Taylor, he couldn't sing either.

We were all self-taught, trying to learn the tricks that Buddy Holly played on guitar. Buddy was the God. He had this guitar that to our eyes looked like a spaceship! A pink Fender Strat. The Everly Brothers were also in Britain at the time, playing Gibson acoustic guitars. They looked fantastic. There was nothing like these guitars available in Britain at the time. Buddy Holly used a capo on his guitar, which we had no idea what it was.

Back at the 2i's, a little guy, who would later become a member of The Shadows, came along and asked if he could sit in. He was a drummer, he said. It was Tony Meehan. He was only 15 but he was brilliant. Then a blonde-haired guy called Jet Harris asked if he could join in. Jet looked like James Dean with his hair and collar up, real flash. He had an electric bass guitar, the first one we'd seen, and he'd also made a step up by playing with Wee Willie Harris on tour.

Clem:

> An agent called Hymie Zahl was impressed with our group, Terry Kennedy's Rock and Rollers, and asked us if we'd be interested in a six-month nationwide tour backing music hall comedian/actor Max Wall. We jumped at the chance. I was engaged to Anna by this time, and although she knew it would be six months or so on the road for me she didn't mind. Max did a skit of Bill Haley which was hilarious, introducing us to the audience as his 'Comets'. It proved to be a great experience.

Terry Kennedy passed away in New York during 1982, news that shocked but didn't surprise Clem:

> Terry was a gambler but whether that had anything to do with his demise I don't know. Going back to our days in the Fifties with the Rock and Rollers, Terry was always cheating us at cards which sounds trivial now, but he was always what we called 'ducking and diving'. I liked him, after all it was Terry who got me into the music business. You always had the feeling that he was after a deal somewhere. He was from Russell Square, a tall good-looking bloke with dark hair. Perfect for the times, perfect for the blossoming rock and roll scene in London. He was never

satisfied though, always looking for a better deal. He wasn't satisfied being just a guitarist and he went on to become a record producer. Always trying to be one step ahead, but his gambling was his downfall. I don't know what happened in New York, but it strikes me as not the sort of place to take liberties. It's funny but my dad never took to him. 'Never trust a man whose eyebrows meet in the middle,' he would say. And Terry's did. Terry was probably the most important individual in my life at that time. He was always pushing us as a band and our breakthrough in 1957, when we were signed up to support Max Wall, was as much as anything, down to Terry's persistence and belief. Max was a great bloke, very funny. He would always talk to us after a show, pointing out how we could improve, which, with hindsight, we must have listened to him too well! By the end of the tour that took us all over the country we were more popular than him. He would bring us into the show by doing his Bill Haley routine, kiss curl and tartan jacket in place and singing 'Rock Around the Clock', but by the end the crowd were shouting for more from us which was a bit embarrassing. It was clear his touring days were coming to an end. These days, notoriety is positively an advantage but back then scandal wasn't allowed, and Max had not long walked out on his wife to be with a young dancer. His antics made the headlines. As the tour progressed Moss Empires became more edgy, and in the end they wouldn't allow him to perform in any of their theatres.

The tour, promoted by Charles Tucker and advertised as a 'Variety Show', opened on March 18th at Brighton Hippodrome and was followed by March 25th Leeds Empire, April 1st Newcastle Empire, April 8th Nottingham Empire, April 15th London Metropolitan, April 22nd Finsbury Park Empire, April 29th Southsea Kings Theatre, May 13th Bristol Hippodrome, May 20th Cardiff New Theatre, May 27th Brighton Hippodrome, June 17th Edinburgh Empire, June 24th Manchester Hippodrome, July 1st Liverpool Empire, July 15th Hanley Royal, July 29th Sunderland Empire and August 12th at the York Regal.

Terry Kennedy's Rock and Rollers were on a bill comprising singing duo Anne Hart, who later married the comedian Ronnie

Corbett, and her partner Frank Potter; an acrobatic duo called Gladys and June Wilkinson, The Five Speedacs, The Six Teenagers and another acrobatic act called The Jumpin' Jax, all travelling around the country by train which meant long journeys of boredom between gigs, playing cards, getting drunk... the era of the motorway was still some way off.

Clem:

> It was during this tour that I fell off the rostrum at the back of the stage and disappeared. It was the only time in my life when I went on stage drunk. Mind you the crowd loved it, they thought it was part of the act! We did two shows a night, six days a week. Nobody worked on Sundays those days and I would always try to get home if I could to see Anna, but it was a nightmare at times trying to travel by train.

> We were on about £25 a week, which was good money. Out of that we would probably pay around 30/- a week for digs, full board. Though they weren't always as salubrious as you hoped for. Often there'd be no facilities in these digs we were booked into and we would have to look around to find a wash house in the town, usually the swimming baths, to have a shower in the morning.

Brian Bennett, then with Marty Wilde's Wildcats, tells of staying in places where there was no food after 9 o'clock; 'If there was, it would be a curled-up ham sandwich.'

Touring by road in the 1950s was equally a nightmare. Crammed into dilapidated coaches or Bedford vans with all the equipment couldn't have been much fun. Not helped either that whoever it was that sorted the schedules was obviously a sadist. Travel before the motorways appeared in Britain was along a myriad of 'A' and 'B' roads in coaches that often had no air conditioning, as Clem remembers all too well:

> You had to get a blanket to put over your knees to try and keep warm. The heating never seemed to work in those charabancs. The seats were hard and uncomfortable, and to compound matters you would regularly find yourself having to travel to one nighters from Brighton in the south to Sunderland in the north,

and then next day back south again to Cardiff or somewhere. It was ridiculous, but somehow we all accepted it as the way it was. Mind you, everything's an adventure when you're that age and we got on with it.

Not everyone accepted it though. Jazzman Chris Barber, who was a little older and wiser, rejected these crazy itineraries:

> I achieved a distinction in Geography at O Level and I wouldn't let them send me on these dreadful tours. I knew where all the places were and I refused to play Land's End one night and Aberdeen the next.

Chris may have been exaggerating on that, but he added,

> I told the agents that it was in their interests as we wouldn't be giving good shows if we were messed about. I insisted that jobs weren't miles apart, that we were booked into decent hotels and that we would have one day off every week.

Tommy Steele, recalling his time on the road:

> Everyone that goes on tour, especially one-night stands, complains that the itinerary hasn't been planned by a geographical genius. It was more like Bingo; the manager would just pull the towns out of a hat. I've done Norfolk and then Ayr the next night, and anyone who tries to get anywhere out of Norfolk is in trouble, but to get to Ayr, wow!

Cliff Bennett: 'Those days it used to take five hours to get to Birmingham from London up the A5.'

Following the Max Wall tour Clem and the boys were approached by Paul Lincoln, who was now managing Terry Dene as well as the 2i's. 'We were asked, along with bass player Brian Gregg, to become Terry's backing band,' recalls Clem. 'We were to be called the Dene Aces on a year-long tour of the Moss Empire theatres along with the Chas McDevitt Skiffle Group. As it happened, I was asked by Jet Harris at the time if I'd be interested in taking over from their drummer Terry Smart in The Drifters. I told him I was going on tour with Terry Dene and it was good pay, so I turned him down. Tony Meehan got the gig. He was later succeeded by my old mate Brian Bennett in 1961.'

Terry Dene, real name Terry Williams, was spotted by Jack Good while singing at the 2i's. Good signed him up for a show he was producing for BBC television, *Six-Five Special*, and also gained Dene a recording contract with Decca through his association with producer Dick Rowe – the same Dick who turned down The Beatles a few years later.

Six-Five Special was a massive hit. Televised live, it went out at five past six on Saturday evening, the first television show to cater for teenagers, even if it was broadcast as more of a variety show, not wanting to dive headlong into the rock and roll craze. The show was introduced by DJ Pete Murray, who coined the catchphrase 'It's time to jive... on the old Six-Five.' Terry Dene, Marty Wilde and others from the 2i's were all given an opportunity to star alongside comedians and dance band crooners. The catchy theme tune, including the frenzied lyric of 'Over the points, over the points', was played and sung by jazz trombonist Don Lang and His Frantic Five over images of a steam locomotive roaring across the Forth Bridge. 'Over the points?' It's not an expression you would hear often nowadays, and most likely it's only dedicated trainspotters who would know what it meant – basically the train passing through the signals. It was all exciting stuff, even if *Mojo* (February 1995) opined *Six-Five Special* was 'a valiant effort but regarded as pretty stiff'.

Clem:

> In that first week with The Dene Aces I earned £70 which was a lot of dough in 1957. The tour also gave me my first glimpse of true pop hysteria, and showed me what pressure and adulation can do to someone who is not ready or equipped to handle it. Terry Dene was being hailed as Britain's next answer to Elvis Presley after Tommy Steele had relinquished the title. Terry had the voice and the looks. What he didn't have was the ability to handle what was coming his way in the next two years. Terry found Decca reluctant to record him singing rock and roll, and

instead released his covers of country and western hits like Marty Robbins' '*A White Sport Coat*', which was his first single. It sold over 300,000 copies in the first seven weeks. Another Robbins cover, '*Stairway Of Love*' remained in the chart for eight weeks.

Like Elvis, who had made his film debut in *Love Me Tender* and followed it with *Loving You*, Dene and The Dene Aces also appeared on celluloid. *The Golden Disc* told the story of a young couple expanding a coffee bar to include a record shop and a recording outlet to help a young singer, and to cash in on the start of the rock and roll era. Dene sang '*C'min and Be Loved*' in the film.

Dene was also part of the entourage that embarked on a voyage to Calais promoted by Paul Lincoln, as documented by Pete Frame in his book *The Restless Generation*:

On June 1st 1957 a Rock and Roll Ferry crossed the English Channel on the *Royal Daffodil* which was described as 'more like a tub despite its noble name'. It was a 16 hour round trip from Folkestone including five hours in Calais. The first rock and roll hooligans in France. Those who made it had a good time, as did Paul Lincoln even though he lost money. The venture was called The 2i's Rock Across the Channel. The bill was as solid as it could have been with Terry Dene and the Dene Aces, Rory Blackwell and the Blackjacks, Wee Willie Harris, Leon Bell and the Bell Cats, the City Ramblers Skiffle Group, The Chas McDevitt Skiffle Group and several more.

The trip was remembered for mainly two reasons, Dene who was due to perform at Calais but was suffering from sea sickness by the time the boat had docked, and a star born with 16 year old Colin Hicks, younger brother of Tommy Steele, who was backed by the Bell Cats. Hicks was signed up by impresario Larry Parnes and his first single '*Wild Eyes and Tender Lips*' followed in November to coincide with a seven week package tour along with the usual acrobats and jugglers, plus The Most Brothers and Marty Wilde. Not everyone shared Parnes' view that he was to be the next big thing though as it was reported that Hicks was bombarded with rotten fruit on the opening night at Finsbury Park from local Teddy Boys who were immediately ejected.

Chas McDevitt:

> The trip was a bit of a disappointment as it happened. The French weren't ready for us, and they didn't know what was going on. There was nothing really organised, we literally turned up and started playing in the street. There's a film clip on YouTube showing us playing opposite a church in Calais where a wedding had just taken place. The bride and groom are looking totally bewildered as we belt out 'It Takes A Worried Man'! They could have thought we were booked as a surprise guest for their wedding entertainment or something, but I doubt it!

The popularity of skiffle had now encouraged the BBC to introduce *The Saturday Skiffle Club* on its Light Programme, with the first airing being on June 1st 1957, simultaneous to the ferry trip. The half-hour show from 10.00 to 10.30am was initially scheduled for eight weeks in place of the regular item for the past eight years, *Organ Recital* fronted by Reginald Dixon.

Saturday Skiffle Club became one of the most successful radio shows of the late 1950s, introduced by Brian Matthew, whose opening line was 'Here it is, the folksy jazz we call skiffle.' The show proved so popular it ran to 61 weeks in total before morphing into *Saturday Club* on October 4th 1958. During its run it featured over 40 skiffle groups, as well as over a dozen special guests.

Following the success of *'Freight Train'*, which reached number four in the charts, the Chas McDevitt Skiffle Group were invited over to America to appear on *The Ed Sullivan Show*.

Chas's career and interest had begun in the unlikely setting of a sanatorium in 1952. Living in Camberley after moving down from Glasgow with his parents at the beginning of the war, he contracted tuberculosis and was confined to isolation for over nine months.

Chas:

> It was while I was in there I became interested in jazz and blues and I used to write letters to Big Bill Broonzy, Sidney Bechet, Josh White and Lizzie Miles, a great New Orleans blues singer. Somebody gave me a banjo while I was there and when I came

out of hospital and went to Switzerland to recuperate, I carved myself a piece of wood with notches on it like a banjo to practice with. I formed a 'group' with some mates when I returned to England and we practiced in a church hall. The group consisted of a trumpet, trombone and banjo, though the brass players couldn't play at all! I was only just getting by after borrowing a banjo chord book off a friend who played in The High Curley Stompers on Saturday nights at a local jazz club. One night we turned up and he said to me, 'You'll have to play instead of me tonight, my banjo's broke'. I said, 'I can't do that, I can't play properly, you can borrow mine.' He said 'You've got a different banjo to me, yours is a Tenor, mine's a G.' So I was thrown in at the deep end and ended up joining them, and for a while after that the band featured two banjos before the other guy decided that we needed a bass and he took up that. That was the basis of the New Orleans-style band which also included what we called the 'Breakdown Band', when we would have a session during the interval with a washboard player, banjo, guitar and vocals. We played numbers like *'Tight Like That'* and *'Down By The Riverside'*. That's how the skiffle thing started. All our roots were in London. When that ran its course I carried on playing with the Crane River Jazz Band which was originally Ken Colyer's band.

The name 'skiffle' came about following Ken's infamous trip to New Orleans in early 1953. Joining the Merchant Navy 'to get a ride over there', Ken 'jumped' ship at Mobile and made his way to the 'Big Easy', where he hoped he'd be able to play with some of the great jazz musicians. He was later arrested after his visa had expired and placed in a cell before being sent back to Britain. It was his brother Bill Colyer who picked up on a term Ken had told him about. In between sets, the New Orleans jazz bands had what they called a 'Breakdown Band' during the interval. There were various terms for these, one was 'The Percolator Band', another was 'Skiffle'. Back in Britain, Ken Colyer's band included Dan Burley and His Skiffle Boys playing the intervals and it was Ken who adopted the name. 'That's what I'll call the music,' he said. Thus the acorn was planted to begin the craze that swept the nation.

My manager Bill Varley had recorded The Vipers and others in his studio in Denmark Street. All the groups were getting signed up except us and I asked him what was going on. He then signed us up with Oriole Records, who were based in New Bond Street. *'Freight Train'* was discovered in America where a singer called Elizabeth Cotten claimed she'd wrote it. She was the maid for Pete Seeger's family at the time. There was no copyright on the song so we published it; if we hadn't somebody else would have. There was a court case, a lot of hassle, but in the end we all had a share of it. This was before Nancy Whiskey had joined us. Prior to this we had won a skiffle contest on Radio Luxembourg six weeks running. Nancy was also on the show, and had made an impression on our record producer. After we'd recorded *'Freight Train'* he said, 'It just doesn't sound any different from anything else, how about getting a female voice on it? That girl who was in the Luxembourg contest?' When we approached Nancy she was reluctant. She was a folk singer and not particularly keen, but we persuaded her to join and we re-recorded *'Freight Train'* and it became a big hit. It could have been even bigger. Oriole was a small independent company and rare in that it had its own processing plant. The trouble was, Oriole was also concentrating on other acts. Russ Hamilton had two hits around that time on Oriole, *'Rainbow'* and *'We Will Make Love'*. Because of this, there simply weren't enough copies of *'Freight Train'* pressed. If there had been, we'd have gone to number one, but it did get us under way.

We played a gig, the 60th anniversary of the Cavern, Liverpool with Chris Farlowe and a number of Liverpool groups in January 2017. It was by coincidence that it was 60 years to the day when we played *'Freight Train'* for the first time at the Metropolitan Theatre in Edgware Road, London. Larry Grayson was the compere on the night, long before anybody had ever heard of him.

The whistling in the song came about when I thought it would add something to the record. Later, when we appeared in *The Tommy Steele Story*, we had to mime to the record and it was a bit silly.

Nancy Whiskey was alright but I had to stand there making out I was whistling and it looked ridiculous. The director said to me, 'Put some expression into it! We can't see your mouth moving', so we did another 'take' and ever since, every time I see that clip it makes me cringe. My head is bopping all over the place!

However, on the back of the success we achieved, we were invited over to America to appear on *The Ed Sullivan Show*. This was seven years before The Beatles' performance on Sullivan's show.

The viewing audience was said to have been over 45 million. The Everly Brothers were also on the show, singing *'Bye Bye Love'*. The show was a great experience, even if Sullivan was something of a square. Due to the musician union rules we had to use American players to back us up. There was only myself and Nancy Whiskey plus Marc Sharratt on washboard. The guitarist Hank Garland, who had played for Elvis, asked us how *'Freight Train'* went and as we didn't have any charts or anything I said, 'Well it goes like this – chung chung de chung...' Hank looked at us with bemusement and said, 'Are you sure?'

Marc Sharratt was insured by Lloyds to the tune of £5,000 for his fingers. It was a publicity stunt but Marc used to flatten a washboard in days, knocking the ridges out! He had a standing order with Timothy White's, the hardware store, for replacements! After a show his fingers were often pitted with zinc chips and bleeding. I had known Marc since we were kids in Camberley. He was tragically killed in a head-on car crash outside Hastings in 1991. We had just returned from a gig in Holland playing with The Searchers and others. Strange thing was, about fifteen years later his washboard and case came up for sale on eBay. I saw it and contacted the seller, a woman who lived in Welwyn Garden City, to try and find out where she had got it from, and also hopefully to buy it to give to Marc's son. The woman told me she had obtained it off a bloke whom, it seems, was working at the scrapyard where the car was taken after the crash. He had obviously snaffled the washboard and kept it. I did manage to get it back; the case still had the Chas McDevitt Skiffle Group name on it, and I was well chuffed to hand it over to Marc's boy.

Nancy was only with us for around six months which was a pity; she could have undoubtedly been an international star but she became pregnant and left. We had loads of auditions for her replacement and Shirley Douglas was the choice. Two years later me and Shirley were married, and we continued to play throughout the 1960s and 70s all over the world in cabaret, skiffle and folk clubs; the Philippines, New Zealand, Europe and America.

In 1958 I opened the Freight Train Coffee Bar in Berwick Street, had it for over ten years. It was next to the Heaven and Hell and 2i's. They were great meeting places. Kids couldn't go into pubs in those days and that's why coffee bars became popular. They were places where youngsters could just get a guitar out and play. We were often top of the bill on shows with The John Barry Seven, though John didn't like to be reminded of those days when he became famous for writing the film scores for the James Bond movies. Later, when rock and roll came in, we were supporting the stars of the day like The Beatles, Gerry and the Pacemakers, Dave Clark Five in theatres such as those at Blackpool and Morecambe. We were on the bill with Terry Dene and The Dene Aces, which included Clem, when there was a fracas in Gloucester following Terry smashing up shop windows. I remember Edna Savage, his future wife, saying to me, 'I don't really know why I'm marrying him, silly little boy.' Terry had his demons, not helped when he tried to get out of doing his National Service.

Back in Soho, the groups used to come back after playing gigs for a late night coffee and wait for their girlfriends and wives to join them, many of whom worked as dancers at the Windmill and Murray's Cabaret Club. Soho was rife with gangsters looking to gain some recompense for 'security'. There was always fights, stabbings going on in the streets of Soho at the time. Live music was provided by groups looking to showcase their talents. It's where I first met Clem. Red Reece, the drummer of our resident group, had left to join Georgie Fame and Clem stepped in. He was the best drummer around. He had this style which I called 'rockashake'. I'm not sure what he called it, but it was unique. Clem joined Shirley and I on tour for a few months before he teamed up with Colin Hicks and then later Johnny Kidd.'

Jack Good, frustrated with the BBC's restrictions and wanting to drop the sport and public-service content from *Six-Five Special* to concentrate on the music, resigned and signed up with ITV to deliver *Oh Boy!*, described as 'the perfect rock TV concept, no variety, no handicrafts moments, no stupid presenters trying to be funny, just hard and fast music with melodramatic lighting.'

Oh Boy!, hosted by Tony Hall and Jimmy Henney, went on air in September 1958. The show was scheduled on Saturday evenings from 6.00 to 6.30pm and broadcast live from the Hackney Empire, featuring Cuddly Dudley, Cliff Richard, Marty Wilde and the Dallas Boys as resident artists. Special guests included Billy Fury, Tony

Sheridan, Terry Dene and The Dene Aces, Shirley Bassey and Lonnie Donegan; US stars the Ink Spots, Conway Twitty and Brenda Lee also appeared. Solo artists were supported by a gang of jazz session men who had a hit with '*Hoots Mon*', they were called Lord Rockingham's XI, even though there were fifteen in the line up! Performers were also backed by the vocals of The Vernons Girls and Neville Taylor's Cutters. *Six-Five Special* and *Oh Boy!* were welcome additions to television's entertainment schedule. The only other show worthy of note was Val Parnell's *Sunday Night at the London Palladium* which on 2nd March 1958 clocked up its 100th performance. To celebrate the milestone the powers that be booked one of America's biggest stars who were over on tour, Buddy Holly and The Crickets.

It was the first time an American rock and roll star had been seen on British television and Buddy was received rapturously by the country's teenagers. They played three numbers: '*That'll Be The Day*', '*Oh Boy*' and '*Peggy Sue*'.

Co-starring comedian Bob Hope, ballerina Dame Alicia Markova and actor Robert Morley, Buddy's performance on *Sunday Night at the London Palladium* was recalled less-than-enthusiastically by Philip Norman in his biography *Buddy*: 'All ATV supplied was a straight-on view of the Palladium stage, containing three rather lonely looking figures in tuxedos, a double bass, a drum kit and an amplifier. The sound on all three numbers was atrocious.'

Despite the ecstatic response to Buddy's performance, whether the sound was crap or not, the show reverted to type with an array of jugglers, acrobats, ventriloquists and headline acts such as singers David Whitfield, Edmund Hockridge and The Beverley Sisters providing the pulse for Sunday night television viewers.

The Palladium had made its bow on 25th September 1955, featuring Gracie Fields singing '*The Biggest Aspidistra In The World*' and American 'singing sensation' Guy Mitchell, who gave the audience '*Chika Boom*'. The show was hosted by Tommy Trinder, whose corny catchphrase was 'You lucky people'. On one occasion when a power failure blacked out the ITV network, Trinder ad-libbed for two hours. His first words when the picture was restored were 'Welcome to Monday morning at the London Palladium'. The audience roared with laughter.

A retrospective of the show later described the format as:

> Based on Old Time Music Hall, a variety bill with an occasional bit of culture to counterbalance the mini-game show, 'Beat The Clock'. The theme tune overtured a typical show consisting of an opening chorus dance routine from the Tiller Girls, followed by a speciality or novelty act (acrobats, tumblers, mimes, puppets), and to close the first half, usually a new or up and coming act. 'Beat The Clock' made up the middle section, and the star of the show would have most of the final segment, with the finale being all the performers on the revolving stage while the credits rolled.'

The revolving stage was famously remembered for The Rolling Stones refusing to participate in what they regarded as nonsense after their appearance in 1967.

The *New Musical Express* of September 26th 1958 reported that Elvis was on the high seas in the U.S. transport ship *General Randall* en route to Germany following his induction into the U.S. Army. Keeping his fans happy was the release of his latest film, *King Creole*. The front page of the *NME* was adorned with photographs of Connie Francis, Tommy Steele, Elvis, Johnny Mathis and a group photograph of The Mudlarks and The Kalin Twins backstage at the Prince of Wales Theatre.

The Top Ten read;

1 *'Stupid Cupid'* – Connie Francis
2 *'Volare'* – Dean Martin
3 *'When'* – The Kalin Twins
4 *'Return To Me'* – Dean Martin
5 *'Fever'* – Peggy Lee
6 *'Poor Little Fool'* – Ricky Nelson
7 *'Mad Passionate Love'* – Bernard Bresslaw
8 *'Bird Dog'* – The Everly Brothers
9 *'Splish Splash'* – Charlie Drake
10 *'Endless Sleep'* – Marty Wilde

The Letters Page included a disgruntled John Waterfield from Devon complaining about Jim Dale, who was compèring BBC's *Six-Five Special*:

> What has happened to Jim Dale? This business of forgetting artist's names is a badly-used gimmick. Or is it that Jim Dale really has a bad memory and as compere can't remember the names? The first programme in the new series left a lot to be desired. I mean, it's all very well giving us new faces, but I wonder how many of these artists have had any real stage experience?

Jack Reid of Ayrshire wrote with dismay:

> I read with disgust that Elvis is recording an album of hymns in memory of his mother. Why doesn't he leave hymns to people who can sing them? I have heard his *'Peace in the Valley'* EP and if ever a record showed how not to sing religious songs, then this is it.

Advertised at the bottom of the page was The Cossor Automatic Record Player boasting a 4-speed change and the ability to load ten records, for the princely sum of 21 guineas. For the less affluent, the Fidelity Record Player was 'Sensational value at only 10 guineas'. Maybe it was, but when you could only play one record at a time, it wasn't exactly in the same league as the Fidelity or the Dansette, which still led the field.

Outside of all this a hula hoop craze was sweeping the nation and giving birth to the Health and Safety culture, following reports that a German chap had keeled over mid-swivel with a heart attack. Warnings were given from medical counsel about the danger, particularly to the neck.

Other news told of a shortage of 'single shillings', with banks running out of 'bobs'. An intricate part of life in the 1950s, the bob was needed to put in the electric meter! If the bob ran out you were up the creek, unless you had one in your pocket. Lights went out, the television went off – a real pain.

The same month, September, saw what many people say was the

first true British rock and roll record released; *'Move It'* by Cliff Richard.

Recalled by Cliff in a BBC documentary:

> I had only appeared at the 2i's for a week when EMI producer Norrie Paramor asked me down for an audition. I went along with guitarist Ian Samwell and drummer Terry Smart to Abbey Road and played a couple of songs in Studio 2. We passed the audition and Norrie recorded us playing *'Schoolboy Crush'*. On the way Ian Samwell had wrote *'Move It'* for what he hoped would be considered for the 'B' side. Norrie liked it that much he swapped it for the 'A' side, and the rest is history, as they say. A tour was set up for October and Hank Marvin and Bruce Welch were recruited in the 2i's to make up the band.

Thus began one of the longest careers in pop music history.

Bruce:

> This guy came down the 2i's dressed like a Teddy Boy, John Foster was his name. He was looking for Tony Sheridan, a guitarist he wanted to back Cliff on a forthcoming tour. John was 18, a couple of years older than us. We told him that Hank was a guitarist if he couldn't get hold of Tony. 'Fine,' he said, 'can you play the intro to Buddy Holly's *'That'll Be The Day'*?' If you could play that, you could get a job with any band! Hank duly played it and John asked if he would like to join Cliff's group. 'Only if I can have my mate along as well,' Hank said. John agreed and he took us around the corner from the 2i's to a tailor's shop in Dean Street where Cliff was upstairs getting measured up for his famous pink jacket. When we walked in he was sitting there, arms spread out. 'Can you come round to my mum's house in Cheshunt for an audition?' Cliff asked. Next day we caught the bus, which took about 40 minutes, and set our gear up in his mother's front room. Terry Smart and Ian Samwell were both there. We ran through a few numbers, passed the audition and a few weeks later we were off on a three-week tour as The Drifters supporting The Kalin Twins, who were huge at the time with their smash record *'When'*. It became apparent how good Hank was, and before long The Most Brothers, who were also on the tour, and the Kalins both asked Hank if he would play for them. The Most Brothers were Mickie

Most, then known by his real name Michael Hayes and working as a waiter in the 2i's, plus his friend Alex Murray. They gave up after a couple of years and Mickie became world-famous as a record producer recording The Animals, Donovan, Herman's Hermits and others.

Cliff had already been signed by Norrie Paramor at Columbia Records and he kept badgering him to sign us as well. Eventually Norrie invited us for an audition, and we went along to the EMI Studios in Abbey Road and carted our gear up three sets of stairs to play in his office. Not the studio. Norrie sat behind his huge oak desk to assess us. We set the drums and amps up and played a couple of songs. Hank and I both sang, we thought we were the Everly brothers, close harmonising. When we heard the tape we then realised we weren't! Anyway, whatever Norrie thought of our singing he signed us and we recorded a song for release called *'Feelin' Fine'*. Sank without trace! A second attempt came with a number Jet Harris had wrote called *'Jet Black'*. That too went down the pan. Third time lucky, and we released *'Saturday Dance'.* Again it was ignored by the public, and we were beginning to get desperate thinking, one more flop and Norrie will jettison us. It was when we were on tour again with Cliff that our luck changed. A singer/songwriter named Jerry Lordan was also on the tour and we were telling him our woes. Jerry told us, 'I've got this song if you'd like to hear it'. We sat at the back of the bus as he played this tune he called *'Apache'* on his ukelele. Well straight away we thought there was something about it and decided to record it as a last try for a hit record. We went to Norrie, and before we could say anything he told us that *'Quartermaster's Stores'* was going to be our next single. Norrie was like our dad. We weren't keen but he was the boss. We recorded *'Apache'* and *'Stores'*, two tracks in three hours, and he insisted that *'Apache'* would do for the 'B' side. We stuck our neck out and argued, and in the end he relented and said, 'OK, tell you what I'll do; I'll take the tapes home and play them to my daughters and see what they think.' And, as things turned out, his daughters agreed with us! *'Apache'* went to sell over a million records! And launch a thousand pop groups!

We discovered that this was a quirk Norrie had. When Cliff recorded *'Move It'*, Norrie wanted to put *'Schoolboy Crush'* on the 'A' side. After they were recorded and Cliff said he preferred *'Move*

It', Norrie told him he'd play it to his daughters first... We were still called The Drifters at the time, but when the American group of the same name heard about us we were informed that we'd have to change our name to something else. By now Tony and Jet had replaced Terry Smart and Ian Samwell, and Jet and Hank went off to a bar for a couple of drinks and to try to think of an alternative. A few things were bandied about before Jet said to Hank, 'You know, on stage, there's only ever one spotlight, and it's always on Cliff. We are always in the background, in his shadow.' And Hank said, 'Hey, that's a good name...'

Throughout 1958, nuclear tests were being carried out on the Pacific islands of Bikini and Christmas by the USSR, USA and Great Britain. Which could be said, with irony, as hardly seasonal joy for the locals. The tests heightened the fears felt around the globe of armageddon as the so-called 'Cold War' went up a notch.

Bob Dylan recalled his feelings in *No Direction Home*: 'We lived in fear that the big black cloud would explode, everybody would be dead. They taught us all at school to dive under the desks. We grew up with that.'

Singer Billy Joel: 'In school we had air raid drills to practice what we had to do if a bomb went off. We'd get under the desk. You were waiting for the mushroom cloud. We thought we were all going to get incinerated by nuclear weapons.'

The tests, stoking up the fears of nuclear warfare, saw the Campaign for Nuclear Disarmament (CND) formed to protest against military action that may have led to the use of atomic, chemical or biological weapons. A massive public meeting was held in London during February 1958, and the first Aldermaston march, with people marching for four days from Trafalgar Square to the Atomic Weapons Research Establishment in Aldermaston, Berkshire, was held on 4-7 April, attracting great attention. The CND symbol was soon to be seen everywhere. From the outset people from all sections of society were involved – MPs, beatniks, jazz musicians, shopkeepers, the odd priest.

Ignoring the fuss over a possible nuclear war, impresario Larry

Parnes began to build his 'stable of stars', rechristening them with dubious stage names and sending them out on 'Package Tours'. Reg Smith, Ronald Wycherley and Roy Taylor became Marty Wilde, Billy Fury and Vince Eager respectively, to name but three. Mostly all accepted the aliases apart from Joe Brown who, when told by Parnes he was going to be known as Elmer Twitch, told him where to shove his name!

Vince Eager was inspired when he heard Lonnie Donegan's '*Rock Island Line*' being played at the local cinema between films and the next day he went out and bought it. Then he formed a band along with Brian 'Licorice' Locking, who would later become bass player with The Shadows:

> I made Licorice a tea chest bass, and on November 24th 1957 we entered a skiffle talent contest in London which was filmed for television. The next day I went to the 2i's and asked manager Tom Littlewood if we could get up and play. The place was packed. He told us to join the queue of people wanting to play, and then I told him cheekily that we were on TV just the night before. We promptly went to the front of the queue and ended up playing three sets through the night. He paid us with a crate of coke and a packet of Blue Riband biscuits! Tom got us fixed up to play a show in Coventry supporting Marty Wilde and the Wildcats. Larry Parnes was there and was sufficiently impressed to sign us. Dickie Pride, Marty, Johnny Gentle were already there; Billy Fury would join later. Larry, who had renamed all these boys, would do the same for me. Roy Taylor may have been a good name for an actor, but not for a rock star! 'You seemed eager,' he said to me, 'so we'll go with that as a surname.' I suggested Vince as a forename as I was a big fan of Gene Vincent and also it was my brother's middle name. Vince Eager sounded more like it, he agreed.

> Parnes contacted Dick Rowe at Decca and gained a recording session for our group and we recorded five songs. On the back of this we joined his 'package tour' and discovered what hard work was! He had us travelling all over the country on a ridiculous schedule in an old bus. It was arduous, tough. Clem Cattini will tell you about driving down from Scotland after a show all the way to the Isle of Wight! This was long before the M1 and

other motorways were built. We arrived with about an hour to spare, exhausted and starving. So much so that Clem bought a bag of chips and ate them off his Tom-Tom! There was a great camaraderie amongst us all. Rivals on stage maybe, all trying to do better, but we were great mates off it. Dickie Pride was the best, he was a great singer, a jazz fan. He was different to the rest of us in that he used to go to the jazz dens and hang out with the jazz players who were all generally heavy into booze and drugs. Unfortunately Dickie got caught up with that which was his downfall. Very sad.

Parnes added Terry Dene and The Dene Aces to his roster and had them working virtually non-stop too, throughout the early months of 1958. The itinerary began on January 6th with a week's residency at the Taunton Gaumont. The show included Chas McDevitt and Shirley Douglas, Miki and Griff, The Two Morlands, Dave Gray – described as 'always gay' – Val and Laurie Aubrey, described as an 'Artistry act', and Larry Grayson the compere. February 9th saw the show at the Tunbridge Wells Embassy, with Wee Willie Harris and The Les Hobeaux Skiffle Group. February 10th at Peterborough Embassy, February 16th at Guildford Odeon with The Worried Men Skiffle Group, The Cossacks and compere/comedian Zom.

As with many 18-year-olds, Terry Dene was faced with the prospect of receiving his 'call up papers' for National Service which, because of his status and fame, was well documented in the press.

Clem:

This coincided with the first time I was on the road with a real rock band. The problem was Terry became a political pawn for the government over the National Service that was everyone's duty at the time. Terry was one of our best rock and roll singers, though he tried too hard to sound like Elvis. Great singer, great voice, but of course he had his problems. On top of the adulation of being a star and his battle to stay out of the army, he married his girlfriend, Edna Savage. It all got too much for him and he turned to the bottle for his escape and couldn't really handle it. He was being pulled every which way, the only time he seemed at ease was on stage. Off stage he was always boozed up. By nature he was quiet, but once he had a few drinks he was transformed. He turned into a nasty character. I remember one night in Edinburgh when it was freezing cold, he was on a binge and he tried to run away from it all, in his vest and underpants! I ran after him and dragged him back to our hotel. Another time he tried to stab a comedian who was on tour with us. He was only trying to give him some advice and help. But he was a nervous breakdown waiting to happen. He was unnerved by all the attention. The rest of the band loved it but Terry found it overwhelming, as if he couldn't understand all that was going on around him. It was an eye-opening experience for me, I loved it. One occasion in Dublin was when we returned to our hotel after a show and thousands of kids were congregated outside shouting for Terry and wanting him to sing. We persuaded him to go out on the balcony and sing 'White Sport Coat', which he did, but he was totally baffled by it all.

The Dene Aces' itinerary saw them on May 19th at Hanley Theatre Royal on a bill featuring Barry Anthony (The Explosive Spark), Sonny Roy (The Funny Boy), Roy Rivers (Music on Wheels), Ronnie Collis (Tap Happy), The McKinnon Sisters (Dance Time) and the Theatre Royal Orchestra. June 9th at Birmingham Hippodrome, June 16th Liverpool Empire, June 23rd Finsbury Park Empire, June 30th Leicester Empire, July 21st Glasgow Empire, and July 28th at Chiswick Empire.

Terry Dene was duly conscripted into National Service and expected to report to Winchester Barracks on July 7th, but his call up was deferred until contractual commitments of the Larry Parnes tour had been completed. Dene's father had been an army officer for the King's Royal Rifles Regiment stationed in Winchester, and Terry was determined to join the army no matter what and to honour his father, who during his service in India had also proudly taken part in Gandhi's security force.

Variety agent Hyman Zahl saw this as an opportunity to glorify Terry's name and career by having a preview of the camp a week prior to him going in, and together with the newspapers arranged for Terry's call-up to be filmed and photographed. Everyone welcomed the idea, including the military, but Terry thought it was a bad idea. When had it ever been heard of a new recruit having a preview of the camp? Not even Royalty had received that red carpet treatment.

Terry felt uneasy and protested, but Zhal had already made the arrangements, explaining that the press were threatening to ruin his career if he didn't go ahead with it. He had no choice. He had a horrible feeling that the objective of the whole thing would end up falling flat on its ass. Everyone present started to realise the animosity Terry would have to face as a result of this publicity stunt, as the shouted threats of both the regulars and the new recruits were now making it clear what Terry's eight weeks' basic training programme was going to be like.

That night in the overcrowded dormitory, where the two long rows of beds were divided by a stretch of corridor, all the hype gone, lights out, the hostility in, Terry laid awake waiting for the threats to materialise, but before they could the corporal was by his side explaining: 'Terry you're not safe here. Come with me.'

He was taken to the corporal's quarters, where he was stationed for the rest of the night. Over the next two days he was transferred to Netley Hospital where he was kept 'under observation' for another two weeks. By this time, with the press haunting him, the authorities were trying to decide what to do with him. They wanted to keep control of the situation, so they sent him to a civilian hospital where he remained for nearly eight weeks. Although it was an open hospital, he was still under military supervision. After two months he was discharged.

He had never entered the barracks again and never really served the service he had intended to serve. Terry was furious, but before he left he was offered a pension for life and when he refused the Sergeant asked him: 'Do you think you will get your career back?' Terry replied: 'You tell me, Sir.'

Before making his comeback with The Dene Aces on a tour which included his wife Edna, Peter Quinton, Hal Roach, Margo and June, Fred Lovelle, Georgette and The Miston Juniors, Terry was a surprise guest on a show starring Dickie Valentine at the Majestic Theatre,

Derby.

Hostility was in the air from the word go after his army fiasco, from disgruntled guys of the same age, the Teddy Boys, who were due to be 'called up' for their own National Service.

On hand to report was the *NME*'s Tony Keniston:

> Terry Dene didn't hear the boos; they booed him, but Terry Dene, making his stage comeback, did not hear! He was making too much noise himself. I travelled to Derby to see one of the most exciting concerts of my life. Backstage the air was electric. Tension was at a crescendo. Dickie Valentine, the star of the show, had not been told until three days before that Dene had been booked as a guest. Terry spent the afternoon before the show nervously fingering his guitar. Every now and then he burst into song and really let rip. There were no temperamental outbursts. He rehearsed with his reformed Dene Aces and made some last-minute changes to his act. The minutes ticked by. Terry remained cool. Outside the cinema, teenagers clamoured at the doors. The first house went as smoothly as Dene's first day in the army. There were even five Redcaps standing by to assist the local police in case of any disturbance. Before he went on, Terry confessed, 'I feel a bit shaky'. Next minute he was shaking, and the girls screamed for more at the end of his act. Singing even better than before his career was interrupted, he rocked out seven numbers. These included the most appropriate '*How Do You Think I Feel?*' When he came off stage that was just the question I was waiting to ask him. How did he feel? 'Pretty good,' he said, stripping off his shirt and rubbing his back with a towel. 'In fact, that was about the best reception I've ever had. I've got a lot of my confidence back now.'

> That was lucky – because he needed it. The second house – like his second day in the army – did not go as smoothly.

> In the auditorium the girls screamed with delight, while the boys shouted insults. Terry, the microphone on his side, whipped himself into a frenzy. The audience couldn't hear him and he couldn't hear them. The biggest battle of Terry's career, out of the army just a month – he won. I don't know how he felt after that, but he looked bewildered. 'I didn't hear any cat calls or booing. Anyway, they've booed before. I know they joined in the hand-clapping, that was good. I think they still like me.'

Frankly, so do I. There was a minority in the audiences who had come with the intention of making trouble.

In their dressing room between shows I talked to Terry's group, The Dene Aces. They were all grateful to me for enquiring after their health, because they discovered a mutual affinity. They were all turned down by medical boards for military service! Clem Cattini told me, 'Marty's (Wilde) feet haven't got a thing on mine.' Clem didn't take off his black and white embroidered socks to prove it, but it did prompt guitarist Tony Eagleton to remark that it was 'something serious' that kept him out of the army. Brian Gregg was also rejected. They didn't tell him why, and he didn't stop to ask. At this point they discovered they were all Grade 4, which sounded like tins of salmon to me, and went to the pub over the road to celebrate.

Dickie Valentine was less than impressed on how proceedings went on the night. On his first solo tour since he left the Ted Heath Band he said 'It's ridiculous, it's hardly fair on people like Billy Anthony and myself who've been entertaining all our lives. Why should one last-minute inclusion on the bill cause us so much anxiety? Even after Terry's stormy spot the crowd weren't very kind to the rest of us. They never settled down.'

Brian Gregg watched everything go wrong for his friend on the tour, which started in Bristol on September 1st, followed by Sheffield on the 8th and a tour of Ireland which saw them at Rush Palladium Ballroom on the 14th, Sligo 15th, 16th Londonderry, 17th Belfast, 18th Waterford, 19th at Arklow, and week-long residencies in Cardiff, Bradford and Chester, and appearing on BBC's *Saturday Club* on October 4th with Humphrey Lyttelton and Johnny Duncan.

'Terry was brought up in London and he wasn't evacuated during the war. It made him very insecure. He should never have gone into the army, conscription was coming to an end and they were worried in case youngsters wouldn't go in the army, so they put Terry in. The other soldiers gave him a hard time. On tour, police were regularly at the front of the stage to keep the soldiers from the local Barracks getting to him.'

Terry Dene himself recalled to broadcaster Spencer Leigh: 'There were fights nearly every night. There were death threats and I had to be hustled in and out of hotels and theatres. I had a great band with Brian Gregg and Clem Cattini. It was really electric and we played to packed audiences everywhere.'

Brian Gregg: 'We came out of a place behind a cinema one night and there were Teds waiting for us and we got hammered. Clem was a big guy who saved the day with his drum stand. They let the handbrake off the van once and it crashed into a car I was sitting in with my girlfriend. The car was a write off. They nearly killed us and they were definitely out to get Terry.'

Joe Brown: 'I did one show with Terry, which was absolutely frightening. Terry was a nice boy but the Teddy Boys wouldn't accept that. They thought it was awful that he wouldn't go in the army. We did a show at Southend and they tried to get to us by battering the stage door down with a telegraph pole they had ripped out! We were sitting backstage terrified. They had to call the dogs to get them off. I got paid ten bob for the evening.'

Clem:

> Ah, the van! We had the name Terry Dene and the Dene Aces plastered all over it. That was probably the worst thing we could have done. Every time we went back to it after a show, it was smashed up! The Teddy Boys took their anger out of their girlfriends screaming and getting excited over us by attacking the van. The other memory I have of that was when I was driving it down for a show in Bath and the fog was a real pea souper. Couldn't see a thing. Terry got out and walked in front of us to guide me. When he got back in he was completely white! Iced up!

> Another time I found myself in trouble was after Terry had bought a Humber Super Snipe car, the dog's bollocks of a car. Terry bought it even though he couldn't drive, or even had a licence. He asked me if I would drive it. We were going to Stoke-on-Trent and I inadvertently went up a one-way-street the wrong way. The police pulled me over and the copper asked me, 'Do you realise you've just gone up a one-way street the wrong way?' I said to him, being smart, 'Well I was going the one way!' 'Didn't you see the arrows?' he asked. 'To be honest with you officer, I didn't even see the Indians!'

It was a good laugh but he didn't see the funny side and I ended up being booked and having to go to court. Making matters worse was that it turned out the car wasn't insured either. Besides that, when the judge read out out a list of previous convictions, they were all my dad's! We both have the same name. I explained to the judge that I must have been about 5 when they were committed! Everyone in the court thought the whole thing was hilarious. He fined me £10 for the indiscretions and another tenner for being funny!

Rock and Roll fans everywhere were in shock with the news that Buddy Holly, Ritchie Valens and the Big Bopper had been killed in a plane crash in February 1959. Holly had enjoyed great success on his British tour the previous year, compered by comedian Des O'Connor, packing theatres out across the land.

Des recalled an incident in a documentary about the tour: 'We were relaxing after one of the shows when a brick came flying through the dressing room window, luckily missing everyone and landed in the middle of the floor. I picked the brick up and saw an autograph book tied to it. 'This must be for you,' I said, handing the book to Buddy. 'I guess the brick is for me!''

June 1st 1959 saw the debut of a BBC television show that became an enduring favourite with pop fans, *Juke Box Jury*. Broadcast live from the TV theatre in Shepherd's Bush the signature tune of the show was John Barry's '*Hit and Miss*'.

The show, inspired by the jukeboxes that graced coffee bars and cafés, was hosted by David Jacobs with a panel of celebrities, DJ Pete Murray, singer Alma Cogan, TV presenter Susan Stranks and singer Gary Miller passing judgement on the chances of a latest record release. Judging them a hit or a miss by pressing the appropriate sound effect button – a buzzer for a hit and a hooter for a miss. Occasionally one of the week's featured recording artists would appear from behind the scenes to create a bit of embarrassment if their record had been deemed a miss. The show became essential Saturday night viewing for years.

Jukeboxes were now a familiar sight in every good coffee bar.

Marty Wilde recalls the impact they made: 'If coffee bars were the temples of the youth, jukeboxes were the altars. With their ability to play at a high volume and fantastic bass response, they made it possible for people to hear rock and roll as it was meant to be heard.'

They weren't appreciated everywhere, all the same. A report in the South Wales newspaper the *Penarth Times* told of how the arrival of a jukebox in the town caused a sensation. An editorial asked the public's view on the matter. Some were for it, though many more were against: 'It was the opening the doors to Sodom and Gomorrah they feared.'

1959 was a big year, for many reasons. Clem tied the knot with Anna, getting married at St Peter's Italian Church in Clerkenwell, with Terry Dene and Edna Savage in attendance. The Dene Aces then split up.

Clem:

> The work was drying up. We had returned from Sweden where we had played a gig without Terry, because he'd gone missing! It was at the venue on the island of Djurgården in Stockholm. He disappeared and we had to do the show without him. It wasn't the first time Terry had done that but anyway, the usual thing in this business, one day you're a star and the next you're deemed passé. Being newly-married, I needed a steady income. So it was back to the 2i's again looking for work. It was stressful, because of the uncertainty of the business, you didn't know when you'd be working next or for how long. Brian Gregg and myself played a couple of gigs with The Playboys for Vince Taylor, and then I joined Chas McDevitt and Shirley Douglas's backing group for three months. It wasn't exactly great money, but it was something. Me and Anna were living with my parents at the time and I had also been to see the doctor because I was feeling run down. He told me to pack it all in! I was a smoker back then, everywhere you went there was smoke and people smoking. I was frequently working late and not getting home until 3 or 4 in the morning, the lifestyle was playing havoc with my health. If we did have to stay overnight after a gig somewhere it would be in the bus; we called it the 'Timpson Hotel' after the name of the bus company that ran us around!

Vince Taylor was arguably an underrated British Rock and Roll star, probably because nobody was sure where he came from! It was generally accepted that Vince was an American and his act was based on Gene Vincent, but Clem revealed; 'Vince was a Yankee from Isleworth!' adding, 'He was a great performer with a good stage presence but he was a bit mad!' A view shared by Cliff Bennett: 'I used to love to watch Vince, but I have to say, he wasn't a great singer.' Which was also the view of Playboy drummer Brian Bennett: 'Vince was amazing but he couldn't sing in tune, keep time... but he was some performer!'

'A memory I have of working with Vince Taylor has nothing to do with the music,' said Clem. 'We were playing somewhere down south and had some time to kill. Brian Gregg suggested we filled it by going horse riding! He knew this woman with horses, so off we went and when she saw us she said to Brian, 'I have a horse for thee', but looking at me – I was around 17 stone at the time – she said, 'I don't have one for 'e'. And that was the start and end of any aspirations I had for a cowboy career!'

Taylor's real name was Brian Maurice Holden. His family had emigrated to America when he was seven. In 1955 his sister Sheila married Joe Barbera, and as a result the family moved to California. Maurice was a big fan of Gene Vincent and Elvis Presley, both influencing him to become a rock and roll singer. Joe Barbera became Maurice's manager, went on a business trip to London, and took him along. First stop was the 2i's coffee bar where Maurice saw Tommy Steele playing, and he also met drummer Tony Meehan and bass player Tex Makins there. They formed a band, calling themselves The Playboys, and legend has it that whilst smoking a packet of Pall Mall cigarettes Maurice noticed the phrase, 'In hoc signo vinces' – and decided on the new stage name of Vince Taylor. Believe that if you will!

Vince Taylor's first singles for Parlophone, '*I Like Love*' and '*Right Behind You Baby*' were released in 1958, followed several months later by '*Pledgin' My Love*' backed with '*Brand New Cadillac*' which was banned by the BBC because of advertising, even though Cadillacs were not available in the UK!

For Clem, things took a turn for the better when Larry Parnes came calling again, looking to put a band together to back Vince Eager, Billy Fury, Dickie Pride, Duffy Power, Johnny Gentle and co.

Along with Brian Gregg, they became members of The Beat Boys, which also included piano player Georgie Fame.

Clem:

> 'A night I'll never forget was when we played at the Trocadero, Elephant and Castle with Vince Eager. There was an area in front of the stage which was an orchestra pit. From the stage you couldn't see hardly anything because of the footlights, you couldn't see the audience because you were blinded. During one number Vince went too near to the edge of the stage and tumbled right into the pit! We all cracked up laughing, looked down and saw Vince holding his ankle, which he'd sprained quite badly. Feeling a right plum he tried to climb back up, it was a near six foot drop, and he grabbed hold of one of the footlights which was red hot and he burnt his hands! And fell back down again! Somebody eventually gave him a hand to get back on stage and the show carried on! Vince was a real trooper!

The opening of the M1 motorway, stretching from Watford to Rugby, by Transport Minister Ernest Marples in November 1959 was greeted with a fanfare of excitement, especially from pop groups! For bands playing up north the journeys to the gigs were stripped of a couple of hours. Standing on a bridge to watch the first cars fly by Marples was said to be aghast and heard to shout, 'Look at them, the fools, they're going to kill themselves!' An observer reported, 'Jaguars and Bentley were the first to show, followed by a wide range of bangers. Cars were being hammered by their owners, bits of cars were falling off, cars were littering the hard shoulders. Breakdown services had their hands full.' Northamptonshire Road Safety Officer Mr. H. Valvova added: 'In the first 24 hours over 100 vehicles had broken down, showing up the weakness in British-made cars.'

Clem:

The M1 made a real difference when going up north and the motorway cafes became great meeting places for the bands. The Blue Boar at Watford Gap near Northampton was the place. You would see everyone in there, going or coming back from gigs, sharing stories, it was a great time. There was a woman working at the Blue Boar who was a big fan of Johnny Kidd and The Pirates. She always gave us extra chips and only charged us half price! Brilliant. A café called Jack's Hill on the A1, the Great North Road, was less than memorable though. They used to give you a ticket there when you ordered your meal and they would shout the number out when it was ready. This particular time the guy who was doing the cooking, I hesitate to call him a chef, shouted out '54' – and I couldn't resist it, I shouted 'House!' I thought it was a scream but he didn't, shouting back, 'Get out!' Obviously he lacked a sense of humour!'

4

Shakin' All Over

'In 1960 British pop was in a critical condition. Rock and Roll had been given a suit and tie and invited onto the variety circuit' – John Peel in the 1990s TV series *Rock Family Trees*.

Peel was mourning the passing of Rock and Roll as he saw it. Elvis returning from the army as an 'all-round entertainer'; the tragic deaths of Buddy Holly and Eddie Cochran. Jerry Lee Lewis banned from the UK after the government discovered that his wife Myra, accompanying him on tour, was his 13-year-old cousin. With Little Richard finding the Lord and Chuck Berry locked up following allegations of his transportation of a 14-year-old girl across state lines for allegedly 'immoral purposes', you can see why Peel was in dismay. However, the picture wasn't as bad as the legendary DJ painted. The Everly Brothers, Roy Orbison and Duane Eddy were all still prominent, and in Blighty there were some great records being made. The Shadows' *'Apache'* and one of the greatest British Rock and Roll records of all time, *'Shakin' All Over'*, featuring Clem Cattini shone through, lighting up an otherwise dull world.

Emile Ford's *'What Do You Want To Make Those Eyes At Me For?'* claimed the distinction of being the first number one record of the 1960s, and by a strange quirk of chart history the second number one was an abridged version of Emile's hit called *'What Do You Want?'* A question Adam Faith hadn't not long before been asking his customers in the 2i's Coffee Bar. Another 'quirk' or useless bit of information, call it what you will, came about this year with two records featuring Shadows guitarist Bruce Welch. *'Please Don't*

Tease' by Cliff and The Shadows, co-written by Bruce, was knocked off the top of the charts by the band's massive instrumental hit *'Apache'*. Thus Bruce knocked himself off the number one spot!

Cliff and The Shadows' popularity was such that their shows were now often accompanied with a cacophony of noise and scenes of hysteria, with teenagers in a frenzy of excitement not witnessed in Britain since the days of Terry Dene.

Bruce Welch:

> The screams became so bad we couldn't hear ourselves think, never mind play. It was a situation that needed rectifying. In this business, when you're starting off you get nothing. When we made our first appearance with Cliff on television's *Sunday Night at the London Palladium*, Vox asked us if we wanted to use their AC15 amps. They looked good but we couldn't hear a thing we were playing. There were near riots everywhere we played with the kids screaming, this was long before Beatlemania. Sometimes I would sidle up to Cliff on stage and say 'Let's have a riot', and all he had to do was swivel his hips and away they would go! After a time Hank asked Vox if they could make a better amp and they eventually came up with the AC30, which became the standard amp for all the groups for years after. Because of our success we were given spare amps, guitars. On tour we would do two shows nightly which was hard work, one nighters all over the country. The lifestyle was tiring, but when you're young it doesn't matter, it's all fun. Our sets were only around 20 minutes long. When we were touring in later years, 'The Final Tours' of the '90s and 2000s, we were playing nearly two and half hours! It used to make me think; we'd be on stage for around quarter of an hour, and have played seven or eight hits! They were all about two minutes long. We had to go through virtually our whole repertoire!
>
> Our trademark Fender guitars came about when Hank said to Cliff that he wanted one like his idol Buddy Holly. We managed to get hold of a catalogue from somewhere, and in the middle page spread was a pink Fender Stratocaster looking like it was something from Mars. There was just nothing like it over here. Cliff ordered one and it came all the way from California. Which might as well have been on Mars those days! It took months! I got the second one a little while later.

During the early months of 1960 the charts included hits by Russ Conway, Michael Holliday and Anthony Newley plus hits by young rockers Billy Fury and Marty Wilde, doubtless helped by travelling the country on Larry Parnes' infamous 'Package Tours'. The impresario's first tour of the Sixties featured American rock and roll icons Eddie Cochran and Gene Vincent on a bill with homegrown stars Vince Eager, Joe Brown, The Beat Boys and Marty Wilde's group The Wildcats, available because of Marty's commitment to the stage musical *Bye Bye Birdie*.

21-year-old Cochran made a huge impression on the tour, which started at Ipswich Gaumont, none more so than on Wildcat guitarist Big Jim Sullivan, who recalled: 'The Wildcats played virtually the whole tour, including a slot on radio's *Saturday Club* and television's *Boy Meets Girl*. When Eddie came into the rehearsal room, opened his guitar case, took out his orange Gretsch guitar and started playing some Chet Atkins stuff, then rock and roll, blues, we were awe struck.'

Clem, on drums with The Beat Boys:

> Eddie was a great guitarist and a great singer, he could even play the drums. He told us in fact that he played the drums on his massive hit '*C'mon Everybody*'. Before he came on stage at the Gaumont we all lined up and formed an archway for him to walk through. The guitars and me with my drumsticks held high. It was brilliant! Gene Vincent though was a different animal. He was the typical brash American. Loud, and to be honest, a real nasty person. He seemed to be forever high on drugs, drink, or anything he could get his hands on! I actually stepped in one time when I thought he was going to kill Johnny Kidd. It was at Wolverhampton Town Hall. Johnny used to love to wear leather gear, it was part of his image and act. Gene Vincent thought he was a cheap imitation of him and accused him of that when he came into the dressing room. He was clearly up to his eyeballs on something and lunged at Johnny with a knife in his hand. As he did I managed to grab hold of Vincent and kept him away. He was too doped up to do anything about it.

Singer Jess Conrad was equally impressed with Cochran and

Vincent as his friend Bip Wetherell, Tornados' keyboard player, tells:

> Both Eddie and Gene had an impact on Jess, who was of course famous for his sartorial elegance and even his best-known hit was a thing called '*My Pullover*', which dented the lower reaches of the charts in 1961. Even if it was ungraciously voted sixth in a 'Worst Records of All Time' poll issued in 1978, which Jess is quite proud of! More importantly, prior to this sartorial foray into the charts, Jess laid claim to pioneering a certain denim legend in Britain. When Gene Vincent and Eddie Cochran arrived here, home-grown rock stars, expected to wear dress suits when 'on duty', were amazed to find the Americans wearing shabby blue canvas trousers. When challenged by the Brits they explained they were known as denim jeans – Wranglers to be specific. Spotting a chance to leapfrog to the forefront of a new fashion, Jess and guitarist Joe Brown each promptly went out and bought a pair of canvas dungarees, cut the bib and braces part of the garment off, buckled a black belt around their waist and stepped out wearing the latest must have garment from the States – namely blue jeans.

Joe Brown: 'Our tour manager Hal Carter used to organise the getaways after the gigs. One night he was waiting with the car engine running, a big Humber it was, and he employed two guys to act as decoys to attract the fans in the opposite direction. For some reason the ploy failed and the fans spotted Gene and Eddie and raced after them. I climbed into the back of the car alongside Eddie, Gene was in the front. Next thing, the fans have opened the door, screaming and yelling, Hal's revving the engine and all of a sudden, we're off... and Gene's lost his pants! The kids had ripped them off! We were staying in a posh hotel in Leeds and we walked in with Gene in just his underpants, a leg iron and a dirty old t-shirt!'

Vernons Girl Sheila Bruce: 'I went to jelly when I saw Eddie Cochran. He was a beautifully-tanned blonde-haired boy with a brown leather bomber jacket on, like the American Air Force, he looked fantastic. Gene Vincent was different. He frightened the hell out of me. He was obviously a very sullen guy, a complex character and not one that anybody really got to know. I was always worried about him.'

Hal Carter: 'Gene used to carry a gun and a knife around with him, which he called Henry. He would say to people, 'Do you want to meet Henry?' and would pull out his knife. He had a street-gang mentality, and I remember one night coming back from Ipswich when he terrorised the tour bus. He ripped the bass player's suit and five of us jumped off at the lights in Romford, even though we lived in north London.'

Vincent was Cliff Bennett's idol, but the singer from West Drayton was taken aback when he met him for the first time in Hamburg with the Rebel Rousers. 'It was our first time in Germany, December 1961,' Cliff recalls. 'I was thrilled to be meeting Gene Vincent. And then when I walked into the dressing room, the first thing he did was to pull a gun on me! It was a Luger. 'You've been messin' with my Margy!' he snarled. Or words to that effect! I crapped myself: 'What? Who's Margy?' My life was passing through me! Margy was Vincent's wife who I'd never seen before, never mind met. Luckily Peter Grant, Gene's road manager was there. Peter was a big guy, about 25 stone, an ex-wrestler who later became manager of Led Zeppelin. He glared at Gene Vincent and said, 'Sit down you c*** before I give you a slap! Cliff Bennett doesn't know your effin' wife... Shut the f*** up and put that gun away!'

'Gene was a bit of a loony,' agreed Joe Brown, 'but I never saw him harm anybody. Great performer though. He was very funny. You never knew what he was going to do. He'd hit the chord of E, and would go 'Wellll...' and you'd see his eyes go blank! And you'd know he wasn't sure if he was going to sing *Be Bop A Lula* or *The Road Is Rockin''* – they all started the same!'

Joe Moretti, who played the lead guitar on Johnny Kidd's *Shakin' All Over*, was also on the tour, but his recall had more to do with promoter Larry Parnes, discovering the entrepreneur's reputation for being parsimonious when he gave him £7 to go to Italy for a television date, but not enough for a return ticket! Joe had to sell his guitar to get home! For the Cochran/Vincent tour he borrowed a Fender Telecaster but, to his dismay, Vincent crashed into him on stage and broke it!

Vince Eager: 'They were all one-night stands, rarely did we have a night off. We were hopping all over the place, it was one of Parnes' typical tours. You could be in Plymouth one day, Glasgow the next day, then Southampton. To hell with the artists, they had to get on with it. We'd travel by coach, by train if the distance was too far. That was when we had more contact with Eddie and Gene, as we'd go up to their car and get the guitars out.'

Joe Brown: 'They travelled in the first-class compartment, Vince and the rest of us were all stuffed in the back! When the ticket collector came round he slung us all out!'

Hal Carter: 'Gene used to drink all the time, but Eddie, who was homesick, spent a fortune on phoning his mum in America. He'd be on the phone for over an hour, two sometimes, on the hotel phone! And we never realised in those days that the hotel would charge you twice as much as you would pay from a phone box. We had a situation at Leeds when Eddie was drunk as a Lord and we had to get him dressed, drive him to the theatre and take him into his dressing room. We gave him some black coffee, then laid him out on the floor and put a leather bag under his head for a pillow. He looked like he was dead on a slab! He was gone. We told the comedian to go on first and then we put the guitar round Eddie's neck, plugged it in to the amp, then when the mic came up through the floor on stage, we propped Eddie up against it for him to have something to hold on to so he wouldn't fall over!'

As the tour progressed, Eddie confessed that he was missing his girlfriend Sharon Sheeley. It didn't help that the tour happened to occur during the first anniversary of Buddy Holly's death. Eddie had wrote a song for Buddy and his two partners in the plane crash, Big Bopper and Ritchie Valens. Titled *'Three Stars'*, it was a heart-rendering tribute. Sinking into the oblivion of bourbon by the day, Eddie's depression still didn't lighten much when Sharon came over from the States. He decided to take a break and head home to see his family in Oklahoma at Easter. First though was the gig at Bristol Hippodrome, recalled by actor Peter Bowles: 'I used to go and see all the rock and roll stars whenever I could. I was appearing at the Old

Vic when Eddie and Gene came over. I went to see the show which, of course, turned out to be Eddie's last. When he came on, the stage was in complete darkness and the spotlight came on as the music started... but it was on his bum – he was wearing a pair of tight-fitting red leather trousers, never seen before. And the spotlight was just on his backside, gyrating. This was wicked. Sexy. The audience was screaming. The other thing I particularly remember about his performance was that at one point he said to the audience, 'I'm gonna do something I've never done before. I've never done this before and I'm gonna do it now. I'm a' gonna do it for you. I'm gonna... I'm gonna...' And we all thought, my God, he's going to drop his trousers! And he said 'I'm a' gonna... smile!' The audience went absolutely mad!'

The tour ended in tragedy with the fatal car crash near Chippenham. Eddie, Gene and Sharon had decided to leave for the airport right after the show.

Hal Carter: 'We'd been using the minicab all week, and asked the driver what it'd cost to take them to Heathrow. He said he'd find out and get back to us, but instead of going to his firm he asked a friend of his to borrow him his car and came back and told us £25. The car set off with the three stars, Pat Tompkins the roadie and the driver and reached the outskirts of Chippenham around midnight. They'd re-surfaced the road that day and it was all small-pebble dusted. The driver hit the brakes, and the back end of the car went. They struck the kerb, the door's flown open, and Eddie's turned to protect Sharon by putting his arm across her. He'd gone forward, hitting his head on the top of the car. He then caught the back of his head on the strut of the door as he was thrown out onto the verge on the roadside.'

One of the first on the scene of the crash was policeman Dave Harman, who later became Dave Dee with his group Dozy, Beaky, Mick and Tich.

Dave: 'The driver and roadie were virtually unhurt but Eddie, Gene and Sharon were lying on the grass injured. There were guitars and gig things all over the road. It was quite clear that Eddie was in a bad way. We had to take everything back to the police station and I realised then that it was Eddie Cochran's Gretsch guitar. He and Sharon were taken away by ambulance. Sadly, Eddie died the next day.'

It was a tragedy that shook the rock world. Wildcat drummer Brian Bennett: 'We weren't employed for the Bristol gig as it happened, and I received a phone call from Norman Riley, Eddie's manager. I was shattered. Eddie was a fantastic guy, taught me some rock 'n' roll drums; he was more than an adept player as well as a guitarist. He'd told me he was looking forward to returning to Britain later in the year and I was really excited about working with him again. It was a terrible tragedy.'

Vince Eager: 'The Eddie Cochran and Gene Vincent tour was a great thrill. We were actually playing in Scotland the night before the tour started in Ipswich, which meant a long, long drive afterwards to get there in time. We just about managed it. After the show Eddie paid me a great compliment when he told me he thought my version of Conway Twitty's *It's Only Make Believe* was the best he'd ever heard! I couldn't believe it. He also said he couldn't believe that I'd never had a big hit in this country and asked me to go over to the States with him in April to record a session with him. Course that never happened. I was actually at London Airport waiting to meet up with Eddie on the night of the crash. On hearing the news I drove down to Bath with a friend to see him in hospital and the surgeon informed us that if Eddie survived he would virtually be a cabbage, or words to that effect. It was terrible. One thing that sticks in my mind though was something that Larry Parnes came out with. Referring to Eddie's record which had been released to coincide with the tour, he said, 'Well Eddie is 'Three Steps From Heaven' now.' I was sickened and disgusted with him. I was going to fly back with Eddie's body to the States and then Parnes made a statement to the national press that rock star Vince Eager is going to accompany Eddie back home. That really peed me off. I saw it as another attempt for Parnes to gain publicity and get his name in the papers. I decided against going in the end to spite Larry Parnes and I finished working with him. I did regret not going to America afterwards though. I felt as if I'd let Eddie down.'

In the cinema, Elvis and Cliff could be seen by their fans in *G.I. Blues* and *Expresso Bongo* respectively. 'New Wave' dramas were becoming a force with *Look Back In Anger* and *Saturday Night and Sunday Morning* inspiring a new direction. Albert Finney's rebellious role as a disillusioned factory worker hit a chord with many, if not the censors who wanted to ban it. Censorship was a weapon used enthusiastically by the establishment, and particularly the BBC. Songs were examined with a fine-tooth comb for anything that might indicate a threat to civilisation as we know it. As far back as 1936 the Beeb banned George Formby's *'When I'm Cleaning Windows'* for being too smutty. The Beverley Sisters' version of *'Greensleeves'* suffered the same fate in 1956 with the Beeb claiming the ban was because the song was too racy – Greensleeves referring to the girl in the song getting grass stains on her dress while lying down with her boyfriend. The puritanical bureaucrats were working overtime. The BBC also didn't like songs about teenagers dying or automobile accidents. Ricky Valance's *'Tell Laura I Love Her'* – the tale of Tommy, a teenager in love with Laura, entering a stock car race to win enough money to buy Laura a wedding ring – only to crash and burn was too much for 'Auntie'. The Beeb decreed that Tommy's dying words 'Tell Laura I love her' were tasteless.

Craig Douglas caused controversy with his *'A Hundred Pounds of Clay'*, which told the story of God creating women. The BBC deemed the song to be blasphemous on religious grounds and that suggesting 'women were created simply to be sexual beings' was outrageous. Like *'Laura'*, it was canned. Most ridiculous of all was the BBC banning Russ Conway's commemorative record *'Royal Event'* from the airwaves following the birth of Prince Andrew, declaring that too was 'in very poor taste.'

Disc jockey Pete Murray gave an insight into the workings and mindset of the Beeb, telling of the time when disc jockeys had to submit a script of their shows to the hierarchy prior to broadcast. 'I wrote one script with the line 'He's a very nice bloke', and the censor sent it back with a side note: 'See Page 4. I think you should change bloke to chap.' I thought, 'Oh God! No.'

Censorship was being tested with the publication of D. H. Lawrence's controversial novel *Lady Chatterley's Lover*, banned in the UK until Penguin won the right to publish the book in its entirety. The book caused a scandal due to its excellent, or should that be, explicit sex scenes, and previously banned four-letter words, and particularly because the lovers were a working-class male and an aristocratic female. The story concerned a young married woman, Constance (Lady Chatterley), whose upper-class husband, Clifford, had been paralysed and rendered impotent. Her sexual frustration led her into an affair with the gamekeeper, Oliver Mellors. During 1959 the government had introduced the Obscene Publications Act stating that any book considered obscene but that could be shown to have 'redeeming social merit' might still be published. This prompted Penguin to print off 200,000 copies with the aim of completing a set of works by D.H. Lawrence to commemorate the 30th anniversary of his death. Twelve copies were sent to the Director of Public Prosecutions challenging him to prosecute, which he duly did. The six-day trial at the Old Bailey gripped the nation. The defence produced bishops and leading literary figures. The prosecution was unable to make a substantial case against the novel, and at one point Counsel Mervyn Griffith-Jones shocked the jury by asking: 'Is it a book you would even wish your wife or your servants to read?' Bookshops all over England sold out of Penguin's first run of the controversial novel, all 200,000 copies, on the first day of publication. London's largest bookstore, Foyles, reported that 300 copies were sold in just 15 minutes and orders were taken for 3,000 more. Next morning, 400 people – mostly men – were waiting to buy the book. Selfridges sold 250 copies in minutes. A spokesman told *The Times*, 'It's Bedlam here. We could have sold 10,000 copies if we'd had them.'

Such was the state of affairs in 1960.

It was the start of a new decade and the end of an era, with the last National Serviceman being called up, the cause of much celebration.

As Adam Faith succinctly recalled in his autobiography *Acts Of Faith*: 'It was as if I'd been on Death Row and suddenly one bright sunny morning someone told me it's ok you can go home, they've abolished hanging!'

Conscription had been re-introduced in 1948. Every healthy man between the ages of 17 and 21 was expected to serve in the armed forces for 18 months, and remain on the reserve list for four years thereafter. Exemption was granted only for those with one limb, no limbs, one eye or those working in coal-mines, farming or the merchant navy, which explains why many teenage lads decided on leaving school to go to sea with the 'Merch' rather than face two years of insults from manic sergeant majors in the army.

In 1958 teenage rock 'n' roll fans had been in dismay when Elvis Presley was conscripted into the U.S. Army. There was the rebellious 'King', shorn of his famous sideburns and locks. If they could do this to Elvis, what chance did the ordinary Joe have? Elvis' term in the army was long suspected to be a co-operative publicity stunt by the 'Administration' and his manager Colonel Tom Parker as a way of setting an example to the youth of America. Portraits of Elvis smiling away as he was scalped at Fort Chaffee, Arkansas, embarking on the *USS Randall* for Europe, driving around Germany in tanks and jeeps, cleaning his rifle, had all been fed into the publicity machine to encourage teenagers to allay their fears of the 'draft'.

With his two years of military service completed, Elvis returned to Memphis from Germany in March 1960, a different man. The King of Rock 'n' Roll had been tamed. Consoling those who yearned for the Elvis of old, RCA released the album *A Date With Elvis* to coincide with his homecoming, with a calendar and the date of his release ringed on the back cover. All the tracks were original recordings from his Sun label days, when 'the hillbilly cat' was at his most vibrant. His first post-army studio album was a moody bluesy collection of songs; *Elvis Is Back!* One of the King's finest. Portraying a more mature and sensitive Elvis, equally at home when racing through the opener '*Make Me Know It*', the melancholic '*I Will Be Home Again*' or the pure blues of '*Reconsider Baby*'. A genuine classic album.

Many would argue *Elvis Is Back!* was the last of what you would call genuine great Elvis albums. *Pot Luck*, *His Hand In Mine*, *How Great Thou Art* and the *Golden Records* series would pass, but for the next eight years Elvis fans had to put up with the dirge that was dished out with his film soundtrack albums. Who can forgive '*Yoga Is As Yoga Does*', '*Finders Keepers, Losers Weepers*', '*Petunia, The Gardener's Daughter*'? A million miles away from '*Jailhouse Rock*' and '*Heartbreak Hotel*'.

Three days after Elvis's demob, on March 6th the Pentagon announced that 3,500 American soldiers were to be sent to Vietnam in South East Asia. The date marks the beginning of a nightmare that would haunt America for decades. The Cold War between the United States and the Soviet Union then went up a notch following the shooting down of an American Lockheed U-2 spy plane by a Soviet missile for encroachment into their airspace. Pilot Gary Powers was captured by the Soviets and pleaded guilty to spying for the CIA. He was sentenced to three years' imprisonment and seven years' hard labour.

Later, during a summit meeting in Paris involving the United States, the Soviet Union, Britain and France, Soviet Leader Nikita Khrushchev walked out and brought a premature end to proceedings after failing to get an apology from President Eisenhower. It was a bad year for Ike, who was also having to deal with the signing of the Civil Rights Act at the time – another problem that would haunt the 'Land of the Free' throughout the 1960s.

With the Cuban Revolution well under way, with Fidel Castro retaliating to a United States embargo by nationalising oil companies owned by Shell, Esso and Texaco after they refused to refine Soviet oil, Eisenhower must have been pleased to see the back of the White House when his term in office came to an end in December.

Aligned to all this was the so-called 'Space Race', which had been kick-started by the Russians in 1957 with the launch of their *Sputnik* satellite. The Soviets then sent 'a stray dog from the streets of Moscow' called Laika into orbit aboard *Sputnik 2*, accompanied with a tin of Chum, on November 3rd. America's response was to launch a chimp called Ham into the sky, explaining it was to test the *Mercury* capsule which was being designed to carry their astronauts into space.

Ham was born in July 1956 in Cameroon, captured by animal trappers and sent to the Rare Bird Farm in Miami, Florida. Which begs the question, how did they know his birthday was in July? Remarkable really. Maybe the chimp had his birth certificate with him. Also, Rare Bird Farm? Somebody needed to go to Specsavers, it seemed. Whatever, the U.S. Air Force bought him and he was taken to Holloman Air Force Base in July 1959 where he was trained under the direction of neuroscientist Joseph Brady to do simple, timed tasks in response to electric lights and sounds. Ham was taught to push a lever within five seconds of seeing a flashing blue light; failure to do so resulting in an application of negative reinforcements in the form of a mild electric shock into the soles of his feet, while a correct response earned him a banana pellet. Animal Rights activists would have been appalled.

Ham was launched successfully from Cape Canaveral, Florida on January 31st 1960 to much acclaim. The capsule did suffer a partial loss of pressure during the flight, but Ham's space suit prevented him from suffering any harm. The only discomfort reported for the unfortunate chimp, apart from sore feet, was a bruised nose. The capsule splashed down in the Atlantic Ocean and was recovered by a rescue ship. Celebrated as a hero, Ham went on to live a life of comfort in the National Zoo in Washington D.C. before passing away peacefully, with his fellow chimps by his side, in 1983.

The race was now well under way and the Soviets regained the lead with cosmonaut Yuri Gagarin, aboard *Vostok 1*, making a 'giant leap', long before Neil Armstrong's stretch on the Moon, to become the first man in space. Gagarin completed a circle of the Earth and returned, like Ham, to a hero's welcome, international celebrity status, and a sandwich.

The news sent shock waves throughout America. Newsreels from the time reveal how frightened many Americans were about what the Russians might do next. Was this the precursor for Russia attacking the United States from Outer Space? The beginning of Star Wars?

With the Soviets rejoicing in the success of Gagarin, America's reaction was to hastily fire astronaut Alan Shepard off the launch pad a month later in his ship *Freedom 7*, but the mission was derided and Shepard's efforts mocked as he returned after just 15 minutes. Blinked and you would have missed it.

Short trip or not, John F. Kennedy, recently installed as the 44th President of the United States, astonished everyone with his announcement that the U.S. was committed to 'landing a man on the Moon' by the end of the decade.

This was science fiction coming to reality, with satellites, cosmonauts, astronauts, dogs and chimps being launched at regular intervals throughout the late 1950s and early 1960s. One particular satellite, Telstar, would capture the imagination of one enthusiast more than any other, a certain Joe Meek from Evesham.

Whilst we were all craning our necks and looking up at the stars, back on Earth another star, Johnny Gentle, had been assigned to a brief if memorable short tour of the Scottish Highlands with an unknown ensemble from Liverpool called The Silver Beetles.

Prior to the tour disc jockey Keith Fordyce gave Johnny a boost with a review in the 'Singles' column of the *New Musical Express*:

> The teenager composer/singer Johnny Gentle has waxed his latest release '*I Like The Way*' on the Philips label. A light and happy rocker that is quite inoffensive and enjoyable, but is not the sort to stick in the mind. The 'B' side, '*Milk From The Coconut*' is cute and has a catchy Hawaiian style. Johnny makes a very neat job of this one. Recommended as worth a listen if you get the time.

The Silver Beetles were just another young band of wannabes in 1960, but different in that they resisted covering current hit records like '*Tie Me Kangaroo Down Sport*' and '*Mr. Custer*'. Instead they favoured the American brand of rock offered by Elvis, Chuck Berry, Gene Vincent and Eddie Cochran. Soon they would be off to Hamburg to work with a rock singer from the 2i's club, Tony Sheridan. For now, though, they were heading north to the Highlands of Aberdeenshire, a seven-day tour arranged by their manager Allan Williams in co-ordination with Larry Parnes.

John Lennon, Paul McCartney, George Harrison, Stuart Sutcliffe and drummer Tommy Moore set off from Lime Street for Scotland ten days after being turned down for Billy Fury because Parnes didn't rate Sutcliffe, figuring he was only in the group because he was a pal of Lennon's but couldn't play a note.

The tour, co-organised with Highland entrepreneur/pig farmer Duncan MacKinnon, saw them playing the circuit of dance halls, church halls and converted cinemas. They met up with Johnny Gentle in Alloa with less than an hour to sort out a set for the gig at the Town Hall.

Johnny remembers: 'They were the roughest looking bunch I had ever seen in my life.'

The pig farmer whose sartorial style was an outsize overcoat and Wellington boots took an instant dislike to them.

'MacKinnon was outraged,' Gentle recalls. 'He saw the five lads from Liverpool playing on stage in the gear that they had turned up in, looking like buskers and thought they were no good and wanted to sack them. He phoned Larry Parnes and told him the band would have to go. Parnes ignored the grunts of the pigman but compromised in that the band would wear some sort of uniform. George had a black shirt in his bag and it was with great reluctance Parnes agreed to buy the others a similar one, except for Tommy Moore who, he reasoned, being at the back playing the drums and virtually out of sight, didn't really need one!'

Next stop on the tour was Inverness, where they were billed along with Lindsay Ross and his Scottish Dance Band in a dual attraction at the Inverness Northern Meeting Ballroom, Ross entertaining the crowd downstairs with Gentle and The Silver Beetles rocking away upstairs.

Gentle: 'Before the show we sat down in a bar and went over the numbers for hours until they got the sound right. They were terribly depressed. My act was only about six or seven songs. I said, 'You know that one, and that one, what do you know that I might know?' We made up an act of Elvis's '*I Need Your Love Tonight*', Buddy Holly's '*It Doesn't Matter Anymore*', Ricky Nelson's '*Poor Little Fool*'. Then they played for about an hour after me, Chuck Berry's '*Rock And Roll Music*' and other American hits at the time. The crowd loved it, the girls loved it; only problem was, Duncan MacKinnon didn't like it!'

Fraserburgh's Dalrymple Hall, Keith, Forres Town Hall, Peterhead and Nairn completed the tour. Their appearance at Nairn recalled by a young female fan:

> 'The music was exciting; they were all dressed in black which was different. Everyone else at the time seemed to be wearing a suit, a collar and tie. The ballroom wasn't very big, it was a cinema and they had taken out the first ten rows of seats.
>
> And that was the dancehall. The stage was up high and it was mobbed. We stood in front of Johnny Gentle, who we thought was gorgeous. Then this lot came on. We didn't think anything of them until afterwards when they became famous. Then we said 'Ach!' We didn't even like them. We'd shared a coke and tea and pie with them during the break.' We couldn't understand what they were saying – because they were from Liverpool. They were just sort of crazy. But nice. Young. Next day I was sitting on top of a sand dune with my friend when we spotted the boys on the beach. So we took a casual walk down towards them, trying to make out we were just passing by. John Lennon asked us where the nearest café was. We said we'd take them. It was about a quarter of a mile away which suited us! He spent his last shilling on two glasses of chilled orange, one for me.

Allan Williams: 'The fee for the tour was something ridiculous, £75 between the five of them. Out of that they had to pay the train fare, van hire, had to live and they had to pay for their hotel accommodation. When they came back they were absolutely broke. They did a runner in one of the hotels and I got the bill! Tommy Moore, who was ten years older than the rest of them, quit when they got back to Liverpool. His girlfriend told him in no uncertain terms, 'You're not playing with those bloody Beetles again. Get a job!' He ended up working at the Garston Bottle works as a forklift driver.'

Tommy Moore's tour nearly came to a premature end when the band was involved in a car accident.

Johnny Gentle: 'Our van plunged into another car and Tommy ended up on top of Lennon who was sitting beside him, asleep. They both ended up under the dashboard. Tommy knocked both his front teeth out and had to go to hospital. Lying in the hospital bed, Lennon kept telling him, 'Get up, we're on stage tonight!' He made it, and sat at the back playing the drums with his teeth missing and a handkerchief on hand to keep dabbing the blood. No wonder he quit when they got home!'

Gentle and the boys went their separate ways at the end of the week, but not before Johnny had given Parnes a glowing report on the band: 'I'd phoned Larry a few times and told him he'd better get up to Scotland to sign these boys. They were getting a far better response to what I was getting. After a shaky start they grew in confidence and had so much belief in themselves. I think they knew that somehow they were going places. Larry Parnes said he just didn't have the time.'

Working for Larry Parnes, Clem Cattini, like Joe Moretti before him, discovered how the money side of the rock 'n' roll world really worked and he wasn't impressed. Stung by the difference a promoter would pay and what he himself would receive as one of the cornerstones of an act, Clem decided he wouldn't sign a contract as part of a band but directly, thus ensuring a fairer payout, even if it meant earning more than his fellow band members.

'It was virtual slave-labour working for Parnes,' Clem said, 'that bad we were often too broke to stay in a bed and breakfast.'

By December 1959 Clem had had enough, and along with Brian Gregg, went to see Larry Parnes at his Oxford Street office.

> Parnes asked us what we wanted and I said, 'More money.' 'Not off me,' he replied. 'If you're not happy working for me then its goodbye!' And that was the end of that! We stormed out and went

to a pub in Soho called The Swiss. I wanted to drown my sorrows, felt sorry for myself. The Swiss was a regular haunt for musicians and it was in there, by chance, that we heard about a guy putting a group together in Willesden... Johnny Kidd.

Kidd was in the process of re-organising his band The Pirates, who had achieved chart success with *'Please Don't Touch'*. Johnny had started out as a guitarist with The Frantic Four Skiffle Group in 1956. They later changed their name to Freddie Heath and The Nutters, and in 1959 had a recording test with HMV which produced their hit record. It was during the session the band were informed that their name Freddie Heath and the Nutters was rubbish and their name would be changed to Johnny Kidd and The Pirates.

The Pirates had now hit the rocks and disintegrated, forcing Captain Kidd to enlist a new crew. Guitarist Alan Caddy remained on board while the rest of the band decided against giving up their day job, feeling that rock and roll was a passing phase and had no future. With Clem and Gregg joining Caddy, Kidd started rehearsals along with a second guitarist, his friend Frank Routledge. Unfortunately for Frank, his wife didn't want him to 'go out on the road' and reluctantly he dropped out, at which point Johnny decided to leave the band as a four piece.

With a name like 'Johnny Kidd and The Pirates' it was obvious the band had a ready-made image. Adorning Long John Silver stage gear, complete with Johnny waving his antique naval cutlass around, Kidd's eye-patch was added following an idea from Clem:

> The story that a broken guitar string hit him in the eye and gave him the idea for The Pirates is untrue. Johnny had a squint in his eye which irritated him, and I said, 'Why don't you get an eye-patch?' He thought it'd be too corny, but I said, 'Well, we are called The Pirates!'

> Our manager Guy Robinson arranged the gigs for us, the band getting £4 and Johnny £8 a show. We were quite happy with that and our first gig was at Hatfield College. The crowd loved us. Guy then got us a record deal with HMV – the first one I ever had. I had never been on a record before, and it was made at EMI, long

before it became known as Abbey Road.

The line-up of Kidd, Cattini, Caddy, Gregg and session man Joe Moretti played on the chart-topping *'Shakin' All Over'*.

'Joe received £1 extra for his efforts,' recalled Clem, 'in addition to his £5 15s session fee which was standard.'

Joe Moretti, speaking in 2002: 'I created the introduction, the backing figures, the solo, and slid Brian Gregg's cigarette lighter across the strings to get that shakin' guitar sound. We had it down in a couple of takes. A week later producer Peter Sullivan rang Johnny to tell him that Jack Good was knocked out with *'Shakin' All Over'* and so it was going to be the 'A' side.'

Joe was born in Glasgow to Italian parents in 1938. He taught himself to play piano, but with the advent of rock and roll bought a cheap guitar and then a Hofner Senator. In 1957 he entered a newspaper competition to find 'Glasgow's Tommy Steele', a contest won by Alex Harvey who later found fame with his Sensational Alex Harvey Band.

Married to Pina in 1958, Joe and his wife moved to London where he frequented the 2i's and jammed with Tony Sheridan and Brian Bennett. After a brief stint with the Colin Hicks band, Joe joined Vince Eager for a pantomime, Vince playing Simple Simon in 'Mother Goose' at the Garrick Theatre, Southport. He then teamed up with Vince Taylor and The Playboys, after which he moved to Johnny Duncan and His Blue Grass Boys and then to trumpeter Eddie Calvert, before concentrating on a career as a session musician.

Michael Heatley in *The History of Rock*:

> *'Please Don't Touch'* was a stunning effort by any yardstick, but the eagerly-awaited follow up was a disappointment. Kidd's crooning of the standard *'If You Were The Only Girl In The World'* was an inexplicable release, since the 'B' side *'Feelin''* had all the hallmarks of a hit. The release of *'Shakin' All Over'* in June 1960, over a year after *'Please Don't Touch'* was well worth the wait for Pirates fans. The magic of the repeated descending guitar figure, echoed by the bass, remains unique, and Kidd's edgy yet insistent

vocals really did 'send shivers down the backbone' of the British record buying public.

Brian Gregg:

The follow-up to *'Please Don't Touch'* did nothing, and the next single was going to be *'Yes Sir, That's My Baby'*, done in a Bobby Darin style. We were told that we could write the 'B' side, but the day before the session we still hadn't come up with anything. Johnny, Alan and myself were in Chas McDevitt's Freight Train Coffee Bar in Berwick Street, sitting on coke crates, when Johnny said, 'Let's write any old rubbish and at least they can see we've made an attempt at it'. We didn't have any instruments with us, but we sang the parts of *'Shakin' All Over'*. The next day we had a quick run through in the front room of my house, and then we recorded it. It was going to be the 'B' side and we were a bit ashamed of it.

Clem:

The *'Shakin' All Over'* session is one I always remember because there was a room at the end of Studio 2 which had an echo chamber in it. There was a rule that you couldn't play after ten o'clock at night, because the flats next door used to moan about the sound. Peter Sullivan informed the engineer that he wanted full echo on our record and was told, 'Oh no, no, I can't do that'. Peter asked him why, and the engineer pulled a book off the shelf which had *The BBC Method of Recording* on it. 'Look,' he said to Peter, 'it's in here, in the book.' Peter looked at him, and told him, 'You know what you can do with your book, put it where the sun don't shine!'

I made a mistake in the middle of *'Shakin''*; I should have played just one bar in the fill, but maybe I wasn't concentrating and I played two. 'Sorry,' I said to Peter, 'we'll do it again,' but he said 'No, it's ok, we'll leave it in.' And it became known as a great piece of work, inventive! We first met Joe Moretti while we were playing in Scotland with Terry Dene. You could see he was a great guitarist and I told him he should go down to London, which he did in 1958. We needed another guitarist for the session, and that's how he ended up playing on *'Shakin' All Over'*. It was Joe too who played on those hits that Jet Harris and Tony Meehan had in

1963, '*Diamonds*', '*Scarlet O'Hara*' and '*Applejack*'. It was Joe who played the twanging bass, not Jet. Jack Good booked us for his brand new ABC TV show *Wham!* on April 10th 1960. Billy Fury, Joe Brown, Jess Conrad, Dickie Pride, Little Tony and Vince Taylor were also on the show. We wore lime-green suits while Johnny sported bright orange, which was a pity as the show went out on black and white television!

Wham! only lasted a couple of months. The show was cancelled in June with a statement: 'ABC thinks there is no longer a public for teenage rock 'n' roll type programmes'.

On June 10th '*Shakin' All Over*' went to number one.

Clem (2017):

In my view, Johnny was one of the finest blues singers ever. If he were alive today he'd be hailed as one of the all-time greats. With the success of '*Shakin''* I really felt part of something. Yes there was the other side, the drink and the drugs, but I never got into that. I was brought up with strong family values and I had a wife at home. Nine times out of ten I'd get home after a gig. I saw what drugs did for Dickie Pride. I was just happy to play. Dickie was a great talent and had recorded an album, *Pride Without Prejudice*. He would surely have gone on to be a huge star, it was so sad. We were suddenly doing interviews for the music magazines like *Record Mirror* and *New Musical Express*. Tickets for our shows were on the black market. We played at High Wycombe once and the tickets priced 2/6d were being sold for £1 by touts. The promoter was so happy with the place being packed, he gave us an extra £5. £2 for Johnny and a pound each for the rest of us. That was a hell of a lot back in 1960. We were heavy with the drink – we weren't angels – and had our scrapes. Me in particular when I was with Alan Caddy, who we called, predictably enough, 'Tea'. Alan drank gallons of the stuff! He was also what we called a 'tea leaf', slang for you-know-what! Not off his mates or anything like that though, his forte was cars and on one occasion there was nearly a huge problem. We were in this huge Vauxhall which Alan had 'borrowed' without the owner's permission, and he went straight into the back of a Rolls Royce. We were out of there double-quick. The demon drink eventually got Alan and he died far too young. Johnny's weakness was gambling. He used to blow his share of the earnings down at the dog track and on another occasion he lost a huge amount in a slot machine. We had done a personal appearance in a record shop in Bradford, and it was agreed that we should stay the night in Leeds, only about ten miles away. On the way we decided to call in at a transport café. I knew there would be a problem when I saw a slot machine in the corner. Johnny had the appearance money on him, around £150, which he eventually exchanged for sixpenny pieces and lost the lot!

We had a change of manager around this time, Stanley Dale, who was also Tony Hancock's agent, took over our affairs. He was an extraordinary character, a rear gunner in the RAF during the war, had one lung and worked from his bed... chain smoking! But he did a hell of a job. He got us a better deal and he was not one to be messed around. Stanley was once so cheesed off with the manager at a venue in Aylesbury, he bought the place so he could sack him!

Johnny Kidd and The Pirates recorded '*Restless*' and '*Magic Of Love*' as the follow-up to '*Shakin' All Over*' on September 5th, with Joe Moretti once again on lead guitar, before commencing a British tour. Released on September 30th, '*Restless*' failed to repeat the magic of its predecessor, reaching just number 18 in the charts.

Four more tracks recorded in Abbey Road – '*Linda Lu*', '*Let's Talk About Us*', '*Big Blon' Baby*' and '*Weep No More My Baby*' – received reviews which were more encouraging.

Record Mirror: '*Linda Lu*' features a jaunty but cool take on the descending '*Shakin''* riff, preceded with a brief vocal introduction before launching into the verse proper. A solo is dispensed with, there appears to be no second guitarist employed to flesh out the sound. As with '*Big Blon' Baby*', Alan Caddy's 'chunky' style can be seen to have evolved rather effectively, the solo on the recording keeping the song chugging along rather nicely without losing the plot.'

New Musical Express: 'A strong and clever performance of '*Linda Lu*', a number that has plenty of difference about it. Johnny lets fly with power and punch, aided by a welcome quantity of inventiveness.'

The itinerary for the tour which followed the sessions was recalled by Brian Gregg as exhausting; 'We travelled overnight all the time and I remember one gig when I virtually fell asleep on stage! I came to in the middle of a song and thought I was going to fall over. I was that knackered.'

The tour began on September 18th in Aylesbury, followed on 20th at Newbury; 23rd Northwich; 29th Barrow-In-Furness; 30th Whitehaven. October 1st in Crewe; 14th Central Pier, Morecambe; 20th Rawtenstall; 21st Leeds; 22nd Barnoldswick; 29th Bury St Edmunds. November 4th Grimsby; 5th Wisbech; 7th in Middlesbrough; 8th Hull; 9th Bradford; 10th Scarborough; 11th the start of a five-day tour of Scotland; 16th York; 17th Warrington; 19th Shrewsbury and finally 20th at Spennymoor.

Clem:

> Some of the places we played and stayed at wouldn't be put up with nowadays. In Spennymoor our digs for the night was a snooker hall, a real rough place. This was mining territory, the arsehole of Britain we called it at the time. We were told it wouldn't be a good idea to go downstairs into the snooker hall, but that was where the toilets were. So we heeded the advice and peed into a big bowl that was hanging from the ceiling light. A year later we were back in that place, and unbelievably the bowl with the pee was still there! That was the sort of thing you had to put up with those days!

> When 'Shakin'' hit number one, I suddenly had a name in the rock and roll world. We were on television, radio, playing to sell out audiences of 3,000 and 4,000 at places like Aylesbury Grosvenor Ballroom. I was on £30 a week, which seemed like a fortune. Life was good. We travelled in comfort in a van with three airplane seats in the back. Years later when I got to know Allan Clarke of The Hollies he told me that they used to travel hundreds of miles to see Johnny Kidd and The Pirates play, which was a great compliment. John Paul Jones of Led Zeppelin once said that 'Shakin' All Over' was his inspiration for going into rock music. Through all of this, Johnny was great. He was a very good singer and in my opinion never got the recognition he deserved before his untimely death in 1966.

November saw the release of the EP *Johnny Kidd*, featuring the band's four hit singles to date: *'Please Don't Touch'*, *'Shakin' All Over'*, *'Restless'* and *'You've Got What It Takes'*.

The sleeve notes by James Wynn, entirely fictional, tell the story of how, whilst tuning his guitar backstage at Wandsworth Town Hall, a string broke and hit Johnny in the eye. Stagehands managed to source a black eyepatch and Johnny fulfilled the show, during which he heard mumblings from a few in the audience that he looked like a pirate, thus he dubbed his band The Pirates, and adorned himself with the name Johnny Kidd – and never looked back!

And as Clem would say – or as the old adage goes – why spoil a good story with the truth?

1960 ended with *'Shakin' All Over'* voted the 7th best British disc of the year. Kidd was the 9th most popular male singer and 11th British Vocal Personality.

The following year, 1961, was memorable apart from anything else for Tottenham Hotspur becoming the first team of the century to win the League and F.A. Cup 'Double'. Not that football fan Clem appreciated this feat too much, being an avid Arsenal fan 'since the day I first heard the Highbury roar when I was just a boy'. Such is Clem's passion for Tottenham's North London rivals that he has been a season ticket for over 60 years, and has been friends and acquainted with many of the Gunners stars throughout the decades.

Football is a passion Clem shares with his good friend, singer/actor Kenny Lynch, an avid West Ham fan and close friend of the late great Bobby Moore.

Kenny grew up in Stepney, East London, one of 13 children. After leaving school at 15 and taking various jobs, he completed his National Service in the Royal Army Service Corps, where he was the regimental featherweight boxing champion. Did Kenny enjoy himself in National Service?

> Did I heck, if I'd been two weeks younger I'd have missed it as well! I don't like people telling me what to do for a start off! So I was never going to be a great soldier. When I went in, I had been boxing for a while as an amateur. One day this guy, Dave Stone,

who was Lightweight Champion of Britain at the time, told me to join the boxing team and from then on, that's all I did, it was great. I used to go home and my mum would say, 'I thought you were in the army?' I'd reply, 'I am,' and she'd say, 'Well how come I never see you in uniform then?' I hardly wore my uniform, I was always in my tracksuit!

After I came out of the army I was singing with dance bands and worked with Ted Heath when Dickie Valentine was ill. 'Get young Kenny Lynch,' Dickie had told Ted. They were a great band, with great jazz musicians like Ronnie Verrell, Don Lusher, Johnny Hawksworth.

A pal of mine then said to me, 'I'm gonna turn pro, why don't you join me? I've been getting good money but getting work is a nightmare so I'm turning pro and going to Archer Street to get jobs, there's plenty of work down there'. That's where the Musician Union's Office was, and the bars where the musicians used to hang out. So I went along, and I became a professional singer. My pal was right, there was loads of jobs everywhere. And I could sing anything. Jazz, Dixieland, Soul. As a kid I loved Ella Fitzgerald, Sarah Vaughan, Billy Eckstine, Carmen McRae and I could sing without having arrangements.

I went to America in 1961 and met a guy who was in control of the Brill Building, Paul Casey. He took me to an office to sign a contract for Aldon Music. 'Contract?' I asked, 'What for?' They were going to give me a grand to sign up! 'Sign the contract,' this guy says. 'Look,' I said, 'I don't write songs'. He said, 'You will'. Then I thought, hang on a minute, I could see this grand disappearing before I'd got it! So I signed. I put the money away and went out with $200 in my pocket, thinking to myself, 'This will take me all year to spend!' Walking down 49th Street, Casey phoned me. He told me to go to Jack Dempsey's Bar and to take the lift to the 8th floor. I met him in this office. 'Sit down,' he said. Big Jewish guy he was, a real Bronx character. He was never off the phone. It kept interrupting us; 'Right, ok, sell, buy.' Dead brash. He was into stocks and shares, full of crap. 'What! I'll need to think about it, give me a few moments, ok, buy!'

Getting down to business, Casey was under the impression I knew everyone. 'Would you like to see...'

I didn't know anyone! So he took me up to this room, 'I'll take you to meet Gerry (Goffin) and Carole (King).' They were sitting in this tiny room with a baby upright piano, like a kid's toy! I couldn't believe it. Is this where they wrote all those great hits – '*Will You Love Me Tomorrow*', '*Take Good Care Of My Baby*' and the rest? Casey then took me to meet Leiber and Stoller, the guys who wrote all The Coasters and Elvis songs. Then it was Mort Shuman. Another guy who along with his partner Doc Pomus wrote dozens of songs for Elvis too. And The Drifters' '*Save The last Dance For Me*', Dion's '*Teenager In Love*'.

'Sit down,' Mort says, 'Would you like to be my partner?'

I said, 'What?'

He said again, 'Would you like to be my partner? Writing lyrics. I get fed up writing effing lyrics.'

'What about Doc?' I asked.

'Don't worry about Doc,' he says.

'I've only been here 40 minutes,' I say.

'No, well more than that actually, 10 more minutes when Casey was here,' Doc said. 'Are you sure?' I asked him.

'Look,' he says, 'you're like me, I can tell. You can do anything you want to. If you want to do something, you do it.' I said, 'Yeah,' and he said, 'You like birds.' I said, 'Right, you got me!'

We ended up writing around twelve number one hits, which were all around the world, in different countries.

I used to go over to the States for four weeks at a time to work with Mort. We wrote songs for Cliff Richard, Billy J. Kramer, The Walker Brothers. We wrote '*Sha La La La Lee*' for The Small Faces in about five minutes. It was actually intended for Amen Corner, but they said it was too simple so we gave it to the Faces. I asked Steve Marriott if he was alright with the key and he said, 'Yeah, no problem,' but when he came to do it he couldn't hit the high notes, so I did the background falsettos! Mort hated the song and told me, 'Don't put my name on it!' When it went to number three in the charts he asked, 'You did put my name on it, didn't you?'

I wrote '*Happy That's Me*', which Wally Ridley at HMV said was going to be the 'B' side of my 1962 single '*Puff*'. It spent six weeks in the charts and reached the dizzy heights of number 33!

Clem, who was on the session, said to me, 'You're a West Ham fan aren't you?'

'I said, 'Yeah, why?''

'Well I'm an Arsenal fan'. And from that day on we've had arguments and banter ever since about football. I also did a few jingles with Clem as well, you never had any arguments with him, apart from the football, he was and is a very good musician.

Kenny's agent was Maurice Kinn, famously known for buying the *New Musical Express* in 1952 for £1,000, 15 minutes before it was to go bust, and then turning it into the world's foremost music paper. When he sold it to the International Publishing Corporation 11 years later, the *NME* was selling 350,000 copies a week.

> Maurice Kinn told me, 'If I want you I'll just phone you in New York,' and one day he phoned to tell me that Sammy Davis was on at The Pigalle Club, Piccadilly, and he'd got tickets. We sat in seats about half way from the stage. I wasn't a big fan but Sammy came on and sang seven songs before saying anything. He was unbelievable, He was on for two and a half hours and I thought he'd only been on for ten minutes! Sammy Davis sang, danced, mimed, impressions, everything... I turned to Kinn and said, 'Thank you, you've just effing destroyed me!'
>
> 'What you on about?' Kinn said, 'You're better than him.'
>
> I laughed, and said again, 'You just effin' destroyed me.'
>
> I felt as if I might as well pack it in there and then.
>
> 'Why?' Kinn asked, 'I guarantee in two years time you'll be bigger than him.'
>
> 'Don't be effn' stupid,' I said.
>
> Kinn kept on, 'Don't worry about that, once you learn to dance...'
>
> I said, 'Look, I'm a singer, not an effin' dancer!'

In 1962 Kenny was one of the contenders for Britain's entry in the Eurovison Song Contest in Luxembourg. Described as a '23-year-old Cockney', Kenny sang a Brian Spiro song *'There's Never Been A Girl'*. He lost out to Ronnie Carroll, who won the contest with *'Ring A Ding Girl'* and came 4th in the Duchy. The winner was a French girl called Isabelle Aubret with her version of *'Un Premier Amour'*.

Then I recorded Mort Shuman's *'Up On The Roof'*, which The

Drifters had released before they came over for a tour which I was also on. Wally Ridley told me he wanted to put my version out, but I said 'No, it's The Drifters' song, I can't do that.' Ridley said ok, and he'd put it on an album.

We were in Macclesfield or somewhere, Johnny Kidd and The Pirates were also on the show, some others. Ridley phoned me; 'Have you looked at the charts?' he asked. 'Charts? What do I want to look at the charts for?' All I was interested in was getting my £60 a week.

'Have a look, it's number 10.'

'What is? Who? The Drifters?'

'No, you.'

I said, 'I haven't got a single out.'

Ridley said, 'I decided to put your version out, it's number 10.' This was December 1962.

Anyway, I received a message to go and see The Drifters in their dressing room. I was dreading it.

'Who is it?' a voice rasped.

'It's Kenny.'

'Come in!'

I opened the door and they were all standing there.

'You bastard!' Rudy Lewis growled.

I said, 'Look, it wasn't me that...' and they all burst out laughing!

'Well done, congratulations!' they said!

And suddenly I went from £60 a week to nearly a grand a night! I followed up '*Roof*' with '*You Can Never Stop Me Loving You*' in June 1963. Ridley told me I now had to have a look at the charts as I was a pop singer. 'No I'm not,' I told him, 'I've only had three records.'

Wally said, 'Go and look at the charts, you've got to start reading them to see where you are.'

I gave in and when I looked, there I was, at number 30. But right behind me, at number 31, was Elvis Presley! with '*Devil In Disguise*'. I said, 'I'm bigger than Elvis!' He was on the way down from having been number one.

In the first week of 1961, Johnny Tillotson's '*Poetry In Motion*' was at number one as Johnny Kidd and The Pirates found themselves back on the treadmill of travelling around the country playing venues such as the now long-gone Central Pier, Morecambe, the Assembly Halls, Melksham... and back in the studios recording 'More Of The Same' and the Etta James classic, 'I Just Want To Make Love To You'. It was whilst playing in Morecambe that 'Linda Lu' was released but if they were feeling good about it, they were brought back down to earth when they were 'surprise' guests on television's popular *Juke Box Jury* in April. Hosted by David Jacobs, the panel delivered a resounding MISS to 'Linda Lu', leaving the boys wincing behind the curtains and hidden from the audience.

The Pirates celebrated Alan Caddy's 21st birthday in February by buying him a AC15 amplifier for a present. They also played at the Majestic Ballroom, Bradford supported by a local group called The Dingo's Rock 'n' Rhythm group, and The Crescent Jazz Band before embarking on a Granada tour with Gene Vincent, Screaming Lord Sutch and The Savages, Johnny Duncan and His Blue Grass Boys, Mark Wynter, Michael Cox, Terry Dene, Danny Rivers, Chris Wayne and The Echoes, Rory Blackwell, Vince Taylor and The Playboys and comperes Mike and Bernie Winters.

Beginning at the Granada, East Ham, the tour's itinerary included February 27th Kingston; February 28th Dartford; March 1st Greenford; March 2nd Woolwich; March 3rd Sutton; March 5th,Rugby and April 14th The Assembly Rooms, Tamworth.

A recording session in May produced 'Bad Case Of Love', 'You Can Have Her' and 'Please Don't Bring Me Down' before an appearance on television's latest 'pop music' show, *Thank Your Lucky Stars*. Hosted by Pete Murray, the show also featured Ronnie Hilton, George Chisholm and The Tradsters, Cleo Laine, Audrey Jeans and The Springfields.

By this time, the feeling was beginning to grow that the best days of the group were over – the hits were petering out, and, over a meal, Alan Caddy, Brian Gregg and Clem gave notice to Johnny Kidd that they were leaving to join Colin Hicks and his Cabin Boys on a tour to Italy. Clem was unsure about it but was persuaded after the others told him that either they all go, or none of them would go.

Clem (2017):

> It was a decision I regretted. I loved Johnny and don't know why I agreed to go, though I suppose I was thinking of job security. Greggy had told us he'd been approached by Hicks but the deal was we all had to go. He had a moody when I said I wasn't going, but in the end, reluctantly, I went. My daughter Giulia had just been born and I didn't relish being away in Italy for three months, but with Alan Caddy being keen as well, I felt sort of pushed into a corner. It was the worst decision I ever made – and I very nearly ended up being conscripted into the Italian army for National Service as well! A letter arrived at my house saying that because of my dual nationality I was liable to be called up. I went straight to the Italian Home Affairs Office and they told me I'd be exempt if I stayed no longer than three months. That was never going to happen! I knew that, after just working with Colin Hicks for three days. He was an a-hole of the first order. For some reason he was massive in Italy and we played to sell-out audiences all over the country. We were on £20 a night and he was earning five times that. In between gigs he just wanted to play poker and take the cash off us. He was a nightmare, like a bully, and more than once I had him up against a wall telling him to leave us be.
>
> There were a few funny moments though, like when I taught our Italian driver English, mainly the swear words, and told him to speak them with a lisp! We were stopped one night because we only had one headlight working on the car. It was hilarious hearing him talking to this Italian policeman trying to make out he was English, and saying, 'This is bollocks, this is bollocks,' with a lisp.
>
> I hated working for Hicks and after a few weeks I'd had enough. I couldn't wait to get home. We came back by train, a 24-hour journey which included a Channel crossing in a very rough sea by ferry. A funny memory of that trip is of eating a meal in the dining room, and I must have been the only one who wasn't feeling seasick. Suddenly a black face appeared in the porthole, a guy was outside trying to get some fresh air and he stood there watching me demolish this meal. And his face turned green!
>
> I came back from Italy with £400 in the bank, a new family to look after, but no job. Then when I got home, Giulia didn't know

me. That did it. I vowed never to be away for that long again. It was looking pretty bleak; Christmas wasn't that far away, and the way things were going it looked like my lovely wife Anna would be cooking egg and chips for our festive dinner. How bad was it? How hard up was I? Well put it this way; I used to collect, just for fun, threepenny bits. Over the years I must have had a good few hundred of them, but towards the end of that year the whole bloody lot had gone – because Anna had used them to keep us in food!

Things were looking grim, but little did I know what was around the corner, that it was to lead me to working with one of the most talented and controversial men ever in pop music – and play on the first British record to be number one in the States.

5

Twistin' with Larry

'Come on, let's twist again' could have been Alan Caddy talking to Clem Cattini, who was sitting at home twiddling his thumbs and out of work since the ill-fated Colin Hicks tour of Italy. *'Let's Twist Again'* was an up-tempo catchy number and had been a big hit in America before twistin' its way over to the UK.

Clem had been pondering his next move when Alan called him to ask a favour.

'When Alan phoned, it was fortunate for me that Arsenal were playing away as that phone call was the one that changed my life,' Clem revealed. 'My escape from the music business over the years was football and whenever I could I would get over to watch Arsenal. Those were the days when they were at home every other week. Alan had seen an advert in the *Melody Maker* asking for guitarists, and he wanted me to go along with him for moral support.'

A record producer called Joe Meek was setting up auditions for a band he wanted to put together at his studio in Holloway Road, which conveniently enough was not far from where Clem lived in North London. When they arrived outside 304 Holloway Road they were somewhat surprised to find it was a leather goods shop.

Clem:

> Above the shop was a three-floor maisonette rented by Meek. The recording equipment, consoles, mics, instruments and cables were strewn all over the place in each and every room. It looked like chaos, but somehow in this maelstrom Meek managed to record some classic hit records of the time there, leasing his master recordings to the big record labels, Columbia, Parlophone,

90

Top Rank, HMV, Decca and Pye/Piccadilly. Joe had lost the services of his house band The Outlaws, who had gone on the road with Mike Berry to promote their latest record *Tribute To Buddy Holly*. My first impression of Joe Meek? I didn't really have one, I was just passing time, helping Alan out with some company. Joe liked Alan's guitar playing, and seeing a drum kit in the corner Alan asked Meek if he wanted to hear me play. 'Go ahead,' he said. I did, and he liked that as well. He then asked me if I'd be interested in teaming up to be part of the band. With a fry up the only prospect for a Christmas dinner I replied straight away, 'Too true!' It was regular work and I had a family to think of.'

Then Heinz came on the scene. Meek was gay and made no secret of the fact. This good-looking blonde guy came into the studio and you could see what was going to happen. Heinz Burt had been bombed out of The Outlaws after piano player Chas Hodges, later of Chas and Dave fame, said, 'No way' to Meek when he heard Heinz on the bass. Meek put him with us instead and the reasons were clear, it was purely personal! He worshipped Heinz, and the two of them didn't have a clue about music. Heinz couldn't sing and he couldn't play guitar, but Joe made him the centre of attention in the group. The line up was me, Heinz, Alan Caddy, George Bellamy and Norman Hale, who only lasted a month. Norman was from Liverpool, a real Scouser, and there was a personality clash with Joe, no doubt about it. Joe just didn't get his humour. He got rid of him and Roger LaVern came in.

Roger:

I went to Holloway Road for an audition and couldn't believe how grotty the place was. The ceiling was falling down in the corner, there were cables, rubbish and machines everywhere, organised chaos really. Joe liked what I did and gave me the job, but what I remember most is walking down the stairs feeling quite pleased when Joe shouted after me, 'By the way Roger, I don't ever want to see you in the studio again with grey hair!' I had to go to the hairdressers and two little women in the back of this shop in Stoke Newington dyed my hair black. I later learned that it was because Heinz was the blonde boy and Meek's favourite – he didn't want anyone else in the group in the limelight. We all had to have black hair so Heinz would stand out.

Clem:

> With sounds and special affects Meek was a genius, no question. He would make stupid recordings like me dropping marbles down the toilet and they would appear on a record somewhere. Joe was paranoid about people knowing his recording secrets – he was convinced people were listening through the walls to discover the secrets of his sound effects. He wasn't the most stable of individuals. However, although he obviously had some talent-spotting qualities, he was far from foolproof. I remember a Welsh guy called Tommy Scott coming to the studio and he was left waiting outside the door because Joe was putting on his make-up. Tommy belted out his number but Joe said, 'No chance, he's never going to make it.' He later emerged as Tom Jones! Rod Stewart sang two songs for him when guesting with his friends in a band called The Raiders, and his reaction was to blow a raspberry in Rod's face and walk out. The man had the social skills of an ape. Another guy came in who was completely different, striking looking, and clearly had something about him. He was David Jones. He went back to his home in South London and later re-emerged, as David Bowie!

Chas Hodges:

> Tom Jones, Rod Stewart and Davy Jones were good singers but not particularly pretty in Joe's eyes. He loved pretty little angelic faces, and that would override everything as far as Joe was concerned.

Better looking or not, soul group Cliff Bennett and the Rebel Rousers were signed up by Meek, despite an inauspicious audition in June 1961. Bennett had been bitten by the music bug, like hundreds of others in Britain, during the mid-1950s skiffle era and started his own band.

Cliff:

> We called ourselves the Rebel Rousers after the Duane Eddy hit. It was the first record we learned and we used to open with it. The original line-up was myself, Mick King, Frank Allen, Sid Phillips and Ricky Winters. Tom Littlewood and Paul Lincoln from the 2i's

were our managers in the early days and got us loads of gigs. One was at a place near Newmarket on the same bill with Joe Brown. 'I've got you £16,' Tom told us. We went wow! That was great money in 1959. We turned pro that year, thinking that we would do it for a couple of years and then we'd go back to a real job.

Regarding Joe Meek... we thought he was mad. We had set all our gear up for the audition and were ready to play when Meek came into the doorway and started mimicking a guitar or sax or something with his voice, trying to explain how this tune he had in his head went. We thought it was hilarious. Sid Phillips and the boys looked at each other and then we all burst out laughing! Meek went mad! 'Right, get out!' he screamed, 'Coming in here and taking the effin' piss! F*** off all of you! Pack up and get out of here!' We were dumbfounded.

Fortunately for the boys, Joe forgave them their ill-manners, signed them up... and continued to display all of his eccentricities.

Cliff:

Meek was so inventive and creative if not temperamental. We were doing a cover of a Jerry Lee Lewis song when I told him I wasn't happy with the sound of Ricky Winters' snare drum. I told him I wanted the dull sort of thud sound that Jerry Lee used to get on his records, so Joe put a cardboard box over it! That was it! That was the sound! He was amazing really.

The Rebel Rousers' debut single was '*You've Got What I Like*' / '*I'm In Love With You*', described in the press as 'Two wild rockers with an out-of-tune honky tonk piano played by Sid Phillips that sounds like a cross between Jerry Lee Lewis and Russ Conway.'

Cliff:

When I first heard '*You've Got What I Like*' on my transistor radio, I almost jumped out of my seat. You didn't get to hear much of that kind of music on the radio in 1961! It was voted a hit on *Juke Box Jury*, picked up considerable airplay, yet somehow it missed the boat. The next single, '*When I Get Paid*', was a straightforward cover of a Jerry Lee Lewis single, but this was relegated to B-side status in favour of '*That's What I Said*'. Jerry Lee told me much later that he thought our version of '*When I Get Paid*' was one of the best covers he'd ever heard of one of his songs, which was a terrific compliment. We recorded a third single with Joe Meek, a thing he'd written called '*Poor Joe*', which received the accolade of 'being one of Cliff Bennett's worst records!' We were dismayed with the song. We wanted our cover of Brook Benton's '*Hurtin' Inside*' on the 'A' side, but Joe Meek got his way. We became disillusioned after that and decided to quit.

May 1962 saw Cliff and the Rebel Rousers in Hamburg for a six-month residency at the Star-Club, signifying that the band had reached the first pop division with their live performances.

Cliff:

We overlapped The Beatles, who were playing the last week of their stint with Pete Best on drums. We were kept being told 'You must see The Beatles,' and when we did, I remember being absolutely blown away with them. I stood at the back of the bar and couldn't believe how good they were. They were brilliant. Three-part harmonies from John, Paul and George, which I'd never seen before. Paul had a fantastic voice. They were doing Elvis stuff like '*I'm Gonna Sit Right Down And Cry Over You*', Little Richard's '*Long Tall Sally*'. This was when we began to change from rock and roll to the soul stuff. We were covering Jerry Lee Lewis, Ray Charles, Sam Cooke. We had a brass section with Sid Phillips, Moss Groves. Later on, Paul told us, 'We really love that sound of yours, our manager Brian Epstein would love to sign you up.' I thanked Paul, but told him to tell Brian that we already had a manager, Bob Alexander. Bob was an ex-wrestler, big, big guy, and we were scared to death of him! But Bob was a good manager. He was close to Johnny Hamp who later produced *Top Of The Pops*, and we had loads of work at the Mecca theatres and universities.

We would do five weeks at a time at the Star-Club, unlike the Top Ten Club where there were loads of bands on, The Searchers, Undertakers, Kingsize Taylor and the Dominoes. We used to do two sets a night. We were the only band from London. At around ten o'clock they'd kick all the teenagers out and a more adult crowd would come in, sailors, gangsters and all sorts.

We played rock and roll, Jerry Lee Lewis, Little Richard, Chuck Berry, before progressing to more soul-type material, Ray Charles and Sam Cooke, who was a big influence on me. I loved all his records. Then I got into Marvin Gaye, '*Can I Get A Witness*', Sam and Dave, '*Soul Man*'.

We were doing '*Twistin' The Night Away*' when Roy Young asked us if we wanted to play at the Star-Club. Roy was the resident piano player at the Star, backing The Beatles, Tony Sheridan, and was responsible for selecting bands from Britain to play Hamburg. He was also a great rock singer. He thought our soul sound was great. 'We get £50 a week each,' Roy said, 'hotels, flights paid for.' I thought, 'Yeah... I'll have some of that... it was mega money!'

We were scheduled to return in two months; time and then our sax player Sid got married and left, and then Frank our bass player left. So, in that two month period the band broke up! I was screwed! I wondered what I was going to do, and then I got hold of piano player Nicky Hopkins and Bernie 'Strawberry' Watson on guitar. Bernie had been with Cyril Davies' All Stars, a terrific guitarist. Trouble was, when we went back to Hamburg we couldn't do the Sam Cooke, Ray Charles stuff! So we played rock and roll. Jerry Lee was impressed, he said to me one night, 'Nicky Hopkins plays better than I do!' Anyway, Roy asked me what had happened to the band. I told him, 'We can't play the soul stuff anymore, the band don't know it so we're doin' rock and roll again, '*Great Balls of Fire*', '*High School Confidential*'. The crowd used to shout out the numbers they wanted to hear. It was brilliant.

After that stint we were due back again in three months' time, by which time Nicky had left, 'Strawberry' had left, Sid came back, along with others, and we had the original line-up back together again! And everyone was expecting to hear Jerry Lee, Little Richard stuff, and we were playing Sam Cooke, Ray Charles!

We did eventually join Brian Epstein and he gave us our first hit record, '*One Way Love*', which reached the Top Twenty. One lesson I learned from him was what to play on our 'B' sides. We recorded '*Slow Down*', the Larry Williams record, and Brian told us, 'Don't do that again. Write your own songs, that way you'll get 50% of the royalties.' If it wasn't for Eppy I'd have never taken songwriting seriously.

Frank Allen, our bass player, had left for The Searchers by this time and we brought in Bobby Thompson from Kingsize Taylor and the Dominoes. Bobby was a great lad, very funny, we used to drink together all the time. When he left a few years later to join The Rockin' Berries I couldn't believe it. Bobby phoned to inform me he was leaving and I said to him, 'You're f***ing kiddin' me!' The Berries were a cabaret, comedy band, good, but I said to Bobby, 'What the f*** you doin'? You're a serious musician!' He did admit a long time after it was the worst decision he ever made. 'I hated every minute of it,' he said.

However, that was some way off from 1962, and the Rebel Rousers were still in Germany, gaining an education working with all the great American artists, Gene Vincent, Jerry Lee Lewis, Little Richard and company.

Cliff Bennett:

Jerry Lee became a good friend and I used to pick him up at Heathrow Airport when he came over. He always stayed at the Cumberland Hotel in Marble Arch. One time he gave us tickets for a show at Birmingham Town Hall. Jerry, who some claimed was teetotal, which was rubbish, always had a bottle of Jack Daniels with him. He was top of the bill with The Viscounts, who opened the show and died a death, and Johnny Kidd, who was also a good friend of mine. We were sitting in the dressing room when Johnny came in, dressed in all his regalia. Pirate outfit, eye-patch, sword. 'God damn!' Jerry Lee exclaimed. He couldn't believe it, kept on looking at Johnny and going 'God damn!!' He couldn't believe that somebody would get dressed up like that to do a show. Well Johnny had come to ask Jerry for permission to do a couple of his numbers. Jerry looked at him and drawled 'Well, Johnny... when I go out there... I'm goin' to rock and roll!' ...and that was Johnny's answer! So he didn't!

Rehearsals with Joe Meek were never straightforward, as Clem explained in *Mojo* (February 1995):

Joe could be very moody. You never knew what sort of day it was going to be when you turned in. Sometimes you wouldn't get more than one note played and you might as well have gone home, cos he'd throw a wobbler. He was a remarkable man, technically, at making records, it's hard to explain, when you're dealing with equipment as sophisticated as it is today. But when you were dealing with the equipment that Joe had, it was like paper and string. The sounds that he got was phenomenal. I saw him wind groups up, his biggest talent was getting the best out of the talent around him, and his downfall was that he could never be wrong. He had this sound and that was it. I had many an argument with him, and many a time I left the studio with a tape recorder or something whizzing past my head! One time I criticised something he had recorded and he threw a metal stool at me. Fortunately it missed! The sounds he achieved was all done from tape to tape. No special microphones. I seldom used a bass drum, I used the case to get a dull thud. He was one of the first producers to close mic the snare drum with an overhead mic above the rest of the kit.

Big Jim Sullivan; *Mojo*:

He would explode and go off in a huff, the landlady downstairs would come up at the wrong time and he'd do his nut, smash things. He was definitely off-centre but he was great, because he worked with us. He tuned the guitar down so I was playing A shapes but playing F, and the sound he got from the guitar was something else. And experimenting with tape echoes. He'd take a note and loop it, and then we'd play a track to it.

Clem:

Musically, we were progressing. The money though came sporadically rather then regularly because Meek couldn't handle his finances all that well. We recorded a single in early 1962 called '*Popeye Twist*', which was the dance craze of the time. It was named after the cartoon spinach-eating character.

Broadcaster Lynn Parsons:

The 'Twist' came out of nowhere, a dance that didn't require you to have a partner. Basically, you had to look as if you were stubbing a cigarette out with your foot. Prior to the Twist, dancing was all about sharing the exercise with a partner. Ballroom dancing, jiving, the Jitterbug, all of which were hard to learn. If you had two left feet you were knackered. The Twist was taken up with all the enthusiasm of being let out of jail. Its simplicity meant that even people with little co-ordination or rhythm could get on the dance floor. It was an innovation, the first time people danced apart.

The first sighting in Britain of this new dance came on television's *Thank Your Lucky Stars,* with host Brian Matthew claiming to be one of the first to demonstrate how it was done:

> The director Philip Jones was always looking for quirky ideas to begin and end the show. I was co-host with Keith Fordyce at the time Chubby Checker came over to Britain to promote his record. Philip Jones brought in dancer Lionel Blair and had both me and Keith doing this dance The Twist with him as Chubby mimed to his song. It must have looked ridiculous but it was a good laugh.

The Twist created a whole new range of fashion items. Twist skirts with lots of layers so they would swirl. Dennison shoes with pointed toes were best for the dance. Burtons tailors joined in: 'Buy yourself a mohair suit to do the Twist.' The craze sparked a whole series of events; Marathon Twist competitions were very popular, some lasting 30 hours. One Essex chap claimed he entered a competition and won the prize money, which was enough to put down a deposit for a scooter. Bands would play throughout the night, with beds laid out in dance halls for rest periods which had a specific time limit. As the shops opened in the morning, hordes of onlookers and shoppers would peer through the windows to watch, and parents would turn up with sandwiches. Journalists and photographers would report and capture images for the newspapers.

The success of '*Let's Twist Again*' triggered one commentator to write 'There was appalling opportunism by record companies to scroll down their roster of artists to see who could possibly make a Twist record. Songs with titles such as '*Peppermint Twist*', '*Ya Ya Twist*' and '*Popeye Twist*' were common. Bobby Darin released an album of Twist songs, and even Ol' Blue Eyes, Frank Sinatra, had a hit with '*Everybody's Twistin*''.

There was also a film made called *Twistin' Around the Clock*, an obvious attempt to cash in on the popularity of rock and roll films at the time.

You can see how, when The Beatles came along at the end of the year, the timing was right and the scene was in urgent need of something new. The Beatles kicked the Twist into touch.

Chub moved on and, encouraged by his record company, continued to make dance records; *'The Fly'*, *'The Mash Potato'* and *'Pony Time'*. Beggars belief really. What was the Mash Potato? Presumably standing in the middle of a dance floor and making movements with your hands as if you were mashing spuds? Can't imagine how that would pull the birds, but maybe it did!

One of the biggest hits of 1962 was *'Wonderful Land'* by The Shadows, a number written by Jerry Lordan, creator of *'Apache'* and adorned with a lush backing of strings from an orchestra arranged by producer Norrie Paramor.

Bruce Welch:

> Norrie was a genius. We had made a demo of *'Wonderful Land'*, which we were quite pleased about, even though we felt it wasn't quite right, we felt there was something missing. We were in Australia on tour a few months later when we received a message off Norrie to call him on our return. When we did he told us to listen to that track *'Wonderful Land'* we'd recorded. While we'd been away he'd recorded an orchestra and backing singers and dubbed them on the record. It was only a two track recording, the guitars and drums on one and the orchestra strings on another. We were blown away. It sounded magical – and it was another number one record for us and a million seller.

Clem:

> *'Popeye Twist'* didn't do much, but we were earning steady money backing Joe Meek's singers, one of whom was Britain's first rock chick, Billie Davis. Until she arrived on the scene, female singers appeared to be of another generation to the record buying teenagers. The Kaye Sisters, Beverley Sisters, Petula Clark. All talented but somewhat distant from the youngsters. Billie was different. She was nothing more than a kid herself, and had a

real quality that appealed to everyone. She was with Jet Harris of The Shadows for a while and had her own female chaperone to accompany her on tour.

In February, 1962, on hearing that Larry Parnes had sacked Billy Fury's backing group The Blue Flames, Meek contacted and offered him The Tornados to back his star. Joe had dreams of developing a team similar to that of Cliff Richard and The Shadows, and believed he was the man to deliver Billy Fury's elusive number one hit. A deal was struck in which Parnes would be in charge of public appearances and Joe would run recordings. Parnes offered The Tornados wages of £25 a week, which Clem, having some previous with the promoter, haggled upwards before signing.

Roger LaVern:

> I went with Clem to Parnes' office in Great Cumberland Place. He was sitting there with a clear desk except for our contracts. And really, he shot us down in flames. It was either do as he says, or do nothing at all.

Clem

> I'd told the boys, 'Look I know what he's going to offer us. Don't sign anything, I've had dealings with him in the Fifties when I was working on his Rock and Roll shows. Just refuse and I know he'll say he'll just get another band in but no way, people knew who The Tornados were and I knew enough people in the press to go and tell them, 'Listen, this is what happened." Unfortunately, George (Bellamy), was worried we'd lose the job and signed. I didn't. I was getting a £100 a week!

It was a deal that would cause ructions and disharmony further down the line with the success and achievement of their number one massive worldwide hit 'Telstar'.

Clem:

> Prior to this we went out on a tour with John Leyton and Billie Davis as The Charles Blackwell Orchestra. He was the musical director of the show, so we were given his name. It was on that

tour that I met the four lads from Liverpool called The Silver Beetles. They were very quiet, very relaxed, confident and cheeky. No airs and graces with them. We could hardly understand their Liverpool twang, it was strange to us southerners but they were great lads, funny. To be honest they were more keen on talking to me about music than the other way round. Billy was from Liverpool and very much a huge name there. 'Are you Billy Fury's drummer?' I remember a Scouse voice asking me, 'What's he like?' It was John Lennon. No mop top in those days, more a real Teddy Boy style. I liked John. He could be sarcastic and surly if he wanted, but he was alright with me. Their drummer at the time was Pete Best. Nice guy. George Harrison – he was a gem, the hardest to understand but what a lovely guy he was then, and he remained that way until he passed away. But the one I really clicked with was Paul McCartney. He seemed a more gentle type of person than the others, and we have remained friends ever since.

Back from the tour, and somehow our band was given the name The Tornados. I can't remember or recall how we arrived at that. I can only think it was Joe Meek, but it was just one day we had a new name. We were still going to back Billy Fury that summer but it was to be with the new name. We recorded an instrumental called '*Love and Fury*' to go with touring with Billy and we started to get some projection. Or rather our bass player Heinz did! It was so obvious. Meek had us all dressed in white and Heinz would be in black or stripes! This may sound cruel, but it is fact: Heinz was by some distance the least talented member of the band. He stood there with a bass guitar, but couldn't play it. He later went on a solo career, but he couldn't sing. Meek was obsessed with him. When we had success later on I was able to afford a Morris 1100. Heinz? He was driving a Ford Zephyr! And as well as that, he had a boat that Meek bought him in Southampton harbour!

Larry Parnes set about organising his next tour, featuring Billy Fury, The Tornados, John Leyton, Marty Wilde, Eden Kane, Karl Denver Trio, Shane Fenton and The Fentones, Joe Brown and The Bruvvers, Jackie Lynton, Ricky Stevens, Peter Jay and The Jaywalkers and compere Don Munday on the 49-night trip.

Advertised as 'The Big Star Show of 1962', the schedule was:

February 19th Kilburn, 20th Sheffield, 21st Manchester, 22nd Derby, 23rd Halifax, 24th Stoke, 25th Leicester, 26th, Worcester, 29th Salisbury, March 1st Watford, 2nd Bristol, 3rd Colchester, 4th Coventry, 5th St. Albans, 6th Loughborough, 7th Preston, 8th Sunderland, 9th Bradford, 10th Norwich, 11th Woolwich, 12th Maidstone, 13th Dartford, 14th Bedford, 15th Aylesbury, 16th Kingston, 17th Walthamstow, 18th Rugby, 19th Mansfield, 20th Grantham, 21st Kettering, 22nd Harrow, 23rd Sutton, 24th Slough, 25th Liverpool, 26th Wolverhampton, 27th Cheltenham, 28th Ipswich, 30th Taunton, April 1st Exeter, 2nd Gloucester, 3rd Southall, 4th Worthing Plaza, 5th Dover, 6th Romford, 7th Guildford 8th Cambridge, 9th Lincoln, 10th Cleethorpes, 11th Hull, 12th Stockton, 13th Carlisle, 15th Brighton, and 16th Plymouth.

The Tornados were given one three-minute solo spot, which was long enough to play their single '*Popeye Twist*'.

Clem:

> Peter Jay and the Jaywalkers were the resident band in Yarmouth when we played there with Billy Fury. Peter was the drummer and could be a bit of a pain at times. He had lights set up in his drum kit which would flash off and on, which the band members would operate during his drum solos. One night I took the bulbs out and put silver paper in the sockets. When he started his solo and the guy switched his lights on, the kit blew up! What a laugh that was! It was just typical of the pranks us musicians would pull on each other, but Peter wasn't amused!

> Some of the places we played were real dumps, the Essoldo Theatres in particular. They were really old and decrepit. I remember John Leyton used to prance up and down the stage and then jump and walk up the side of the wall, like you used to do when you were kids. This particular place, John leapt up and his leg went right through the plasterboard! He was left dangling while we played on! A year later I was back playing that theatre, and the hole was still in the wall!

In 1995 Larry Parnes was talking about his Package Tours and whims of the artists to broadcaster/writer Spencer Leigh: 'The tours were organised like a military campaign. We would take our own stage manager, assistant stage manager and lighting person. It wasn't a big crew, and you always had an artist or a group who were not totally satisfied with the way things were arranged.'

Clem:

> Our welfare didn't matter to Parnes. He regarded us as pieces of meat, and the show must go on and all that. I had bronchitis once and really couldn't do the show. He sent a doctor round to give me some shots to get on with it. The tours were exhausting. I fell asleep during a New Year's show at Boston Gliderdrome; I slumped over the drums, Alan Caddy gave me a bump to wake me up! When 'Telstar' was in the charts Parnes had us dashing up to Blackpool on a Sunday during the season we were doing at Yarmouth. He told us he was going to fly the band up, but then changed his mind and only flew Billy Fury up north. He hired two campervans and a couple of drivers to take the rest of us and the gear. It was that knackering, on the way back in the early hours I suddenly found myself upside down along with everybody else in a ditch! The driver had fell asleep!

The 'space race' continued to capture the public's imagination, with America's John Glenn and Russia's Gherman Titov both sent up to circle the Earth. This was all *Boy's Own* stuff, but the next significant launch into space was the satellite they called Telstar. Able to transmit live images from across the other side of the world and right into our homes, Telstar was launched from Cape Canaveral in July 1962. The first images were received by a satellite dish on Wednesday 11th July at Goonhilly, near Helston in Cornwall, and relayed to our television screens in time for the evening news. Watching was the technology-minded Joe Meek. Next morning he claimed he awoke with a melody in his head.

Clem:

> Meek had planned for us to record '*The Breeze And I*' as another attempt to get in the charts. But on the grapevine I had heard that The Fentones, Shane Fenton's backing band, had beaten us to it. We were in Yarmouth at the time with Billy Fury and I rang Meek up to tell him. 'OK,' he said, 'no problem. I have another tune I

want you to record. We will go with that instead.

The Tornados drove from Yarmouth after a Saturday night show and reported to the studio on the Sunday morning, and worked for 12 hours to put down rhythm tracks for Joe's two inspired melodies. Clem:

> I can't say I was too pleased at the prospect. Sunday was the one day I would get with my family after six days a week in Yarmouth, but Meek was insistent. Joe had this melody in his head and hummed it to us. We tried to work out what he was getting at and did the arrangements. Joe told me he saw it like a rocket going off so I played a moving rhythm on the drums, Alan figured out some chords and we put it down, and I don't think we ever got the recognition or respect as musicians we deserved. I don't think we even knew the name of the tune at the time, and after we'd done our bit he said he was going to put some effects to it. The Americans had just launched the communications satellite called Telstar and he was to name the tune after that. I wasn't that concerned to be frank, I just wanted to get home to Anna and Giulia and then get ready to return to Yarmouth.

Meek's friend Geoff Goddard was brought in to play on the clavioline, to tinkle on a piano that had drawing pins stuck into the hammers, and to provide vocal sound effects. At the time, the effects were believed to have been the actual signal from Telstar, but in truth they were more down to earth – the 'rocket lift-off' was said to be Meek flushing his toilet.

Thus was born '*Telstar*', the biggest-selling British instrumental single of all time. The record topped the charts in England and, even more amazingly, in America as well, and The Tornados were in a unique position in the world of British pop/rock. Initial reviews of the record were very dismissive. Even keyboard player Roger LaVern wasn't too impressed initially: 'Quite frankly, I thought it sounded like Mickey Mouse music. But when the fame started, I got to like it.'

Melody Maker: 'Billy Fury's backing band ought to be able to produce something less monotonous than this.'

David Jacobs on his *Juke Box Jury* show: 'I am sorry to have to play this. It sounds like music from a third-rate ice show.'

Roger: 'Jacobs was a typical BBC pompous-type. His comments were arrogant and belittling. Brian Gregg was going to lump him in the bar after the show.'

Radio Luxembourg disc jockey Tony Prince met Jacobs around the same time and gave this insight on him in his autobiography: 'David was a charming English gentleman who was just as you saw and heard him on the media, but don't ask me how he got into teenage radio because this was one square fella in a very round world. Yet he was voted Best DJ every year in the *NME* readers poll.'

David Jacobs was an old-school disc jockey and his comments weren't forgotten. Clem saw him at a charity show The Tornados were playing at in the 2000s and couldn't resist having a go at him:

> I said to him, 'You don't remember us do you?' He said, 'No, should I?' I said, 'Yes, we're The Tornados and you were the very rude man who slaughtered us about '*Telstar*' when we were on your show at the time. You've probably forgotten that, haven't you. The thing is, people still know us – but there's a lot of people out there who don't know you!'

Roger LaVern:

> I actually phoned David Jacobs in 1995 to ask him if he would attend a charity show I was involved in. His response was 'Why on earth would I want to come to boring Bromley?!' That summed the man up for me.

Joe Meek was asked by *Melody Maker* for his response to critics saying '*Telstar*' was a banal record. He replied with more than a hint of contempt: 'If it was played by the Hallé Orchestra it would be hailed as a great piece of music. Okay it was cooked up and had some gimmicks on it, but so have the Trad records in this country haven't they? I wrote '*Telstar*' one midnight. I think it's good but I suppose it could nag some people.'

Whatever Jacobs thought, the record went to the top of the charts within weeks, much to the surprise and delight of the band.

Roger:

> We were in Yarmouth and I had gone down to the administrative office near the seafront to pick up any mail we had. The receptionist said, 'Oh there's been a phone call from Chris Hutchins of the *New Musical Express*. He's been trying to contact someone from the band. Said he's going to phone back.' So I hung around for a bit and the phone call came through. 'I've been trying to get hold of one of you, your record is in the charts at number twelve!' Well, I was just a little old country boy, this was incredible. I was so excited. He was coming down to Yarmouth for a meeting and then he rang back, 'Roger, I made a mistake, '*Telstar*' is at number ten!' I went looking for the rest of the boys, we all split up during the day, and the first one I came across was Alan Caddy. 'Alan,' I said, 'guess what? We're at number 10 in the hit parade!' And he went.. 'So what?' which deflated me somewhat, but I suppose though that Alan had already been there, and top of the charts with Johnny Kidd and The Pirates.

Clem:

> Alan might have been winding Roger up, as a week later Alan came up to my room in the hotel and was banging on the door, 'Clem,' he shouted, 'have you seen this?!' He had the *Daily Mirror* in his hand, it was a Thursday and I remember this because it was every Thursday they printed the Top Twenty. There it was, The Tornados and '*Telstar*' at number five! We were in shock with the excitement! A week later it was number one. It was all too much to take in. Suddenly the phone calls started to flood in. I must say I still feel proud to be part of that record. And I will also say that Joe Meek did a fantastic job on it with the sound effects. I believe it was also Margaret Thatcher's favourite record, though I'm not sure if that is something to brag about! Better news was to come. The Americans loved it! Because Telstar was their project, they were delighted to have a tune dedicated to it and we became the first British band to have a number one record Stateside. They also wanted us to go over on tour, and that was a major compliment back then I can assure you. If we had been able to go we'd have been a very wealthy outfit, but the last

word was with Larry Parnes. I'd had clashes with him earlier in my career when I told him to stick his job. Clearly he had a long memory. The problem was that Meek had contracted us to do a tour the following January, February and March with Billy Fury, and Parnes insisted that if we went to America, then Billy had to go as well.

With Fury, The Tornados' stage presence was restricted to playing *'Telstar'* for two minutes, either side of which they faded into the background, 'looking pretty behind a top-flight singer who they were outselling by at least two to one.' Clem hated the whole experience, as he revealed to Spencer Leigh:

> We carried on with Billy and other singers right through until 1963. I was usually on a rostrum, I didn't like people watching me in case I made a mistake. A lot of the stages had rakes on them so people could see you better. They would put in wedges for the drums, but they could come out and some drummers ended up in the footlights. That happened to me and I was lucky not to tip into the pit. I remember Billy looking at me in wonderment. Billy was a good singer, very underrated in my view, but the Americans had never heard of him. They said, very firmly, 'No.' It was just The Tornados they wanted. Parnes was just as emphatic. 'No Billy Fury, no Tornados.' End of story! We did make a few bob out of *'Telstar'*, even if it took me 30 years to get the full royalties from the record! Joe Meek later claimed he'd made £30 grand out of *'Telstar'*! But we could have made, with no exaggeration, millions if we'd been able to go on that tour. But Parnes was adamant.

Whilst this was all going on, a crisis was escalating between the two world super powers, the United States and Russia, culminating in what became the Cuban Missile Crisis. The world was on the precipice of nuclear war. Suddenly, who was at number one in the Top Twenty seemed irrelevant. The world was holding its breath as Khrushchev and Kennedy decided who was going to push the button first. Looking back all these years later it seems far-fetched and exaggerated, but at the time the fear was for real. Doom-mongers had a field day... 'The World Is Nigh' was a favourite placard to be seen at the time. Monks were apparently climbing to the highest hilltop in Nepal.

Bip Wetherell, Tornados keyboard player in the 1990s, remembers being at school and worrying whether this was going to be his last day on earth, never mind school; a feeling shared by millions of people around the globe.

Not the Tornados though. They carried on regardless. and recorded an EP of songs in October which included the theme music for a series of Edgar Lustgarten films entitled *The Scales of Justice*.

The Shadows, unfortunately, were caught up in the crisis when they were in America with Cliff promoting their film *The Young Ones*.

Bruce Welch:

> We were in Miami when the crisis was at its peak. Tanks were lined up on the beach facing Cuba. There was nobody around, everyone was seeking shelter, it was scary. We were playing halls which were virtually empty because of the crisis. Cliff and us played live the first half, and the film, renamed *It's Wonderful To Be Young* in America, was shown in the second half. It wasn't wonderful at the time!

Russia's influence in Cuba was a deep concern for Kennedy, and he sanctioned the CIA plan to overthrow communist leader Fidel Castro with the invasion of the Bay of Pigs. It proved to be a disaster and an embarrassing episode for the United States, an episode which only strengthened the position of Castro's leadership, making him a national hero. Khrushchev reached an agreement with Castro to place Soviet nuclear missiles in Cuba to deter any future invasion attempt. Kennedy ordered a naval 'quarantine' of Cuba and demanded the Soviets dismantle the missile bases already under construction or completed, and return all offensive weapons to the U.S.S.R.

The message was unmistakable; 'It shall be the policy of this nation to regard any nuclear missile launched from Cuba against any nation in the Western Hemisphere as an attack by the Soviet Union on the United States, requiring a full retaliatory response upon the Soviet

Union.'

Khrushchev responded by calling the U.S. 'blockade' an 'act of aggression', and stated that Soviet ships bound for Cuba would be ordered to proceed. Kennedy told his advisors it appeared only a U.S. attack on Cuba would remove the missiles, but insisted on giving the diplomatic channel a little more time. The crisis had reached a stalemate, but took a dramatic turn when ABC News correspondent John Scali reported to the White House that he had been approached by a Soviet agent suggesting that an agreement could be reached in which the Soviets would remove their missiles from Cuba if the United States promised not to invade the island.

Khrushchev sent Kennedy a message; 'If there is no intention to doom the world to the catastrophe of nuclear war, then let us not only relax the forces pulling on the ends of the rope, let us take measures to untie that knot. We are ready for this.'

U.S. Attorney General Robert Kennedy met the Soviet Ambassador Anatoly Dobrynin, and the next morning Khrushchev issued a statement that Soviet missiles would be dismantled and removed from Cuba.

The crisis was over. And Bip Wetherell went back to school the next day...

The Shadows returned home to 'Dance On' and continue to roll out the hits with *Wonderful Land* and *Guitar Tango*.

Having teetered on the brink of nuclear conflict, the superpowers began to reconsider the nuclear arms race and took the first steps in agreeing to a nuclear Test Ban Treaty. The crisis remains one of those epochal moments in the lives of all those who lived through it.

The height of the 'Cold War' precipitated what was one of the 'coldest' winters ever recorded in Britain.

During the winter months of 1962 and '63, a report from the Met Office told of how Britain was plunged into an Ice Age:

> It began just before Christmas. A belt of rain over northern Scotland on 24th December turned to snow as it moved south, giving Glasgow its first white Christmas since 1938. The snow-

belt reached southern England on Boxing Day bringing a snowfall of up to 30cm. A blizzard followed on 29th and 30th December across Wales and south-west England, causing snowdrifts up to six feet deep. Roads and railways were blocked, telephone lines brought down, villages were cut off for several days. Farmers couldn't get to their livestock, many animals starved to death.

For the next two months, until early March 1963, much of England remained covered with snow. The cold spell caused lakes and rivers to freeze, sea water in some of England's harbours turned to ice.

It was during this time, in November 1962, that Bob Dylan first paid a visit to the UK to appear in a BBC drama, *The Madhouse On Castle Street* by Jamaican playwright Evan Jones. Few in Britain had heard of Dylan at this point. Bob was still making his way in New York, but word was spreading. Director Philip Saville had seen the Woody Guthrie disciple performing in New York and was amazed by what he heard and saw. 'I thought this is too good to be true... I was determined to cast Dylan in *Madhouse*.'

Those tuning into the *Wednesday Night Play* would never have believed that the lonesome-looking figure of Dylan would become such a huge part of our lives. Dylan was down to play the lead role of Lennie, 'an anarchic young student who wrote songs', but at the first script reading he told director Saville; 'I don't know what I'm doing here. These guys are actors. I can't act!' Saville's response was; 'Great, now is the time to tell me.'

Nonetheless, Dylan did feature in the play, screened on the BBC on 13th January 1963, pitched against ITV's *Sunday Night at the Palladium*. Dylan would be left with one speaking line – 'Well, I don't know I'll have to go home and think about it' – and the chance to sing. 'It worked a treat,' Evan Jones recalled. 'I don't think I was at too many rehearsals after that. I saw the first run through of the play, which begins with '*Blowin' in the Wind*' and it was absolutely mind-blowing.'

Dylan performed three other songs: '*The Cuckoo*', '*Hang Me, Oh Hang Me*' and '*The Ballad of the Gliding Swan*'. During the trip Dylan was introduced to the English folk scene, meeting and becoming a close friend of Martin Carthy, who later wrote; 'His time in England was actually crucial to his development. If you listen to the *Freewheelin'* album, most of which was made before he came to England, and you listen to his next album *The Times They Are a-Changin'*, there's an enormous difference in the way he's singing, in the sort of tunes he's singing, the way he's putting words together... Bob Dylan's a piece of blotting paper when it comes to listening to tunes... the visit had an enormous effect on him.'

As 1962 turned into '63 a Rhythm and Blues boom was developing, with Alexis Korner's Blues Incorporated proving an influence to many aspiring blues musicians. The *Melody Maker* wasn't too impressed, as was likely expected, and went as far to ask if the so-called 'R&B Boom' was 'Trend or Tripe'.

> Are the signs pointing to a boom or a bandwagon existence? Boom will mean true recognition for genuine R&B, bandwagon spells the story of Trad all over again. The number of bands who are making reasonable money can be counted on the fingers of one hand. Innocuous-looking Cyril Davies, who emerges from his giant overcoat in a jazz club to shout blues with the best of them, sang and played harmonica with Alexis Korner, one of the kingpins of British R&B. Cyril moved on to form his own group, which opened at The Marquee. He had some interesting points to make: 'How do you tell the difference between rock and R&B? Well, I admit it's a close thing in many cases, but I think material is all important. If it comes over with feeling, it comes over well whether it's loud or anything. It has to come right out of the pot, then it's good.'

> Alexis Korner's view on the trend/trash question was lucid. 'With every trend there is a certain amount of danger. There is bound to be a limited number of good groups, and a great many bad groups. The point is – the ones that were first in can't be responsible for the second class outfits that come into the field. I think there is room for several types of groups playing several types of R&B and if the purists consider this wrong – well...'

> Can we really expect to see rhythm and blues, either the gutsy stuff of Cyril Davies' wailing harmonica or Alexis and his rasping

saxes ever making the Top 50? From one of the newer faces on the R&B scene, Mick Jagger, came a thought-provoking suggestion: 'It has got to move out of London. Only two or three clubs are making any money at the moment and it has to spread to live. That's the only way it can become popular, and retain its form at the same time.'

Maybe he's right. The New Year will bring all the answers.'

And looking at the Top Twenty as 1962 came to a close, it was clear there *was* some room for a bit of Rhythm and Blues. Great records they were but nonetheless... Nat King Cole's '*Ramblin' Rose*', Sinatra's '*Me and My Shadow*', Rolf Harris' '*Sun Arise*', Stan Getz with '*Desafinado*'... '*Telstar*' was still in there at number 8 though! And Elvis saw 1962 out with '*Return To Sender*' at the top.

6

A Change is Gonna Come

It's 1963, and the fear of us all being blown to Kingdom Come has subsided. The Soviet Union and United States finally got their heads together, screwed the nut and signed the Test Ban Treaty and we all felt a little better.

Relief may have been tangible, but the 'Cold War' was still omnipresent with the fears and mystery heightened by espionage novels from John le Carré, Len Deighton and Ian Fleming. The films *Dr. Strangelove, From Russia With Love, The Spy Who Came In From The Cold.* Exposure of Cambridge spies Philby, Burgess and Maclean. The Greville Wynne story, the John Profumo Affair and the assassination of President Kennedy. It was some year this.

Apart from the aforementioned, we also had to deal with a chap called Dr. Beeching decimating our railways. Later in the year there was the gang of bank robbers relieving the Glasgow to London Express of its bounty.

The Space Race went up a gear, with Russia taking the lead yet again over America by sending a lady, Valentina Tereshkova, into orbit aboard *Vostok 6*. Tina returned three days later to a heroine's welcome. The excursion caused much debate about whether a woman would suffer more stresses than a man when being launched into the stratosphere. Royal Air Force Wing Commander Peter Lloyd suggested otherwise: 'Surely the stresses are going to be the same despite, if I may use a non-medical term, a woman's innards are different to a man's.' Impressed or not with Valentina's achievement, America would leave it for a couple of decades before they sent a femme into space, Sally Ride aboard the space shuttle *Challenger* launched in 1983.

'*A Change Is Gonna Come*' was written by Sam Cooke following an altercation in a 'whites only' Louisiana hotel, compelling him to comment on the Civil Rights struggle in America. The song became an anthem for the movement led by Dr. Martin Luther King. It could also have been an augury for what was to come in the United Kingdom. And we haven't yet mentioned the arrival of The Beatles.

'*A Change Is Gonna Come*' was what everyone was praying for at the beginning of the year as Britain shivered through the winter and we dug ourselves out of the snow. Records tumbled as the white stuff, blizzards, freezing fog and temperatures brought the country to its knees. 'Iceberg Island' was how the RAC described the situation. On Boxing Day 1962 the Glasgow to London Express – which by a quirk of fate was the train that would be robbed the following August – ploughed into the back of another passenger train during a snowstorm outside of Crewe. Twenty people lost their lives.

On the M1, there was a pile up of 27 vehicles near Toddington. Casualty departments in hospitals around the country were overrun. Driving tests were postponed. Ice on the River Thames became so thick a car rally was held on it. Factories and schools were closed because of the freezing temperatures. Householders fighting the bitter cold stoked up the coal fires, and the energy-sapping electric and gas meters went into overdrive. Single shillings, the food for these machines, were gulped down at such a rate banks were soon reporting a shortage. 'We can't cope,' they whined.

Memories from those miserable pre-central heating days are ingrained. Icicles on the inside of windows. Paraffin heaters stinking the house out. Ploughing through two feet of snow to get to school. 'Wellies' chapping the backs of legs. Snowball fights and slides all the way. There was some fun to be had!

On the sporting front just three F.A. Cup Third Round ties survived the atrocious weather: Preston v Sunderland, Tranmere v Chelsea and Plymouth v West Brom. With no games being played, the Football Pools companies came up with the idea of a 'Pools Panel', comprising former footballers Ted Drake, Tom Finney, Tommy Lawton and George Young, plus former referee Arthur Ellis, to argue who they thought would win, lose or draw the scheduled games. In case they were to fly off the handle they were kept in order by the chairman, Group Captain Douglas Bader.

Also falling foul of the weather was a Granada 'Package Show' starring America's Johnny and The Hurricanes, cancelled 'due to circumstances beyond our control,' as were the last seven dates of a nationwide 'Jukebox Doubles' tour, with promoter Don Arden explaining; 'It's the culmination of a number of things, not least the weather'. Jukebox Doubles featured artists that would nowadays be called Tribute Acts. The weather may well have been a contributing factor, but it's a fair bet that poor ticket sales was the main reason, as fans weren't willing to leave their firesides and pay good money to see Brad Newman as Elvis Presley, Steve Francis as Billy Fury, Sally Green as Brenda Lee, Dev Douglas as Adam Faith, Dru Harvey as Gene Vincent and The Jokers as The Shadows.

Due to the on-going antipathy between Larry Parnes and Joe Meek, The Tornados' tour of the United States to back up their number one hit 'Telstar' unfortunately failed to materialise. Instead, The Tornados returned to the recording studio with Billy Fury to cut tracks for what was to become the Billy Fury and The Tornados EP. What could have been perceived as a snub to Joe Meek, record producer Mike Smith was booked by Larry Parnes for the session. Eight tracks were recorded, some with a view as a possible follow up record to 'Telstar'.

Clem:

> Following up 'Telstar' was always going to be one hell of a task because the record was so good and the tune was so memorable. Even now it hasn't dated. You sometimes hear it on the radio and I challenge anyone to pinpoint it to the 60s. There were a couple of attempts as a follow-up but nothing came near. 'Ice Cream Man' was one, and I feel that could have done better if he hadn't have been for the title. It was too childish for me, not enough credibility. The most successful was 'Globetrotter' which I hated,

and didn't rate at all. It was too much like '*Venus In Blue Jeans*' by Mark Wynter, and I couldn't stand that! When we recorded '*Globetrotter*', Joe Meek asked me what I thought of it and I said to him, 'I don't like it'. He went off his head and threw a stool at me!'

The *Melody Maker* wasn't too convinced either; 'Tornados go Globetrotting' was their heading in the reviews for new singles on January 5th. 'Tuneful – though not quite as tuneful as '*Telstar*' – and danceable. A hit of course – but will it orbit like '*Telstar*'?'

Clem:

> Of course, what '*Telstar*' did give us was a name. We had achieved fame, and that gave us good billing the following summer at Blackpool. It also gained me a contract to write a weekly column for *Record Mirror*, and there was one group who got frequent mentions that summer. They were The Beatles and they also had a new drummer, Ringo Starr.

Larry Parnes was never far from controversy and he caused a furore with the Royal Albert Hall leisure committee over a concert called 'The Top of the Pops' after they refused Billy Fury top billing, which was reminiscent of the dispute over the lost Tornados America trip. Arguments carried on for months before Larry pulled Fury from the show and organised a show himself to be recorded at Decca studios, which would also produce a 'live' album. He placed an advertisement in the music papers telling those who had bought tickets for the Albert Hall and were disappointed because of Fury's omission should retain their ticket to gain entry into the studio concert in April. Three hundred fans took advantage.

Clem:

> They had a great big studio at Decca where they recorded the classical stuff, and they decided to put a few chairs in there and hold a concert. I really enjoyed the show. There was a few problems at first because the screams drowned out the music, but the result of this recording was *We Want Billy!*

Repeated here is Clem telling Peter Jones of the *Record Mirror*

(November 1963) the story behind the session as they listened to the album;

'It took all day,' said Clem, 'We had two separate audiences, but ran through both sides of the album for each gathering. First off, Tony Hall introduced each Tornado. Then we swung right into 'Sweet Little Sixteen' and Billy slipped quickly out of a door by the control panel. You can hear the screams. Fantastic.'

Clem listened to the opener for a moment. 'Such a lovely feel to Billy's voice. No getting away from it. He really gets to grips with this Chuck Berry number. Course being in the box, we couldn't hear all that was going on with the earphones and so on. But I like Bill better on this kind of material. I think he enjoys doing it more than the usual single-type ballads.

'Now hear 'Baby Come On'. We didn't know this one until the morning of the session. Bill's just fine. Next comes 'That's All Right'. He starts it slowly... you can feel the tense excitement build up. It was Bill's idea to speed up midway. I have to follow him on the beat and tempo. Out front, Billy was grafting hard. The effect got us going. We all got the audience going. 'Sticks and Stones'? Yes, Bill dug this one up from a Ray Charles album. Listen to that feeling in his voice again. He does all these numbers from time to time on stage, except 'Baby Come On'. Now comes 'Unchain My Heart'. Get that coloured approach to his singing. And you know, every movement he makes counts. A lot of them, I have to follow with a bang on the bass drum. You know Billy completely loses himself when he's working. Kind of gone – you think he's oblivious to everything. Here comes 'I'm Moving On'. Used to be his closer on stage. He builds and builds like mad. He can't stop himself writhing like a snake. A Hank Snow number of course. You hear those screams even when he's not singing? It's just a movement made by Bill. He can control an audience beautifully.

Working with Billy is really an experience. I don't think any singer has shown so much improvement over the years. Fans who just hear him on his singles don't realise how good he is on the Chuck Berry and Ray Charles sort of stuff. He's the sort of bloke who knows exactly what he wants, musically. He works on his own intuition. He really is a shy person, you know. But he loses himself completely once he gets the rhythm going inside him. This one's 'Just Because'. He used that too, as a stage closer. More of that coloured-style of singing. The double ending is effective, too. He just stops dead... says 'Ha'... and off goes that riot of reaction. The second side has his old hits. Working with Bill is really hard work. We were whacked by midway but a satisfied kind of whacked, if you see what I mean. Of course, we were nervous. You can't help that feeling. Now we come to those early hits. Like 'Halfway To Paradise', 'I'd Never Find Another You', 'Once Upon A Dream' – all with a special key change link. We just went straight through the lot. Then right at the end we used the intro to 'Sticks and Stones' to get Billy off. Everybody just joined in on the 'We Want Billy!' chant. Fantastic and ear-splitting. Bill didn't hang about though He'd have been mobbed. By the time the fans got outside, he was probably back in his flat having a cuppa. He's a thorough professional. That's a lot rarer than you'd think. I think he's one of the most exciting performers on the scene – and I'd think so even if we weren't working with him.'

Clem:

On stage Billy did stuff like blues and country, all the stuff we did on the live album was rock and roll. In my view Billy wasn't given the right material to record. That's what he was really good at. He had a great rock and roll voice, he was a great singer and one of the finest rock singers of that era. He was more the Elvis Presley of Britain than anybody else. Don't get me wrong, I think 'Halfway To Paradise', 'Jealousy', 'I Will' were great but I don't think they reflected what he did.

Despite the success of the We Want Billy! album, Billy was in a fury with The Tornados, finding the constant changes in the line up irritating as it meant more and more rehearsals. Joe Meek had extracted Heinz from the band to launch his solo career, and The Outlaws' Chas Hodges and then Tab Martin stepped in at short notice when they were due to appear in the film Just For Fun. Brian Gregg then rejoined his old mate Clem in the band when Tab left to form the jazz/soul group The Peddlers with organist Roy Phillips and drummer Trevor Morais.

If the merry-go-round on bass guitar was annoying for Billy Fury, when Roger LaVern departed through illness midway through a tour the same month, ending up in Kidderminster Hospital, he must have wondered if the carousel of musicians would ever stop.

A number of recordings by The Tornados were released this year including *'Ridin' The Wind'*, *'Dragonfly'* and an EP entitled *Tornado Rock*. LaVern, Bellamy and Gregg then departed in August and were replaced by Jimmy O'Brien, Bryan Irwin and Ray Randall, leaving Clem and Alan Caddy as the only remaining original Tornados.

We Want Billy! was released in October 1963 to critical acclaim, but to a backdrop of acrimony with Parnes and Meek still not talking to each other and rumours that Fury was ready to ditch The Tornados and concentrate on a solo career.

Clem:

> Joe Meek wanted Heinz to be the next big star, but to be honest it was never going to happen. He just wasn't good enough. He went solo and had a hit with *'Just Like Eddie'*, a song dedicated to Eddie Cochran, but after that it all went flat for him.

Released in July '63, *'Just Like Eddie'* made it to number five in the hit parade. You would have expected Heinz to be well pleased with the way his career had taken off, but in the *Melody Maker* he revealed frustrations, stating that he thought ballrooms, the traditional venue for pop groups apart from the package tours, was the kiss of death for artists like himself: 'I am turning down £2,000 worth of offers every week. Ballrooms are the kiss of death and I won't have anything to do with them. The audiences at ballrooms just want a sound, they're not interested in any work the performer puts into an act and it is very depressing. I'm sticking to concerts.'

The Outlaws, with Ritchie Blackmore on lead guitar, became Heinz's backing band for a season with comedian Arthur Askey in Rhyl following a British tour alongside Gene Vincent and Jerry Lee Lewis, which must have been a startling contrast – one minute playing with true legends of rock and roll, and the next supporting a music hall comedian whose catchphrase was 'Hello playmates'. Heinz's shows were far from being described as successful. He had a tough time on tour from mostly male audiences, some of whom threw cans of baked beans at him. Failing to follow up *'Eddie'* with anything substantial, Heinz soon became a side note in music history and was left on the shelf like so many others in the wake of The Beatles' arrival.

The relative failure of *'Dragonfly'* and rumours concerning Billy Fury's association with the band begged questions, which journalist Art Johnson asked Clem, who remained very upbeat about the progress The Tornados were making with the new boys:

Art: 'Is anything going wrong with The Tornados on the disc scene? Their last single, *'Dragonfly'*, buzzed into the charts and then just as fast buzzed out.'

Clem: 'There was a strike at the Decca factory which didn't help much with the sales of *'Dragonfly'*. But I think we've been a bit upset by the changes in personnel of the group. Heinz was a pretty big draw with that blonde barnet shining all over the stage, and then Roger LaVern had to leave because of his back problems. So there was a kind of uncertainty about the whole set up. But I honestly think The Tornados have never been better than now. There's so much enthusiasm in the group with the new members. Rehearsals are turning out to be a lot of fun as well... and the touring with Billy Fury... well that's always an exciting experience for all of us. Every so often you get these rumours that Bill is looking for a new group and that tends to react against us. But this new spirit will show through on discs eventually, I'm sure. Then look for us up at the top again. We are keeping our fingers crossed anyway.'

Art: 'Clem and Alan Caddy have become the elder statesmen of the group, father figures to the three newcomers Clem calls 'Son Number One', 'Son Number Two' and 'Son Number Three'. The three – Jimmy O'Brien on organ, Bryan Irwin on guitar and bassist Ray Randall – have added a stack more personality in the line up too. Jimmy wags his head all over the organ as he plays and his technique – picked up largely on trips to the beat clubs of Germany – adds depth to the sound. He uses a fair whack of echo on organ which means getting away from the dry sound you usually get... and Ray Randall is proving another big favourite with the fans. Young boy face, wide grin, mop of fair hair and a rather shy approach. The group were mobbed by a crowd of fans up north not so long ago, and most of them made a beeline for little Ray.'

'Poor bloke, he looked terrified,' said Clem. 'He went all white-faced and looked as if he was going to faint. We moved in to try to protect him but that didn't really work. They nearly shoved me through a plate glass window! It was a funny experience for all of us really, because The Tornados have never usually been the sort of group to get such treatment. Still it kind of boosted our egos!'

Between the years 1960 and '62, a Trad Jazz revival occurred with the Acker Bilk, Chris Barber and Kenny Ball bands much to the fore and The Temperance Seven's *'You're Driving Me Crazy'* hitting the number one spot. Duffel coats, goatee beards, pipes and St. Bruno were all back in vogue.

One musician less than enamoured with the 'boom' was Clem Cattini, who confessed:

> I must admit I was turned off by the jazz scene. I remember when *'Telstar'* was number one and we were invited to a midnight jazz concert as guests of honour. I forget who the drummer was, but he was a black guy and it came to his drum solo. Now it was at that period when the jazz attitude was to turn your back to the audience and play what you wanted to play, to the point of ignoring the audience. This guy did a twenty minute drum solo playing the 1st and 3rd beat of each bar, and that's all he did throughout his solo and this went on and on and I thought, hang on, I think you're extracting the Michael. I understand he had to impress the few in the front who were going 'Wow, yes man,' but that really wasn't for me and I got up and walked out, it was pure self indulgence.

The first indication that a change was on the horizon came when The Beatles had sneaked into the top twenty with their self-penned *'Love Me Do'*. There was something distinctly different about the sound and the group that was piercing through the Frank Ifields, Acker Bilks and Pat Boones. The name must have rang a bell in Larry Parnes's ear... the group he rejected in 1960 called The Silver Beetles.

Having spent the last few years flogging themselves in the clubs of Hamburg, The Beatles were ready for world domination. Their arrival was perfect timing, and an antidote to a world consumed with fear. Suddenly the world looked a little less dull.

The Beatles were in the vanguard of what was dubbed a 'Merseybeat' boom. Gerry and the Pacemakers, The Big Three, Billy J. Kramer, The Fourmost, Cilla Black and Tommy Quickly were all signed up by Liverpool's answer to Larry Parnes, Beatles manager Brian Epstein.

Coinciding with this was a TV police programme called *Z Cars*, which was set in a fictional suburb of Merseyside called Newtown. Police constables 'Fancy' Smith, Bert Lynch and Jock Weir driving around in Ford Zephyrs in search of hub caps was essential viewing.

Liverpool instantly became fashionable. Music moguls from the south were all making a beeline up to the north west to see who they could discover. The Searchers, Merseybeats, Hollies, Mojos, Herman's Hermits, Undertakers, Wayne Fontana and The Mindbenders, and The Swinging Blue Jeans were amongst the cream of the crop signed up.

Signed to the Parlophone label, The Beatles' star continued in the ascendency with the release of '*Please Please Me*' and '*From Me To You*'. What made them different from the normal line up of three guitars and a drummer was that no one was the particular lead singer. Producer George Martin is on record as saying that at first he couldn't figure them out. Every group had a 'lead' singer: Cliff and The Shadows, Joe Brown and The Bruvvers, Marty Wilde and The Wildcats. That was the traditional line up of bands all round the country. The front line of The Beatles – McCartney, Harrison and Lennon – all sang, a result of working hundreds of hours in The Cavern in Liverpool and Hamburg, where they all had to share the duties. Another result of this was the harmonies they excelled at, gelling together like the Everly Brothers.

These early days are affectionately recalled by Bruce Welch:

> The Shadows were firm friends with The Beatles with a nice

rivalry. We had a party one night in my house when we were all there. I remember sitting on the stairs with John and playing our guitars. John asked me what we had for our next single and I played him 'Dance On'. 'What's your next single?' I asked John – and he started belting out 'If there's anything that you want...' 'From Me To You'. I went 'Wow!' These were the early days and they were something else, fantastic. You just knew they were going places and were going to leave everyone else behind!

We went to see The Beatles when they were second billing to Roy Orbison on tour at the Slough Granada in early 1963. Roy was a lovely guy, a real gentleman. After the hysterics, following The Beatles must have been daunting for Roy, but he walked out on stage, stood stock still, hardly moved, and absolutely paralysed the audience with his singing. What a performer, amazing. His range was unbelievable and he was so quiet and modest. He was a huge superstar, and a brilliant guy. We played at the *New Musical Express* Poll Winners Concert when everybody was on. The Beatles, Stones, Tornados, Gerry and Pacemakers, Hollies, Roy... and incidentally, nobody got paid! It was a right rip off, but a showcase for everyone I suppose. In the backstage area where there was a dining area for the artists, Roy came over to us and I couldn't believe it when he asked, 'How's it going Bruce?' We had only met him once briefly a while before this, and he remembered our names. It was so sad when he lost his wife in a motorbike crash and then his kids in a house fire. When he died at the age of just 54 it was probably a result of years of grieving that brought about his premature demise, even though he'd married again.

With our success in the early Sixties we were able to buy ourselves villas in Portugal, which became an escape from the hype and mayhem of the pop business back home. Talking to Paul McCartney, he was telling us how bad it was for The Beatles. 'We can't go out of the door,' he said. 'We just can't go out for a walk to the shops or a stroll without getting mobbed or chased by fans or photographers.' I told him to get himself a villa like the rest of us, in Portugal. I said to him, 'Come over to our place,' which was remote in the south of the country. You had to fly to Lisbon those days and hire a car for a five hour drive but when you get there, nobody in the village will know who you are and they won't care. So he came over, he was taking the villa for a couple of weeks after we were leaving. I met him at the airport, he was with Jane

Asher at the time, and on the way down he was scribbling down lyrics for a melody he had in his head, on some sheets of A4 paper. When we arrived at the villa, he borrowed a guitar and strummed out the song that would become the most recorded and covered track ever, 'Yesterday'. Amazing!

The Beatles were featured in a March issue of the *New Musical Express*, where they were mentioned in the same breath as the current top pop idols Cliff Richard and The Shadows who were releasing two hit albums on the Columbia label.

The Beatles have recorded three new titles, including their next single at the Abbey Road studios. They are also booked for a charity show at the Liverpool Grafton on June 12th, where they are giving their services free in aid of the NSPCC. They have also revealed that they very nearly made a mistake when releasing 'Please Please Me', which is at number one, as their second single. It was a big moment for the Liverpool band. 'What made it more exciting,' said John Lennon, 'was, we nearly abandoned it as the 'B' side to our first single 'Love Me Do'.' Producer George Martin advised the boys to leave it for another time and 'to try and tidy it up a bit.' Lennon revealed: 'We changed the tempo, altered the lyrics a bit, added the harmonica and by the time the session came round we couldn't wait to get it recorded.' Once it was done they went off to a West End restaurant to celebrate and found themselves causing a stir because of their distinctive hairstyles and taste for suede clothes! As they were hardly known outside of Liverpool in this country, they decided to impersonate The Shadows! A job made easier by John wearing heavy-rimmed glasses in the style of Hank Marvin, though he doesn't wear them onstage because he doesn't want The Beatles to be accused of imitation. Their witticism came through when ordering meals: 'Will you order, Hank?' and 'Brian, did Cliff mention...' A short distance away, a young man and his girlfriend were watching and after a while he came over to ask if they would sign their autographs, a request that was met with much laughter! 'You are The Tornados, aren't you?' he asked.

If there's one thing The Beatles are determined on, it's not to move to London. They've a great fondness for their home city, Liverpool. 'We love the place,' said Paul. 'We all met at school there, it's where we had our first breaks, the fans were, and are, terrific.' In their early days the band played regularly in all the Liverpool clubs. Paul; 'We used to work at a club in Upper Parliament Street, playing for a striptease girl. We played behind her, but at the end of her act, she would turn round, and... well, we were all young lads and we blushed like mad! Four blushing lads in pink mohair suits! She brought sheets of music for us to play her arrangements, things like Beethoven and the Spanish Fire Dance. We can't read music, so in the end we said 'Sorry', but instead we can play the '*Harry Lime Cha Cha*', which we'd arranged ourselves, and '*Moonglow*'. She had no choice!'

The Beatles are looking forward to the release of their debut album, which George Martin is enthusing about. 'Incredibly, the boys recorded non-stop for 12 hours even though most of them had heavy colds.' And after the final scorching number, a pulsating version of '*Twist and Shout*', George Martin looked down from the control room in sheer amazement. 'How could anybody achieve such a fantastic sound after so long? The tougher the conditions, the better they get!'

The Beatles were added to the bill for a BBC Albert Hall concert on April 18th, Del Shannon headlining a show which also included John Leyton, The Bachelors, Susan Maughan, Matt Monro, Kenny Lynch, Julie Grant, Shane Fenton and the Fentones, The Springfields, The Vernons Girls, Hall and MacGregor and The Chris Barber Band.

Clem:

The Beatles were awesome. They had such incredible talent and it frightened the rest of the music industry to death. We all knew there was a new era on the way. They were so special. You could hear it in their voices and you could hear it in the music they wrote. Basically, they put the kybosh on everyone else's career. This was a new genre of music coming through and we all knew it. At the start of 1963 The Tornados were a bigger name than them. They were asking me questions. By the end of that year, many pop music acts were history. They killed off The Tornados and many other acts as well because of the kind of music they inspired.

Clem came to meet and become lifelong friends of The Beatles during the summer of '63 when they were playing in Blackpool:

The town was buzzing. It was the day The Beatles were playing their weekly concert at the ABC Theatre. Thousands of teenagers from all over the North West of England, and even as far away as London, treated Blackpool like some kind of Mecca in those days. They queued for hours to get in to see them, some waiting overnight to ensure they got into the venue. Many would settle for a glimpse of the four young men who were to revolutionise music, not only in Britain but all over the world. What those kids didn't know was that they were already there inside the theatre. I know, because I was with them – tucking into a roast Sunday lunch! Such was the hysteria surrounding them they had to be smuggled into the ABC early that morning. For them, ordinary life was over. They had to get there early and leave late, and I would meet up with them for a chat and a lunch – roast beef, lamb, chicken and sometimes fish and chips. And while there we would chat about the column I was writing for the *Record Mirror*. 'Hi folks, this is Clem in Blackpool here...' that is how it would always start. 'This week I am chatting with the Fab Four again...' And I would relay to the thousands of Beatles fans what the four of them had been up to in the last week. The readers lapped it up. I realised I was in something of a privileged position because they were not giving interviews to anyone else, no papers – certainly not on a regular basis. So how come they would talk to me so freely? It all stemmed back to five years earlier when I was in the backing band for Billy Fury. The Silver Beetles, as they were then, were scratching out a living playing at the famous Cavern. Billy was from Liverpool and something of a local hero to John, Paul, George and Pete Best, who was the drummer at the time. They would come backstage to talk to the band and I got on really well with them. Especially Paul. He was like me, clearly family-orientated and we struck up an immediate rapport. It was the foundation of a friendship that has lasted some 50 years on. Of course I went on to play for Johnny Kidd and The Pirates and then The Tornados, so that helped my credibility with them, because of the worldwide success of '*Telstar*'. They were highly impressed that I was one of the first Brits to top the charts in America. I had heard their record '*Love Me Do*' the previous October. It wasn't a huge hit, but I knew there was something there. Then in February I heard the sound that would change the face of pop music when they released '*Please*

Please Me'. It came on the radio and I thought there and then, 'This is different, this is new, this will wipe the rest of us off the face of the planet!' And I was right. Quite simply, they had the indefinable quality – genius.

They had liked the stuff Billy Fury used to play on stage, a lot of real Rhythm and Blues stuff, Ray Charles songs, Billy did a lot of that in his act and was a lot more versatile than people would think if they just listened to his records. We would talk about the major influences on their music when we had our Sunday get-togethers in Blackpool. Perhaps we got on so well because it was musician talking to musician. We were on the same level. There was no hero worship or anything like that. One particular topic of conversation was their forthcoming trip to America. Many of their songs before those written by John and Paul were taken from American groups like The Marvelettes and Chuck Berry.

Many people thought the boys were mad going to America, they reckoned they would flop because they were taking American songs back to America. Taking coal back to Newcastle, as the old expression used to go. I never had any doubt.

So, what were they like back in those days? I'll start with John Lennon. I never really got close to John, but I don't think anybody really did. He always had a barbed comment to make in any conversation, always a kind of smart remark. He wasn't rude to me, not at all. But while the other three were family-orientated, John wasn't and I had the feeling that he was a wee bit envious of those who did have family ties. John was abandoned by his father when he was very young, lost his mum through a tragic accident and was brought up by his aunt. I think in a way he resented the fact that he didn't have anyone to fall back on. It was like the heavy sarcasm was a kind of safety barrier for him. He seemed afraid to get too close in case, I reckoned, he got hurt again.

Ringo was a lovely guy, but I can't say I ever really got to know him. But I'm not alone in the opinion that he wasn't the best drummer around. John Lennon agreed. Asked if Ringo was the best drummer in the world, John replied, 'He's not even the best drummer in The Beatles!'

George was so laid back. Really gentle. As it turned out, we got a lot closer many years later. We were at the same event and George asked me if it was true I was the drummer with Johnny Kidd and

The Pirates. When I told him I was, he was really impressed. 'I loved them, they were so good. I used to travel miles to watch them. I really want to know what Johnny was like. Can we meet up soon to talk about it?' I said that wouldn't be a problem, but unfortunately before we could he died of lung cancer. What a great loss. Lovely man, excellent guitarist.

The Beatle I came really close to was Paul. Somehow it was obvious he was the leader of the group. He was fascinated by Joe Meek and his production methods, how he managed to create sound effects on '*Telstar*'. You could see he was like the unofficial chief, the man who was organising everything, the man with the most input. He was also a big family man and I think that is one of the reasons we got on so well. I have been married to my wife Anna for over 50 years and he liked the fact that in an industry in which marriages don't last five minutes, I and Anna had stayed strong. There have been so many myths about Paul over the years. All I can say is, I don't recognise any of them. Tight? You are joking. He offered me the chance to work with him as part of his band Wings but I turned it down. Why? Because the work I was doing by then paid better, and I didn't have to tour and leave home. He couldn't have done more. He made it clear that when we went on tour to the States, Anna would be coming with me. All flights and hotels would be paid for, no problem. But I explained that I didn't want to be away from my kids for so long, so I turned it down. He really respected the fact that it was for family reasons. Linda McCartney was a lovely person. She made a point of seeking me out whenever she knew I was around, in a recording studio or on *Top Of The Pops* or some other television show. If ever Wings were playing somewhere like Wembley Arena, through the door would come the complimentary tickets with backstage passes. More recently I have heard gossip about Paul being a wife-beater. That cannot be the man that I have known for more than 50 years. He just isn't capable of it – and I stand by every word of that. That is not Paul McCartney.

The drummer Paul recruited for Wings was American Denny Seiwell. Denny was raised in Pennsylvania, had enlisted into the United States Navy and played in the Navy Band. Later moving to New York, Denny played with Zoot Sims, Art Garfunkel, Janis Joplin, James Brown, Billy Joel, and John Denver amongst many others.

'New York was such a great place in those days,' he recalled. It was where Paul McCartney, then in the process of forming a new band with his wife Linda, saw Denny play and decided he was the man he wanted.

Denny (2018):

> I did a record with Paul called *Ram* and it was after that album Paul asked me to continue on and form Wings. The salary was low but we were promised more in the way of royalties. That didn't happen, because of legal problems left over from The Beatles break up. It was the only bad thing about those days and corrected later. The band with Denny Laine (ex Moody Blues) and Henry McCullough (ex Joe Cocker) was like one big family living between London and the McCartneys' farm in Scotland.

Denny, interviewed by *Ultimate Classic Rock* editor Nick DeRiso in 2013:

> 'The *Ram* recording sessions were just an extraordinary experience for everyone, including Paul, I believe. There wasn't really a lot of pressure. Every day he would come in with a song that he wanted to record, and we'd sit around and add some parts that would really make it shine, and start recording. At the end, we'd say, 'My God, this is some really great stuff.' It was just the three of us at any given time, Paul, sessions guitarists Hugh McCracken, David Spinozza and me. Paul was playing guitar or piano, so we didn't get to hear bass parts or any of the finished songs or vocals. We worked with a pilot track. So it was really bare bones, and when I finally heard the final product, I was really knocked out.

Nick DeRiso: 'At the time, *Ram* was roundly panned, but it's grown in critical stature over the years. Why do you think it took so long for people to recognise that project as being one of McCartney's better solo records?'

Denny: 'I think a lot of people were just mad that he was leaving The Beatles, and going off and doing his own thing. I think that had a lot to do with it. I know the critics really did not see the value in that record, but I just thought it was a masterpiece. It's the best record I ever made, and I've made a lot of records.'

Henry McCullough, who joined Wings along with Denny Laine in December '71 before they recorded the second album, *Wild Life*, had less fond memories of his time with the former Beatle, recalling to Clem Cattini the band being treated like second class citizens:

'They were given living quarters in an outside building on the farm, Henry told me, and told by Paul and Linda there was a good café in town where they could get some food,' says Clem. 'You would have thought that bonding together and rehearsing was all part of the package, but it seems the band members were kept at a distance. I liked Paul, but he did have a reputation for being parsimonious.'

Which Denny Seiwell admitted, 'was mostly true.'

Denny Seiwell appeared on Wings' debut album *Wild Life* as well as the follow-up *Red Rose Speedway*, the chart-topping '*My Love*' and the Oscar-winning '*Live and Let Die*' before leaving on the eve of McCartney's sessions for *Band on the Run*.

Denny (with Nick DeRiso):

> Paul kind of pushed Henry into the corner about him playing his part the same way, every time we played – the solo from '*My Love*' as an example. I think Henry had just had enough of it, and he left. I had no plans on leaving, but at that point I felt like we had really gone to great lengths to become a band, and to go down to Lagos and record *Band on the Run* without Henry – it was just going to be a bunch of overdubs again like *Ram*. I tried talking to Paul into postponing it for a month, and breaking in another guitar player. He didn't go for that. Then some of these other problems started coming to the front, and I said: 'It's time for me to leave, too.' I was really pushing for an agreement; we were all working on a handshake. We had no contracts or anything like that in those days. I don't think we could have even had one that was legal, because of the Apple receivership and the court case that was going on at the moment. So I was there at the best, and the worst time, if you will. It's one of the few regrets that I have in my life – that I didn't sit Paul down and say: 'Hey, we gotta talk about this.'

Denny eventually moved to Los Angeles, where he has resided since 1975. Henry McCullough suffered a heart attack in November 2012. He died at his Northern Ireland home in 2016 following a long illness.

Clem:

Collectively The Beatles were phenomenal, but individually you couldn't get four more diverse characters. There were better musicians and singers, but there was a chemistry between them. Their style was one that had never been seen or heard before. Until then it had all been 'Moon in June' stuff, 'stars in the sky'. They changed all that. But it needed those four to make it happen. An example came when they went on tour to Australia and Ringo was taken ill with tonsillitis. Unable to go, a replacement was found to stand in, Jimmy Nicol, a far superior drummer technically but you know what, without Ringo, it just wasn't the same. No – there was a blend of individuals in that group that made them unique. And it was as if they knew they were destined for great things. Not in an arrogant, big-headed way. The opposite, in fact. I had seen what stardom and fame had done to Terry Dene. Great talent that he was, he just broke down when it came to handling the big-time. I had seen others turn to drink and drugs. The Beatles? They weren't fazed by any of it. They were aware of the hysteria whenever they played, but they didn't seem the least concerned. Nor should they have been. The ones with the worries were people like Cliff Richard, Marty Wilde, Mark Wynter, Joe Brown and Adam Faith. They were about to be blitzed, their days were numbered, mine too. I remember talking to Bruce Welch of The Shadows; 'Have you heard them?' I asked. 'Oh yes,' he said, 'life is going to get difficult I think mate.' How right he was!

They merged black music with what was traditionally regarded as white music. They captured the mood and the spirit of black music like no other white group had done before. Only Buddy Holly ever came close.

The Beatles inspired a whole new explosion of new talent, and it was quite a compliment to us that in 1963 we were voted second to The Shadows as best instrumental group in the *New Musical Express* poll. Every year there was a concert and we shared a dressing room with The Beatles. Some experience that was! There was a lot of time to kill and John Lennon would spend most of it drawing and doodling. A very good artist he was. His favourite was always drawing Ringo, with a cymbal on the end of his nose! That aggravated the life out of Ringo which, of course, made John do it more. Anyway, before we left the dressing room Brian Gregg, our bass player, decided to go round and clear up all the mess, including dozens of drawings by John Lennon. He just dumped them in the wastepaper bin. What would they be worth now? I dread to think how much was tossed away that night.

Joe Meek saw the signs, his magic in the studio was becoming dated, the hits were drying up and he was also becoming infamous rather than famous for his sexual persuasions. Society wasn't as tolerant back then as they are now, and to be gay was almost a crime. Obviously as the group were always associated with him and in that era, it didn't do us any favours, none at all. By the end of the year The Tornados were finished, and Joe Meek was struggling to come to terms that his career was finished too. He died tragically in 1967. He shot the landlady at the flat above the studio and then shot himself. I knew Meek would not die a natural death, that there would be something controversial about it, sadly I was proved right.

Arthur Howes signed The Beatles up for their first UK nationwide tour, which lasted from 2nd February to 3rd March 1963. They were fourth on an eleven-act bill headed by 16-year-old Helen Shapiro. Other acts on the tour were The Red Price Band, The Kestrels, The Honeys, Dave Allen, Kenny Lynch and Danny Williams. They were also joined briefly by Billie Davis during the latter part of the tour. The reaction from teenagers, particularly the girls, for The Beatles stunned everyone, prompting journalist Rex Makin of the *Liverpool Echo* to call the mayhem 'Beatlemania' after thousands of hysterical screaming girls followed and chased the boys everywhere after their shows, bringing city centres to a standstill.

The Beatles were soon edging up the bill and headlining. The hysteria became intense, but what was it that caused such an outburst of unparalleled emotion? The world was in a dark place at the time, fear of nuclear war paramount. Was this a release from the tension? A realisation of one's mortality? A craving for excitement?

The crooners and rock and roll stars of the late 1950s and early

60s were trailing in these emerging artists' wake. '*I Like It*' sang Gerry and the Pacemakers, '*I'm Telling You Now*' sang Manchester's Freddie and The Dreamers. Suddenly the world was becoming aroused.

Bemoaning the demise of the crooners was singer Kenny Lynch, who expressed his frustrations in the *Melody Maker*. 'We're Brainwashed By The Charts' Kenny claimed:

> From the day you enter showbusiness in this country, you're trapped. You've got to live with the trends. If you can't be a shrewd midget until you're 40, you're out. Everybody has to play up to the charts. If you want to keep going, you've got to go on churning out hit after hit – consisting of anything the masses can whistle – it's a stifling business. A singer in this country gets absolutely no chance to mature. There just aren't the venues where a bloke can play to the audiences who respect his style. After The Pigalle, The Talk Of The Town, and The Room At The Top, there are just the concerts left. The cabaret places draw the sort of people who go for the sing along stuff. A singer like Matt Monro even has trouble doing what he likes. The cabaret audience in this country likes the type of jolly Alma Cogan laughing-voice song. If an agent brings a big American jazz act into the country there's only a limited string of big cities where it can play. Nobody can do a Darin here, with no pandering to the charts. People are brainwashed by the charts and in a way, the singers are brainwashed into believing that the public only want to hear the charts stuff.
>
> The only bands doing anything are those like Acker Bilk and Kenny Ball's. And they don't want pop singers with them. It's sad.

Kenny:

> My first impression of The Beatles was like most people's, I thought they were great. At the time leading up to that tour with them and Helen Shapiro, I'd been appearing on a TV show for Granada, a nightly current affairs-type thing, *Scene At 6.30*, introduced by Michael Parkinson. I was asked to sing a few numbers with their jazz trio led by Derek Hilton. They were great players, won all the awards up north every year. The Beatles told me they'd watched me on the Parky show, it went out in the Manchester and

Liverpool area. 'We thought you were a great singer,' John Lennon said, 'can we play for you on the tour?' I told them that I would have loved that but they'd already put Sounds Incorporated with me. They wrote the song '*Misery*' on the bus. Helen Shapiro was offered it but she didn't want to record it, so I said I would. And I became the first one to cover a Beatles, Lennon/McCartney song! Mind you, when I told John Lennon that Bert Weedon was on guitar he wasn't particularly amused! Bert was a legend but old school. I gave it a much more pop-oriented arrangement than The Beatles would use when they recorded '*Misery*' themselves on their debut album, *Please Please Me.*

Beatlemania created a groundswell of interest in the music and fashion world. Magazines sprung up out of nowhere. Designers caught on, realising that everyone below the age of twenty wanted to dress like Beatles with polo neck shirts, Cuban-heeled boots, collarless suits. Dresses became shorter, the mini skirt caused nothing less than seismic shock when it was introduced by Mary Quant. Rising hemlines equalled rising blood pressure for the generation who had fought through the war and struggled through the 1950s.

At the forefront of fashion in 1963 were Y-Front Underpants. 'Fit For A Man' posters were to be seen everywhere; on the Underground, in the newspapers, magazines, advertising hoardings. 'Men like the Y-Front because they have the unique contour cut that makes for a perfect fit, the clean cut fit that a modern man demands. At only 7/6d a pair.' Whether you thought it was load of balls or not, they were here to stay.

The Beatles may have been all that everyone was talking about, but on the front page of the March 8th issue of the *New Musical Express* Derek Johnson was asking the question: 'Do we want Elvis here?'

The rumours are rife again. The annual springtime whisperings concerning an impending visit to this country by Elvis have started again. Should we ask ourselves the highly pertinent question: 'Do we want Elvis here?' Much of the romance, which is the essence of the Presley cult, is derived from the fact that he is a remote, aloof almost mysterious figure. He might conceivably be a fictional or historic character so far as the vast majority of fans are concerned. Herein lies the secret of the Presley appeal. The insurmountable barrier separating him from his British fans has boosted the legend out of all proportion. Presley's periodic disc releases and film appearances are sufficient to whet the appetite and catch the imagination – but never to completely satisfy. If Presley were to dumbfound the cynics by making appearances in Britain, he would undoubtedly cause the biggest wave of fan hysteria in the history of showbusiness. Everyone would want to see this phenomenal figure who has dominated the pop music scene for years.

But after it was all over, after the 'mystery' was 'solved', what then? Would Presley return to the States, confident that he consolidated his position in Britain and had in fact secured an even larger following? Or would the fans, their exuberance suddenly fulfilled, begin to lose interest once they had achieved their most cherished ambition – that of seeing Elvis in person? Whichever way you look at it, this must be regarded as a risk. Another point of view is if he doesn't eventually put in an appearance, Elvis will lose many of his British fans on the grounds that he is neglecting them. But risks are heavy. He wants to concentrate on films and records, his attitude is that in this way, millions can see him throughout the world rather than to spend time playing concert dates which would only benefit a few thousand fans. There never has been such a powerfully appealing personality on the international scene as Elvis – and I'm inclined to think that the legend is indestructible. Evidently, RCA think the same way, judging by the new ten year deal they have made with Elvis. *'One Broken Heart For Sale'*, his latest offering, is far from a scintillating disc, good by anyone else's standards, but indifferent Presley material. Del Shannon is among those who believe that Elvis would be ill-advised to visit Britain. 'If he did go over there, I'm sure the fans would love it,' he admitted, 'but then they would say – 'Well, we've seen him now' – and it would kill the image they have of him.'

Following the success of *'One Way Love'*, Cliff Bennett was keen on a track called *'Sha La La'* to be the follow up:

I fell out with the engineer Norman Smith over this. 'That's a great song,' he said to me. And he gave it to Manfred Mann! I said to him, 'It was a great song for Manfred Mann then... but not for me!' I never got on with him after that. I went to see Ron White, head of EMI, and told him I wasn't happy. 'What's up?' he asked. 'I'm not happy with the producer Ron, I want to produce myself.' He thought for a minute and then asked, 'Do you know Norrie Paramor?' Well of course I did. Norrie, producer at Columbia Records, was as famous as George Martin. 'Norrie's nephew David wants to get into the business. Why don't you give him a try? Take him under your wing?' And we worked together for the next six or seven years. We got on great together.

Nicking my songs seemed to happen a lot to me. I used to go to a record shop in South London called 'Froggy's' with Screaming Lord Sutch and we'd listen to all these great American imports this guy used to get in. One was '*Just One Look*' by Doris Troy. The Rebel Rousers were playing with The Hollies one night and Allan Clarke asked us afterwards where we got that song from. They released it as a single and it kicked off their career! When we were in the Star-Club we did a fantastic set, '*Some Other Guy*' and others... and Kingsize Taylor copied us. I said to him, 'You're doing our set.' Kingsize, who was a gentle giant, replied, 'Yeah... but you don't own em!' I wasn't going to argue!

In early 1966, we were booked as an opening act on The Beatles' last European tour. Paul said to us one night, 'We've got this track which would be great for you to do.' They were recording their *Revolver* album and one of the tracks was '*Got To Get You Into My Life*'. Right away I thought it was great track, and was excited to be given it. Paul produced it for us at Abbey Road. We spent a good few hours on it and it was getting late when Paul called it a day. I was up for finishing it off, get the vocals down, but Paul said, 'No, leave it, we'll come back tomorrow with a clear head.' He only lived around the corner. Next morning we were in the studio when Paul walks in... in his pyjamas and slippers! And that's a lasting memory I have of '*Got To Get You Into My Life*'!

The result was a number six single that was a double triumph for Bennett, his own original song '*Baby Each Day*' gracing the B-side.

Changes are part and parcel of the business. Roy Young had become a permanent member of The Rebel Rousers in 1964, but by 1968 Cliff had decided he wanted a fresh start and he left to leave

Roy to carry on with The Rebel Rousers as The Roy Young Band.

Martin Luther King Jr made his famous 'I have a dream' speech in the shadow of Lincoln's monument on 28th August 1963. It would be flippant to suggest that the fight for Civil Rights and the March on Washington commanded less press space than a report that surfaced in Britain from a gentleman called Dr. Beeching, but the doctor managed it, wiping everything off the front pages when he decimated the entire United Kingdom rail network with a stroke of his pen.

The doctor, later to become better known as Baron Beeching of East Grinstead, was appointed Chairman of the British Railways Board in 1963 and immediately set up an investigation as to why some railway lines were running at a financial loss. The railways were the arteries of the country, serving thousands of hamlets, villages, towns as well as the cities, providing employment for millions, but apparently the railways was seen as old hat, out of date and costly. Transport Minister Ernest Marples, who appointed Beeching, was well-known as a 'car' man, more interested in building motorways, which was commendable, but to disregard the livelihoods and community spirit the railways gave was short-sighted, when you look at the gridlocked roads and giant car parks which are the motorways in the 21st century. 'Freight Train, freight train, run so fast...' sang Nancy Whiskey and Chas McDevitt just six years previously. Once Dr. Beeching took over, the freight trains were going nowhere.

Beeching axed a third of Britain's 7,000 railway stations along with 6,000 miles of lines and 70,000 jobs. Years later he acknowledged, 'I suppose I'll always be looked upon as the axe man, but it was surgery, not mad chopping.'

If this was regarded as a robbery, it was surpassed in August this year with the infamous Great Train Robbery featuring a cast of Bruce Reynolds, Buster Edwards, Ronnie Biggs, Gordon Goody and a host of others. The Glasgow to London mail train was held up at a bridge near Aylesbury and relieved of just short of £3,000,000, catching the imagination like a present-day Jesse James gang. Most of the robbers were eventually rounded up and sent down for considerable spells of detention at Her Majesty's Pleasure.

By April, a climate change was coming on all fronts. The weather was finally relenting its grip, and on the political front, the appointment of Harold Wilson as Leader of the Opposition Labour Party in succession to the late Hugh Gaitskell, who passed away in January, was significant. Pipe-smoking Harold appealed to the working classes on this threshold of political upheaval. It probably helped that his constituency was Huyton in Liverpool, coinciding with the rise of *Z Cars*, The Beatles and the Merseybeat phenomenon which the country was embracing.

While Wilson was settling in to his new role of Opposition Leader, the Conservative Government was being dragged and screaming into a scandal that would rock the establishment to its foundations. Secretary of State John Profumo was caught with his pants down and embroiled in a three-way courtship with a young lady called Christine Keeler and Captain Yevgeny Ivanov, a Soviet naval attaché, which during this period of Cold War hysteria wasn't a wise thing to be doing. The world was paranoid enough as it was. Somehow it was appropriate that, ironically, one of the biggest hits at the time was Billy J. Kramer's *'Do You Want To Know A Secret?'*

As recently as November 1962 British businessman Greville Wynne, recruited by MI5 to make contact with a senior Russian military intelligence officer Colonel Oleg Penkovsky, was arrested by the KGB at a trade fair in Budapest. Penkovsky, a goldmine of intelligence for the West having access to thousands of secrets is often referred to as the 'spy who saved the world'. Penkovsky regularly met Wynne in London and Paris to hand over material and they went out drinking together. Wynne was put on trial and received an eight-year sentence. Penkovsky was shot by a firing squad.

Whilst all this was going on, the so-called 'Third Man' in the Cambridge spy ring, Kim Philby, defected to the Soviet Union from his base in Beruit.

So, on the back of all this, Profumo's dalliance with Miss Keeler was dumb to say the least... the tabloids had a field day. John Profumo was described as a randy politician, homophobic strait-laced Tory who had a brief affair with Christine Keeler, a topless showgirl in 1961. What he didn't know was that she was also sleeping with a Soviet spy.

In a report that would have done *The Sun* proud, it was said that Profumo's wife Valerie didn't care for the cut of her husband's trousers. 'Surely there must be some way of concealing your penis,' she apparently wrote to hubby, the Secretary of State for War. In 1963, the concealment of Profumo's penis – the denial that it was where it was said to be at the times in question – was the premise of the greatest sex scandal of post-war British politics.

Reports tell that by 1963, media allegations that Profumo had fallen into a honey trap in which Keeler was manipulated by her osteopath friend Stephen Ward (damned by hacks as a reckless libertine with MI5 and Kremlin contacts) into luring her Tory lover to blab nuclear secrets that were passed on to the Kremlin became so ubiquitous that the minister felt compelled to make a statement to the House. His sex lie – 'There was no impropriety whatsoever in my acquaintanceship with Miss Keeler' – destroyed not only Profumo, but also the government: Prime Minister Harold Macmillan's ill health was exacerbated by the Profumo affair and he resigned that October.

The issue became a public matter once it was claimed national security had been compromised. Profumo stood up in the House of Commons in March to deny the affair. During April and May the politician kept up a front, suing foreign publications that had relayed the rumours.

Eventually, on June 5th Profumo confessed to Parliament that he had lied, and tendered his resignation. Three days later the *Sunday Mirror* printed a letter from Profumo to Keeler that had been circulating among journalists all Spring. Known as 'the Darling letter', it made it clear the pair had been lovers.

The Tornados, meanwhile, were traipsing up and down the country again on a variety of tours arranged by taskmaster Mr. Parnes. The first was promoted as 'Your Lucky Stars' and featured Joe Brown,

Susan Maughan, The Tornados, Eden Kane, Shane Fenton and The Fentones, Jess Conrad, Rolf Harris, Peter Jay and The Jaywalkers, Daryl Quist, Peter Lodge, Mike and Tony Nevitt, and The Diggeroos with Al Paige as compere.

The programme gave fans an insight into the stars on parade, including this on Jess Conrad:

> Born in South London, Jess has a family connection with show-biz through his father being a former Jazz pianist. He went to school in Dulwich and Brixton and was said to be not too disappointed when he had to leave at the age of 15. Jess's first job was as an assistant with a stainless steel merchant in Kingston. He then left to take up a position in his father's florist business in Shepherd's Bush. While there Jess gained work as a film 'extra' and was given a small part in a film. At the time, a producer was looking for an unknown to play the part of a Rock and Roll singer in a play. Jess got the part and was a tremendous success. Offers flowed in but he turned them all down, maintaining that he knew nothing about singing and he was an actor only. Eventually he went to see Jack Good and told him that although he wasn't a singer, he had a big fan following as a result of the TV play. Jack listened to him sing, agreed that he couldn't, but 'he did have a certain teenage quality' and booked him for his show *Wham!* A recording contract followed, and through his increasing popularity as a singer he started to get better parts in films. On TV he's appeared in *Probation Officer*, *Dixon of Dock Green*, *No Hiding Place* and *The Human Jungle*. Jess has also starred in the films *Rag Doll* and *The Boys.*

Meantime, Jess returned to Decca to re-record four tracks he had waxed some months before his recent switch to Columbia, re-dubbing his voice on the tracks, which came from an episode titled 'The Flipside Man' in ABC TV's series *The Human Jungle*.

Others on the tour worthy of note were The Diggeroos from Sydenham, London, 'making a name for themselves in Ballrooms.' Canadian Daryl Quist was seen by Larry Parnes when he was in the chorus of a Tommy Steele pantomime in Liverpool. Peter Lodge was a keen cyclist and reader, and a gentleman's hairdresser given an audition by Parnes for one of his Yarmouth shows.'

The troupe kicked off in February at the Southend Odeon on the 15th, before hitting the road for shows on February 22nd Derby (Gaumont), March 15th Plymouth, 16th Bournemouth (Winter Gardens), 17th Cannock (Danilo), 18th Guildford (Odeon), 19th Wakefield (Regal), 20th Halifax (Odeon), 22nd Bradford (Gaumont), 23rd Stockport (Essoldo) 24th Birmingham (Hippodrome), 25th Stockton (Hippodrome), 26th Scarborough, 27th York (Rialto), 28th Southampton (Gaumont), 29th Taunton (Gaumont), 30th Huddersfield (Odeon), and 31st March at Liverpool (Empire)

Missing from the tour was Craig Douglas, who had recorded 13 hits in the four years since he had made a breakthrough in 1959. Craig had suffered a bout of tonsillitis earlier in the year and feared that his showbiz career had come to an end. His manager Bunny Lewis told how, after the operation in March, Craig had an audition to see if he would be able to make a package tour being lined up by Larry Parnes. Craig admitted beforehand he was desperately nervous and tensed. 'My throat is in a terrible state after the op.'

Bunny Lewis was forthright about his chances of recovering, telling the *Melody Maker*: 'I listened to Craig's pathetic attempts to sing properly, he hasn't got the same voice. I'm cancelling £2,000 worth of bookings. He couldn't face an audience right now.'

Craig, despondent when revealing that 'Over 100 fans have asked me for my tonsils as a souvenir,' had gone from being a £5-a-week milkman in the Isle of Wight to a £500-a-week singing star, but now faced an uncertain future. 'The future looks grim,' he admitted. 'It could be back to the milk. I've lost over a stone in weight following the operation and I haven't felt right since. I can't swallow properly, I hope I can pull through,' adding with a hint of self-deprecating humour, 'I have a Jaguar to support.'

Just four years earlier, in August 1959, 17-year-old Craig Douglas was billed as 'Britain's newest singing sensation' in the *New Musical Express* of August 7th 1959, with two songs – '*A Teenager in Love*' and '*Only Sixteen*' – in the charts:

In less than a year, the talented youngster has gone from being a milkman to one of the brightest emerging stars in the country. Described as quiet, unassuming, Craig's popularity has already reached startling heights. And he's genuinely bewildered. Craig began his recording career last year with Decca, before they told him to stick to delivering milk. Snapped up by Top Rank, he's proved the doubters wrong and, like the proverbial cream, has risen to the top. Craig's career is being guided by Dick Rowe, who says of his protege's meteoric rise in showbiz: 'I always knew he would make the grade and everybody at Top Rank has worked extremely hard on his behalf. Craig realises this and is sincerely grateful. We put out three records by him in under four months, which is a very dangerous thing to do, but we wanted him to get off the ground. I think we've done the trick.'

Craig is an ambitious fellow who is not content to just sing. He's currently taking piano lessons, learning to dance and taking elocution lessons as well. Dick Rowe adds: 'His heart is really in the business and he should go a long way. I think he can forget about going back on the milk.' His popularity has been boosted with appearances on television shows *Cool for Cats*, *The Jack Jackson Show* and *Lunchbox*. At present, 16 fan clubs have started up, two of which are in the Isle of Wight where they are proclaiming him as 'the local boy done good'. Lined up for the rest of the year is a Pop Prom Concert at the Albert Hall and at Christmas he will make his pantomime debut in 'Aladdin' in Doncaster.

The Tornados' ties with Billy Fury were formally severed in December, by which time there was only Clem and Alan Caddy of the original line up left.

Clem:

Working with Billy had been a great time. He knew how to work an audience, he was a master. We were on a tour of Ireland one time and during the first show he started to wiggle his hips, which immediately got all the girls going. He was warned then that if he did it again, they'd close the curtains. Well Billy did, and they did close the curtains! Another time, in Scotland on New Year's Eve, Billy was doing his usual gyrations and this guy looked up at him on stage and warned him, 'If you wiggle your ass again I'm goin' smack yer one!' So Billy did, did it on purpose, and as we finished our set and came off stage, this guy came up chasing him, and I got my bass drum and put it behind the door of the dressing room to stop him! That was the sort of thing that happened.

Road manager Hal Carter:

Everybody got the impression that Billy was mean and moody, but he wasn't. Offstage he was actually very inoffensive, quiet, very shy! Before he went on stage he'd be very nervous.

Clem:

The tours were constant and manic; we would do Spring tours lasting months, Summer seasons and then what they called Autumn tours. Billy wasn't the healthiest guy, he'd had scarlet fever as a child which had left him very weak. On tour he always looked very pallid, and I've seen him looking totally exhausted .

On November 22nd the world was stunned with the news that President Kennedy had been assassinated in Dallas. Conspiracy theories have proliferated ever since over who it was that killed JFK. After the Cuban Missile Crisis some twelve months before had been reconciled, the world appeared to be a better place. What occurred that afternoon in Dallas, Texas brought all the fears right back again.

Top of the charts at year's end was '*I Want To Hold Your Hand*' by The Beatles, with '*She Loves You*' at number 2.

They were soon to be heading off to America which was still reeling in a state of shock over the Kennedy killing, The Beatles arrival in February was perfect timing. The US needed something to lift the gloom; it wasn't expected to be a band from Liverpool that would do it though!

As far as Clem was concerned, he had said before that 'the writing was on the wall.' Things were changing. As 1964 beckoned, Clem was already looking ahead...

7

It's All Over Now

'It's New Year's Day, It's Number One, It's *Top of The Pops!*' – DJ Jimmy Savile's opening salvo on Wednesday, January 1st 1964, broadcast for the very first time from BBC Television's studio in Dickenson Road, Rusholme, Manchester. *Top Of The Pops* was starting out on a journey that would last for over 42 years.

If he was sitting at home watching, Clem Cattini may have been forgiven for thinking his time had passed for appearing on this show that would become an established weekly event for the next four decades. Was he destined to become consigned to the waste bin of pop history with a host of other pre-Beatles artists? Clem couldn't have dreamt that by the end of the decade he would become a major component of the show as resident drummer with The Top Of The Pops Orchestra for over thirteen years, and play with a multitude of superstars as diverse as Michael Jackson, Tom Jones, Stevie Wonder, Abba, The Wombles and Benny Hill.

The Times They Are a-Changin', Bob Dylan's third album, was released on January 13th 1964. That they certainly were. The Vietnam War was escalating and more and more US servicemen were being drafted and sent to South East Asia; many never to return home, many maimed for life. Images seared across our television screens brought the horrors of 'Nam right into our living rooms. Our ignorance can be bliss. How many can own up to not even knowing where Vietnam was back in the early Sixties? America had problems. The Civil Rights Movement Act was passed in July, but violence and murders in the southern states continued. The Governor of Alabama,

George Wallace, backed by the Ku Klux Klan, fuelled the trouble with his infamous speech 'Segregation now, segregation tomorrow, segregation forever', as the fight for desegregation gathered apace with Martin Luther King Jr at the spearhead.

The Times They Are a-Changin' included songs of injustice and hard times: *'The Lonesome Death of Hattie Carroll', 'The Ballad of Hollis Brown'. 'Only A Pawn In Their Game'* told the story of American civil rights activist Medgar Evers, who worked to overturn segregation at the University of Mississippi and to enact social justice and voting rights. He was murdered by a Klansman in 1963.

With all of this going on, was it any wonder that America, still deep in shock over the Kennedy assassination, embraced the coming of The Beatles and the 'British Invasion' of pop groups this year as a twinkle of light in an era of abject gloom? The Beatles took America and the world by storm. Beatlemania went into overdrive as they released a succession of hit singles, albums and their film *A Hard Day's Night*, which featured a brief cameo appearance from Clem Cattini on the soundtrack, something The Tornados drummer had long forgotten about until it was recalled by an unnamed studio engineer in the 1990s:

> It was during the scene when the 'man on train' was taking a seat in The Beatles' passenger car, and infringing on their rights by closing the window and forcibly snapping off Ringo's radio. During the six seconds that the radio is on, a generic instrumental rock song is heard. It was suspected that this incidental bit of music was actually played by The Beatles themselves. Film producer Walter Shenson stated that this was the case, claiming the music was performed and recorded by The Beatles during sessions that occurred around a week prior to when they started filming *A Hard Day's Night*. If we take Shenson at his word, it would be John Lennon who played a boogie-type rhythm on guitar and George Harrison who adds an energetic lead solo over it. Ringo Starr, when asked about the track, said he didn't remember it at all – he wouldn't have done. It was, in fact, Clem Cattini playing the drums on the track.

When asked for his recollection, Clem's recall was as vague as Ringo's:

> I do remember working with George Martin at Abbey Road, doing some instrumental stuff which was used in the *Hard Day's Night* film. The main thing I remember though was doing a whole session with George and getting fed up with him continually calling me 'drummer'. In the end I got the hump and told him, 'Mr. Martin, this 'drummer' does have a name!'

Such was the popularity of The Beatles their return from America was reported live on Saturday afternoon's *Grandstand* sports programme, with presenter David Coleman on hand at London Airport to greet them. Showjumping and wrestling fans weren't amused.

The inaugural *Top Of The Pops* kicked off with The Beatles' so-called rivals, The Rolling Stones, performing Lennon and McCartney's '*I Wanna Be Your Man*'. In a set list that read like some sort of agony column, Dusty Springfield followed with '*I Only Want To Be With You*', The Dave Clark Five with '*Glad All Over*' and The Hollies with '*Stay*'. The Swinging Blue Jeans then rocked things up with '*The Hippy Hippy Shake*', after apparently enjoying a punch up with the Stones over a ballpoint pen for signing autographs. Urban myth, embellishment or whatever, when asked about the incident on the Derek Jameson Radio Show in 1986 guitarist Ray Ennis said: 'It was probably Ralph Ellis who was the protagonist. Ralph was a robust type of guy, not unknown for jumping off stage to fight someone,' before adding with typical scouse humour; 'That's how Mick Jagger got his lips!'

Ralph gave his version of the incident in 2018:

> It was blown up out of all proportion by the press. Keith Richards asked to borrow my pen and when I later asked him for it back, he said he didn't have it. He was being cocky, trying to take the piss. The Stones thought us northerners were numpties from the sticks. I grabbed him by his throat and threatened him. Mick Jagger, who I thought even then was effeminate, handed it back.

Thing was, I was brought up in a tough area of Liverpool, Scotty Road. You had to be tough to survive there. I was brought up without a dad. He was killed in a motorbike accident when giving a friend a lift home from Lime Street when I was a kid. My mother was left to bring me and my brothers up on her own. It was hard. You soon became streetwise, growing up in that environment. The Stones may have thought they were something else, coming from London, but they didn't impress us up here. They were pussies by comparison, but to be fair we did some tours with them later and became good friends.

The *Top Of The Pops* show was completed with film clips of Cliff Richard and The Shadows, Freddie and The Dreamers and The Beatles playing the week's number one, '*I Want to Hold Your Hand*'.

Whilst the Jeans and the Stones were losing their heads over a biro, over in Denmark the Danes too were losing their heads when it was discovered that the head on their famous Little Mermaid statue in Copenhagen Harbour had disappeared. A 500 Danish Krone ransom note for the return of the decapitated head was given to a newspaper, who forwarded it on to the Police. Whether it was paid or they just screwed another head on the mermaid is not known.

Other items in the news included a robbery at the Turkish Baths in Jermyn Street, Piccadilly, London when two men walked in and snatched the spectacles off the desk attendant, told him to turn a blind eye, and robbed his till of £76.

And Britain's obsession with the weather was illustrated when it was revealed that over 500,000 telephone calls had been made since the previous October, from people wanting to know if it was going to piss down.

Under the guidance of manager Andrew Loog Oldham, The Stones were rolling along nicely. Casting them as the bad boys of rock was a clever ploy by Oldham, who encouraged them to be sullen, unkempt and a polar opposite to the clean cut and witty Beatles. They followed '*I Wanna Be Your Man*' with a clear indication that they were in it for the long term with their second hit, Buddy Holly's '*Not Fade Away*'. Their first number one, '*It's All Over Now*', in July 1964, a Bobby

Womack song, signalled the end for many of the Fifties stars, being railroaded onto the cabaret circuit.

Eric Haydock, bass player with The Hollies who were also on the first step of a career that would continue into the millennium, recalls with some amusement the first time they encountered The Stones, and the perceived altercation The Stones had with The Swinging Blue Jeans:

> They did have a barney on the *Top of The Pops* show, but it was more of a handbags job really. The Stones were smug, had a bit of an attitude, but the lads from up here, up north didn't get too bothered about it. 'They're alright,' they'd say, 'they're just pussycats'. Oldham knew that musically they weren't that good. Brian Jones was a good leader and musician, but he had too many daggers in his back. They were big in the London area but Bill Wyman recalled to me the first time they played up north. 'We were the new sensations,' Bill said, 'then we played this gig in Middlesbrough. We had all our gear set up, guitars, AC30 amps, drums, mics. It looked impressive and then this band from Manchester came in, one of the guitarists carrying a sideboard. 'What's that?' Bill asked. 'Thats my amp,' he said. Bill asked him, 'What do you mean?' He opened the cabinets in the sideboard and there were two 8" speakers in them! Then he opened a drawer and there was a little Linear amp in there! Then another guy came in with a tea chest. 'I've got a 15" speaker in there,' he said to Bill. Toe rags they were, said Bill! They then went on before the Stones and tore the place up. Story goes that later, when they were back in London, Oldham told Mick Jagger, 'Mick, I was at the gig with the Manchester band and I tell you what, I'm not being funny but, Mick, you'd better learn to dance! Quite frankly, for the rest of your life, you've got to dance your effin' arse off! Because you'll never be able to sing like those lads! Never in your natural!'

The Animals, another northern band, from Newcastle, exploded on the scene in 1964 with their version of the tale of a New Orleans whorehouse, 'House Of The Rising Sun', expropriated from Bob Dylan's self-titled debut album. Produced by Mickie Most, it was feared at the time that the record, being over four minutes long, would suffer from lack of airplay due to the BBC's stringent rules of songs being no longer than the regulated three minutes. Somehow it slipped through the net and became a landmark similar to that of athlete Roger Bannister's gut-busting effort in breaking the four minute mile in 1953. '*Rising Sun*' became the first record to break the four minute barrier in pop music!

The Tornados were still hanging in there with their debut LP *Away From It All*, released in August 1963, a somewhat ironic title with hindsight, but the scene was rapidly changing and the album was described in *The All Music Guide To Rock* as 'out of date, a humdrum affair with weak material that can't overcome their trademark outer space roller rink organ and Joe Meek's usual, at times clichéd, bag of tricks production'.

Guitarist Alan Caddy obviously agreed, and decided that he too wanted to be 'Away From It All', throwing in the towel to leave Clem as the sole survivor from the original line up. Alan released a single, '*Tornado*', which, despite his apparent disenchantment, sounded like The Tornados, on the HMV label. Alan later became an arranger and session player for Dave Dee, Dozy, Beaky, Mick and Tich, The Spencer Davis Group, Kiki Dee, The Pretty Things and Dusty Springfield.

Stuart Taylor from Screaming Lord Sutch's Savages replaced 'Tea' to fulfil one final Tornados engagement with Billy Fury in Amsterdam, later rated by Clem as one of the best gigs they ever played. It was a nice way to part company with Billy, who was determined to pursue a solo career. Unfortunately for the former Tugboat man, another twelve months and Billy was sunk as the music scene continued to progress in a constant flux of fashion and change.

Clem:

> Around this time we went to Hamburg which was, quite honestly, a disaster. We were absolutely the wrong band to play over there at the time. It was all R&B, Rock and Roll, vocal groups, not an instrumental group they wanted. My main memory of Germany though is being met at the airport, taken to the Star-Club in Hamburg and just as we arrived, a guy came running out of the club, followed by another, who promptly shot him! That was a surprise to say the least. Welcome to Grosse Freiheit! We were

also given red bags with the Star-Club logo on and told to take them everywhere. It was a security measure. 'You'll be recognised and left alone,' we were told. Hamburg was worse than Soho. Gangsters, spivs, you name it. Soho was tame by comparison.'

Clem called it a day

...primarily because I was tired of the line up changing every five minutes. Interestingly, the guy who took over from me in The Tornados was future Jimi Hendrix Experience drummer Mitch Mitchell. So I was jobless again, drinking coffee in The Giaconda, Denmark Street, and wondering which direction my career was going to take next, and if I had made the right decision to quit The Tornados. Maybe I wanted the best of both worlds: to work in music on a regular basis but still be based in London with my family. What I didn't want to be was to be associated with just one group, albeit the one who became the first act from this country to top the charts in America. Which was one hell of a market to crack until The Beatles came along. I had also seen the other side of fame though and what happened to people when the fame suddenly disappeared. There is no rhyme or reason for it. One minute you are number one in the country, the next, no one wants to know you. I have seen it drive people crazy, and to the bottle. I could see why drink and drugs became a huge problem in the pop music world.

Johnny Kidd, for example, was one hell of a good singer and for me, never received the recognition he deserved. When you get real quality musicians like George Harrison and The Hollies telling you they travelled hundreds of miles just to see him, you know he was special. Johnny just faded from the scene. The record-buying public stopped shelling out for his music. It's a cruel business and Johnny just couldn't understand. It made him really down and depressed. I had also seen it with people like Karl Denver. He was a merchant seaman from Scotland who was suddenly in demand because of the success of his big hit 'Wimoweh'. He had one hell of a voice, no question. But he couldn't resist the drink. He had no airs and graces and never looked at ease in the world of showbusiness. It wasn't his world, he wasn't comfortable. He was happier with a glass of scotch in his hand and that developed into something of a problem for him and I am sure that contributed to his premature death.

Quite often groups would do two shows and finish really late, regularly after midnight. In that scene you can't just switch off and go to sleep. With the adrenaline pumping, you just feel so wide awake. The drink and the drugs were always there and always available and it just seemed a natural progression for many of the stars. I had learned my lesson early when on the Max Wall tour. What helped me later was I always drove home so the adrenaline kept me alert, and the police those days didn't have much of a clue about the drugs. I remember Tony Secunda, later the brains behind Black Sabbath, getting out of the car while we were driving across Blackfriars Bridge, and asking a policeman if he had a light. For a joint that must have been four inches long! And on top of that, the copper obliged!

Unless you were part of a supergroup like The Beatles, Rolling Stones, Kinks, then you tended to be part of a fad rather than something lasting, but people always wanted musicians who could play on demos or be part of studio recordings. The first two guys I met who were involved in the studio productions were John Carter and Ken Lewis, who became better known as The Ivy League. I was doing demos for them and others at six pounds a time and it soon added up. I was now involved in the session scene and on my way to the number one spot 41 more times following 'Shakin' All Over' and 'Telstar'.

We – myself and other session players like John Paul Jones, Jimmy Page, Big Jim Sullivan – would be in The Giaconda, chatting away over a coffee and someone would come in with a song they'd wrote and ask if we could make a demo for it. Many a time, they would come back and ask if it was possible for us to record a master for their song. We did that many times, not knowing who the artists were or what the song was. It was like a production line. When the Stones' first album was in the process of being put together Andrew Oldham was in Denmark Street looking for session men to make demos of a handful of songs Mick Jagger and Keith Richard had written. I played on a few demos for The Stones, one I remember was 'Heart of Stone' which was on their *Out Of Our Heads* album.

Oldham, in his biography *Stoned*:

Regent Studio was booked and Big Jim and Clem were there. I was using session men because I couldn't ask Brian, Bill and Charlie to work on their day off for free. There really was nothing special about Mick and Keith's songs, apart from a ballad they weren't too confident about, '*As Tears Go By*'. They got something down all the same and of course later it broke Marianne Faithfull into the big-time. We recorded the first album in about ten days. We'd decide to do a tune, but if Mick didn't know the words, he would run around to Denmark Street to Carlin Music to pick up the words to something like '*Can I Get a Witness?*' He'd come back 25 minutes later and we'd start.

Bass player Bill Wyman:

On the first album, we cut everything in mono. The band had to record more or less live in the studio, so what was on our record was more or less our act, what we played on the ballroom and club circuits. It was really just the show we did onstage recorded in one take – as it should be.

Clem:

The name Andrew Loog Oldham was a selling point, it would sell records. The fact that it was a Andrew Loog Oldham production carried a lot of weight. Andrew was like Joe Meek in that respect, very inventive and innovative. He would do things that supposedly you couldn't do. Maybe to other producers in the business he was crazy, but among the musicians... I never thought he was crazy, I thought he was clever. If you walked in and it was Andrew, you knew you were going to enjoy the session and have a good laugh. He would ask for contributions from you whereas a lot of producers wouldn't. That's what is written, that's what we want and that's the end of it. All you really were was a musical navvy. With Andrew you could put forward your ideas which, as a working musician, is good for you. You feel as if you are part of something, you feel as if you've contributed something as opposed to being a machine. Plus with Andrew I always knew I was going to play with Jimmy Page, John Paul Jones, Big Jim Sullivan and Nicky Hopkins. Let's face it, if you can't enjoy that, you might as well pack in.

Clem's session work allowed little time for preparation or reflection on what he played:

> I remember thinking that my playing constituted the 'flavour of the month' and that contractors would tire of me as soon as the next competent drummer arrived on the scene. If I'd known it was going to be that important 40 years on, I'd have played better in the first place. When you're involved in it you don't realise the importance of what you're doing at the time. All I was doing was earning a living. You know, it was like, we want a road dug today, so get a spade and a shovel. This was the thing. Dig it and earn a living.

John Aizlewood of the *Evening Standard*:

> Session men would go in, they would be given a song, they would play it, they would pick up their fee, they would go home. Big Jim Sullivan, Vic Flick, Jimmy Page (sometimes called Little Jim), Joe Moretti and Joe Brown all began playing in bands until their technique, knowledge and sound brought them to the attention of producers and of contractors. Similarly, bassists Alan Weighall, Herbie Flowers, John Paul Jones, Eric Ford, Ron Prentice established their reputations as live performers before becoming denizens of the sunless world of recording studios. Producers turned to drummers like Clem Cattini, Bobby Graham, Ronnie Verrell and Andy White because they had learned how to read music, how to hold a band together on stage, and when to play (and when not).

Andy White, who famously played on The Beatles' '*Love Me Do*' and the Billy Fury album *The Sound of Fury*:

> When contractors couldn't get a particular individual, musicians would often recommend a replacement. I used to dep for Clem when he was doing the Herman's Hermits stuff with producer Mickie Most. Clem was the drummer on '*Silhouettes*' and '*Can't You Hear My Heartbeat*'. The only member of the Hermits to play on those records was singer Peter Noone. Session men learned arrangements quickly, played flawlessly and usually could read music in a world where recordings took place in strictly limited

three hour sessions. Musicians like Vic Flick and Clem didn't panic when tapes were rolling.

In fairness, Hermit guitarist Keith Hopwood explained the reasons behind the use of session men on their recordings during an interview on Sky Arts television:

At the time we were constantly touring America after we had made a breakthrough over there. Mickie Most was always looking out for songs that he thought would suit us and we'd often come back to find that he had recorded the tracks with session men Clem Cattini, John Paul Jones, Vic Flick, whoever, and all we had to do was go in the studio and lay the vocals down. Then we had to learn how to play them before we went back out on tour.

Eric Haydock:

Clem was and is a great drummer, there was an elite then, a group of them, class drummers. Clem, Brian Bennett, Phil Seamen, Tony Meehan, Ginger Baker. They did sessions as well as play with bands. The studios would call these guys in to get the job done quicker. The managements were signing everybody up at the time. All the bands were going down to London for a session and you had to get it done in the time that was allowed. They'd say there's three bands in today, you've got to 1.30. The Hollies recorded in Studio 2 at EMI and I remember them saying to us, 'Come on lads, The Beatles are in at 2 o'clock and they've got priority!' Thing was, the bands wouldn't be used to playing in a studio or recording. The singer might get it after a couple of takes, the bass and guitar might too, but the drummer, that was a different thing. They couldn't keep time, they would have to speed up and the producers would say, 'We can't have this, get Clem in,' or Tony Meehan or whoever.

That's what happened with our first drummer Don Rathbone. It was the management who decided Don should be replaced and he went into that side of the business. Clem would come in and ask 'What have you got?' They'd say, 'Here, look at this, listen to the demo,' and Clem would say, 'Right, that looks ok,' and he'd get it done in one take. Piece of piss! Then pick up his £12! 'Here, sign here.' You had to sign everything at EMI. Clem would take his £12 and he'd be off, probably to another session at another studio! When Bobby Elliott came in to replace Don, The Hollies never used session men afterwards. Bob was a great drummer, bit flash, he'd swing his arms, crash the cymbals from below, twiddle the sticks. It was all show, but Bob was great. It was all in his wrists. You never saw his arms move, unless he was putting on a show! Brian Bennett was the same, and Clem, Tony Meehan. Technicians.

Typically, the major studios had three standard session times a day: 10.00am–1.00pm, 2.30–5.30pm and 7.00–10.00pm. Contractors like Charlie Katz might book a musician to play a morning session at the EMI Recording Studios in St. John's Wood, an afternoon session at Decca's West Hampstead studios, and an evening session at Pye's studios near Marble Arch. Musicians might also be engaged to record a commercial before the morning session or after the evening session. Other studios such as Olympic, Regent Sound, Trident or IBC had more flexible hours, but all had to work around the system established by the majors.

In the first half of the Sixties, production crews and musicians generally presumed that in a three-hour session (which did not include arriving in time to set up your equipment and to allow the studio staff to position microphones) a singer and musicians would be able to produce at least four completed recordings. Allowing a few hours for musicians to find the right groove for a song did not figure as part of the schedule, unless stars like The Beatles were involved, and even they might end up recording late at night to avoid scheduled day use of EMI.

Many of the best-known recordings of the era by The Dave Clark Five, Herman's Hermits, Them, Peter and Gordon, Dusty Springfield and Cilla Black feature these musicians, whether acknowledged or not. Producers (commonly known as artist-and-repertoire managers in the early 1960s) and music directors relied on session musicians to realise their often unspecific ideas about a performance in the studio. Music director Reg Guest came up with at least two different arrangements for the recording of '*The Crying Game*' (the orchestral version was never released), but it was Jim Sullivan's musically and technically inventive guitar playing delicately embroidering Dave Berry's vocal that distinguish this disc. Using a DeArmond foot pedal to play with tone and volume, Sullivan painted tears onto Geoff Stephens' song.

Shel Talmy, an American record producer, brought in extra musicians for sessions, a practice he used on many recordings – because he knew from experience there was no guarantee that young, new groups were competent enough on their instruments to make a decent enough recording:

> One of my very best friends was Clem Cattini who was wonderful, he had a great sense of humour. Not only is he a great drummer, but he lifted a session because he was so funny. The session musicians for The Who's 'I Can't Explain' and 'Bald Headed Woman' included John Carter, Ken Lewis and Perry Ford of The Ivy League who supplied the high-voiced backing vocals. The Who didn't do backing vocals or, to be more precise, they did them badly. Perry Ford also played piano on the song. Clem was brought in but Roger Daltrey, Pete Townshend and John Entwistle insisted they wanted their own drummer Keith Moon on the session and wouldn't budge. The other session man was 20-year-old Jimmy Page.

Entwistle, from Dave Marsh's *Before I Get Old*:

> We arrived at the Pye studio and found ourselves out-numbered by Talmy's session people. He didn't like our backing vocals so he dragged The Ivy League in. He was also unsure of Pete Townshend's ability on lead guitar and Jimmy Page played on the recording instead. Talmy always kept a drummer and other spare parts in reserve, I'm quite certain if Talmy could have pulled it off he'd have had Clem Cattini on drums instead of Keith Moon as well.

Pete Townshend (*Before I Get Old*):

> Shel Talmy was a great believer in making groups who were nothing into stars. He was also a great believer in pretending that

the group didn't exist when they were in the recording studio.

Shel Talmy:

> It was just work. I wasn't there to win popularity contests. I was out to make hit records, not hang out with the guys. They thought I was aloof and stand-offish, which was probably true, but if we'd have been all mates together, nothing would have been accomplished.

Zoot Money and The Big Roll Band, who had a big hit in 1966 with '*Big Time Operator*' reiterated Entwistle's gripe about record producers. Zoot:

> '*Big Time Operator*' was produced by Johnny Harris. Our drummer Colin Allen had to step aside because Harris wanted to use his session man Kenny Clare. They were all the same, it was jobs for the boys basically. They wanted to get the recordings done with guys who could follow the dots to save time and hope that they could put whatever feel they could into it. They didn't want a band coming in and spending half the time arguing over arrangements and whatever. Although I never worked with Clem, over the years we'd run into each other at festivals and the annual lunch of reprobates at the Barnes Restaurant. Clem was always good company and one of the more proficient drummers in the rock world. Wonderfully self-effacing and musically knowledgeable. I did work with his granddaughter Michelle, who is an actress, on the TV series *Get Back* with Ray Winston in the 1990s. Michelle also appeared in the popular TV series *Shine On Harvey Moon* and *Goodnight Sweetheart* too.

Clem:

> Not that he would have remembered, but I first met Keith Moon in a club in Manchester when I was part of Lulu's backing band. It was about midnight and the show had finished when in came The Who. Three of them were merry but Keith Moon was as high as a kite. On what I don't know, drugs or drink, maybe both! He wanted to play on my drums and was getting quite insistent about it. But there was no way I was letting him anywhere near them in the state he was in. I could see them getting trashed and broken

in pieces. In the end Moon got the message. He was in no state to argue. He was obviously someone who liked to live life to the full and I have to say it was no surprise to me that he died the way he did at the age he did. I met up with Roger Daltrey a few years later at a function connected with Arsenal Football Club. 'You know I'm the drummer you didn't want, don't you,' I said. He claimed not to remember but I reckon he was being polite, because it was mentioned in a book about the band! Moon wasn't the only victim of the booze, two of the original members of The Shadows were gripped by it. Both Jet Harris and Tony Meehan were kicked out of the group because of their drinking. It was said at the time that they were leaving to do their own stuff, and they did have a couple of big selling singles '*Diamonds*' and '*Scarlet O'Hara*'. The truth was though that The Shadows couldn't control the drinking and it was beginning to impact on their career. Further down the line Jet realised he was an alcoholic and disappeared off the scene for a few years while he recovered. He even worked as a bus conductor for a while. Jet is proof of just how pop musicians, especially those in high-profile groups, are liable to succumb to a life of booze. When I was in the Top Of The Pops Orchestra in the Seventies I could see the effect booze and drugs was having on Keith Richards of The Stones. I've said before that I didn't care for them as individuals, though I did like Bill and Charlie.

Their talent I never doubted, but with their college background they were just not like the majority of bands who came from working-class backgrounds. Keith deteriorated unbelievably over the years. He was a good-looking guy and talented with it. But he became old long before his time because of the drugs. His face was lined and his speech slurred. He looked drawn and haggard. With the money he and the band were earning he should have had a stress-free life with the lifestyle they had. Instead he looked twice his age when he was 35. The joke was that they were laughter lines – but nothing could have been that funny! It was when I saw what happened to people like Keith I knew I had made the right decision to become a musical navvy.

Swinging Blue Jeans guitarist Alan Lovell saw how booze affected their singer Ray Ennis:

Ray liked a drink, which caused a lot of problems and came to a head at a gig in Budapest, Hungary. Because of Ray's inability to co-ordinate, we ended up playing virtually as a trio. He couldn't even hold the neck of his guitar! He was messing about, making out he was twiddling the knobs on the amp. It was embarrassing and I was really upset about it. I had been in the band around ten years at this point and decided then to take control of the band's future. This had been bubbling under for quite a while and we were also getting tired of playing the same set every night, the same old songs, which were great, but musicians get lazy. If you came out with an idea about playing something new or something from the back catalogue, it would get thrown out without any thought given to it. I managed to change things when I dug out 'Ol' Man Mose' and 'Angie' from the *Blue Jeans A-Swinging* album which was released in 1964. I said to Ray and the boys, 'Let's rehearse these and a couple of Chuck Berry songs.' We did, and Ray thought they were great! He hadn't played or heard them for years!

Alan's move to take over the band was later a subject of some controversy. During an interview on Tameside Radio with DJ Francis McMahon in 2018, Ray Ennis told his side of the story:

By the '90s we were now on the 'chicken in a basket' circuit, there had been a number of changes of personnel over the years and then we lost Colin Manley and Les Braid. Both had succumbed to the deadly disease of cancer. They had both been my friends for many, many years and I was really down. I felt despondent and on the 'Flying Music' tour in 2010 I decided I wanted a break and told the rest of the boys in the band, Alan Lovell, Pete Oakman and Graham Hollingworth, I was going to take a year off. It was my 70th birthday this year and with the tour ending in Liverpool, where I first started, there was a kind of going full circle about it. It felt right. They immediately fired back, 'You're retiring then!' I said, 'No, I'm taking a year off.'

Alan Lovell had joined the band on the recommendation of our manager Hal Carter to replace Colin. We were playing the Regent Theatre, Ipswich, Hal gave Alan some tapes of our songs, he learnt them, it felt good and he joined up. When I was having my sabbatical, Alan Lovell decided to register the name of the band in his name! The band had been in existence for over 50 years, we'd had a number of hit records in the Sixties, been through many stages, the guys in the band at this time weren't even from Liverpool and Alan Lovell had the nerve to go and claim the name! When we were in the charts he was still at school! I didn't find out what he had done until some time after. By all accounts, by law, you're supposed to inform the rest of the boys in the band of your intentions and you then have six months to contest it or oppose it or whatever. He never told anyone! I took the case to court and the judge was on my side. He was really blunt and told Alan Lovell that what he had done was totally immoral and disgusting. By the word of the law though, the judge's hands were tied. 'Legally,' he told Alan Lovell, 'you're in the clear and unfortunately, I can't do anything about it but judge it in your favour.' So he had the Swinging Blue Jeans name to continue working.

I did start playing again, I hired some local lads and we go out as Ray Ennis and the Original Blue Jeans. As long as I don't use the word 'Swinging' it's fine. I have heard a number of times that Alan Lovell's band are not as well received now because there are no original members left. Tribute bands are alright as long as there is at least one original member still playing. And I have to say, we are getting great receptions when we play on the Sixties Rock n Roll tours.

Pop music was still limited to *Top Of The Pops* and *Ready Steady Go!* on the television and *Saturday Club* and Sunday afternoon's *Pick Of The Pops* on the BBC Light Programme, plus the wretched reception of Radio Luxembourg. It was all about to change with the advent of what the press labelled 'pirate radio'. Broadcast from the high seas off the coasts of Great Britain, Radio Atlanta began broadcasting from the boat *Mi Amigo*, anchored off Frinton-on-Sea, in July 1964, before it merged with Radio Caroline. The *Mi Amigo* was a German-built schooner which had survived the second world war and, during the Sixties, the war with the establishment, but sadly it sank in 1980.

24 hour music was on tap and the youngsters lapped it up. 'This is Radio Caroline on 199, your all-day music station,' would announce DJ Johnny Walker. The up-beat disc jockeys, rather than the staid drones of the post-war broadcasters on the Beeb, the jingles and commercials all added a freshness to an exciting music and fashion

scene.

Founded by Irish businessman Ronan O'Rahilly, Radio Caroline, named after the daughter of J.F. Kennedy 'to symbolise the new generation', was anchored just outside the three-mile limit of British shores. By the end of the year O'Rahilly would claim that Caroline had more listeners than the BBC. One journalist, who was obviously a fan, wrote, 'There is something irresistibly romantic about a radio ship wallowing lazily in a slight swell on the North Sea'.

Not that disc jockey Tony Prince would agree, as he stated in his biography *The Royal Ruler & The Railway DJ*:

> Some days we bobbed up and down like a cork in an ocean. One time we had a transmitter failure and was off the air for three days not long after the launch. The gales made it impossible to climb the 160 foot mast to carry out repairs. Wrapped up against the cold biting weather, playing cards to pass the time, suffering with seasick, wasn't romantic!

The BBC had a launch of its own in the Spring, a second television channel called BBC2 which had an ignominious start when a power failure in West London put paid to the broadcast.

During this period the terms 'Swinging London' and the 'Permissive Society' were coined, and it was as if the shackles of the 1950s had finally been cast off. Everyone, it seemed, wanted to visit Carnaby Street, the King's Road in Chelsea; The Marquee Club, Bag O' Nails, Flamingo, Cromwellian, and other night clubs opening up in London. Fashion designer Mary Quant and hairdresser Vidal Sassoon were making headlines, Mary boldly declaring 'Paris is out of date.' Rudi Gernreich introduced the topless dress, to the glee and disgust of a cross-section of the public. Two models were posing in the topless dress when Rudi asked a gentleman if he would like to see his wife in it. His reply was, 'I wouldn't mind seeing someone else's wife in it!' Conversely, an elderly woman was aghast; 'I think it's absolutely disgusting. A girl who gets dressed like that deserves a blinking good hiding!' Tantalisingly, a dry cleaner's shop in Manchester saw an opportunity and advertised an offer of 'Mini skirts cleaned at twopence an inch,' which wouldn't have set many back!

The media was taking a keen interest in developments, and one reporter visiting a hairstylists in Knightsbridge was taken aback: 'I walked in and thought I'd made a mistake and gone into a ladies' salon. 'Take a seat sir,' I was told, 'while I attend to these gentlemen.' Sitting in the chairs were these long-haired boys in the group they call The Kinks. It's difficult enough to tell who is a she or who is a he, but when both sexes are wearing the same hairstyles as well as the same clothes it poses a lot of very disturbing questions.'

Branded 'Mods' and 'Rockers', teenagers were making most of the headlines in 1964, albeit if they were for the wrong reasons. Mods followed The Who, Small Faces and rode around on their Vespa and Lambretta scooters. Rockers tore around on Triumph Bonnevilles and BSA motorbikes, leather-clad like Marlon Brando in *The Wild One*. Clashes were inevitable, and on Bank Holidays fights and riots broke out at the holiday resorts of Brighton, Clacton, Margate and Hastings. Terrorising holidaymakers, they smashed windows, threw deckchairs at each other, fought on the beaches, fought with the police... causing an outcry which the tabloids made hay with, splashing their front pages with massive headlines. This wasn't on a par with the outbreak of World War Two, the Cold War, or the Cuban missile crisis... but a fight between youngsters on a beach! The headlines gave the impression that the country was in a total state of anarchy. Partly to blame of course, declared the editors, was the music:

'Clacton's terrifying experience last week at the hands of the Wild Ones was all tied up with purple hearts and beat music. The degeneracy of the younger generation has a lot to do with beat music, and the violence that these groups incite among the audiences.'

'Beat music is mainly responsible because it causes the youngsters to become aggressive, because the music is beefy and aggressive.'

Melody Maker ran a feature asking the stars for their opinions on the matter.

John Stokes of The Bachelors: 'We don't agree that any form of music is responsible for this sort of thing. People get carried away because they are the sort of person who gets aggressive. For sure, 'Diane', 'Charmaine' and 'Ramona' are never going to drive the kids into a frenzy, maybe the old man and old dear, but not the mods and rockers.'

Hilton Valentine of The Animals: 'A load of yobbos go to these places like Clacton with the intention of having a go. It has nothing at all to do with us. Music attracts people, but so do a lot of other things. These people are just making exhibitions of themselves. What's that got to do with beat music?'

Graham Nash of The Hollies: 'Beat groups do nothing but good for the kids. If they didn't go to ballrooms and concerts they'd go to places like Clacton and let off steam in the way those people did there. Our fans are not fighters anyway, they're girls mainly. What really can cause trouble is drink. A couple of fans get stoked up with drink and there can be trouble. Is that our fault?'

Clacton bore the brunt of the battles. Police reinforcements from all over Essex were called in to quell the riots. 97 arrests were made as the mob overturned cars, stoned the police and fought with each other. The loutish behaviour was condemned by Margate Magistrate George Simpson: 'These long-haired, mentally unstable petty little sawdust Caesars seem to find courage like rats, by hunting only in packs.'

A report concluded: 'It really has come to something when people can't take a short holiday without the threat of long-haired youngsters with knives indulging in an orgy of hooliganism. They come to the seaside resorts on their motorcycles at weekends and on Bank Holidays, dressed up in Carnaby Street get-up, ready for the mayhem that is to follow.'

A BBC radio reporter asked one teenager in Clacton what fun they got from 'smashing things up.' He replied: 'Well, we get a kick out of it, you know, it's something to do, there's nothing much else to do on Bank Holiday Monday is there? So we smash things up'.

'How old are you?' '16.' 'And what would your parents say if they thought you were doing this sort of thing?' 'They might go a bit mad. But I couldn't care less as it happens.'

A woman standing nearby, overhearing this, was irate. 'I feel they ought to have their bicycles confiscated and their licence suspended! When they came swarming onto the beach, I was terrified.'

'Put the Mods and the Rockers altogether in one section of the beach so they can fight amongst themselves and it might be ok,' said another.

Disc reported on The Beatles working with producer Jack Good for a 'TV Special':

> 'It has been a terrific thrill to work with them,' Jack said while stating he is convinced the boys are the natural successors to The Crazy Gang. 'Take the Shakespearean sketch; The Beatles are acting a six-minute sketch in full costume from *A Midsummer Night's Dream* with Paul as Bottom, George as Moonshine, John as Thisbe and Ringo as the Lion. Thing is, when they first saw the script they didn't like it. Thought it just wasn't funny. I had a hard job persuading them to do it. I was amazed at how quickly they picked it up and learnt their lines. At the start of the show they wear herald's costumes to play a fanfare on the trumpets. They all had their costumes on and once they got hold of the trumpets it was riotous. All four of them started busking *'Can't Buy Me Love'* – it sounded like a street band down on Shaftesbury Avenue!'

Away from the stage, Ringo was rumoured to be engaged to Dusty Springfield! This was doing the rounds when Dusty arrived in the Hawaiian Islands for a holiday. The islands were buzzing with the news. If that left Ringo bemused, in America news was breaking that he was also engaged to actress Ann-Margret! *Disc* wrote 'Ridiculous American publicity reaches new heights of absurdity with Hollywood claiming the song *'Anna'* on The Beatles' debut LP is dedicated to her!'

Top of the charts were The Searchers with *'Don't Throw Your Love Away'*, with The Bachelors at number two with *'I Believe'*. New releases included a Tommy Quickly record unfortunately titled *'You Might As Well Forget Him'*. For those interested, *Disc* also included the top ten from other countries. Number one in Spain was *'If I Had A Hammer'* by Trini Lopez. In Holland it was *'Vous Permettez*

Monsieur' by Adamo and Norway's number one was '*La Meg Vaere Ung*' by Wenche Myhre. Which undoubtedly fascinated everyone.

Gerry Marsden was featured, telling of how he'd been flying around that much, every time he saw a plane his elbow started flapping! And his brother Fred hated flying; 'He just sits there very quietly when we're taking off and looks straight ahead. All the way until we land. Then he looks pleased – and surprised.'

The Letters page included an interesting observation from R.F. Matthews of Bristol: 'Surely it's time your readers realised what a 'gimmick' is? It seems obvious to me that a gimmick is something used by artists to attract attention to their act and should be something easily removed by an artist on leaving the stage. Johnny Kidd and The Pirates with their pirate rig have a gimmick, but to say that The Rolling Stones' long hair is a gimmick is rubbish, since they don't remove their hair off stage!'

The economy and cost of living were improving, as could be seen by the Bank of England issuing £10 pound notes for the first time. The average weekly wage was revealed to be £16, which probably made session men baulk. As Clem admitted, 'You didn't know at the start of a week if you would make £6, never mind £16!'

Advertised as 'The car that asks to be abused, only then you will appreciate its durability and longevity,' a brand new Volkswagen 1200 would turn you over for only £625. The Austin Mini would set you back £493, and the Triumph Herald 1200 was yours for £579 7s 1d. Yes, 7/1d tagged on the end of the bill!

If you wanted to smarten yourself up, a suit from Burton's tailoring - 'You can't beat style,' they promised - cost you £11 19s 6d.

Clem:

> My decision to adopt a 'have drums will travel' approach paid off as far as I'm concerned. I had two sets of drums. I recorded loads of stuff at the Olympic Studios in Barnes, also at Decca, Pye. Eventually, having to take my drums in the car got too much, the traffic was getting worse, so I got myself a roadie who would go ahead and set one kit up at Decca say, ready for me to start, then go off to Pye or wherever and set the second kit up for an

afternoon session. Then he would go and pick the first kit up at Decca and take them to EMI! Ok it did stop me hitting the big-time and making mega bucks that I could have made if I had been in one of these so-called supergroups, but I just wanted regular work and the chance to play with some of the greats and I realised that dream. I was able to mix with hugely-talented people like Johnny Gustafson and Billy J. Kramer from the Merseybeat explosion. Billy was a nice lad, though too full of himself for my liking and into that category I would put The Animals. Eric Burdon had a voice to die for, he was tremendous, he sounded like a black soul singer. The keyboard player of course was Alan Price, who always wanted his own way. He apparently had an aversion to flying, which cost the group dear. He riled the rest of the group because of what he did when 'House Of The Rising Sun' came out. The song was an old negro spiritual, but Alan changed the words to make it a sweatshop where a girl was working rather than a brothel, which was the place in the original. The rules are that if you change the words you can keep the royalties. Alan did. He wasn't always the easiest person to work with, very selfish. The coach taking the group would leave when Alan said it would leave, and would stop when he said it would stop. Manfred Mann was another arrogant individual. The rest of the band were great though. I got on well with Paul Jones and then later Mike d'Abo. Tom McGuinness and Mike Hugg were also great guys. A group I got to know really well was The Kinks, but they had their moments. I think they used *Top Of The Pops* to learn from experienced musicians like myself. I remember Mick Avory asking me once how I tuned my drums for '*You Really Got Me*'. I had played on the original when it was recorded. I explained it to him – then the next week he was in the *Melody Maker* answering a reader's letter about tuning drums! Cheeky sod! I thought. But then I suppose, who was the mug? After all – Mick has the swimming pool!

Mick Avory had joined The Kinks after passing an audition following an advert he placed in the *Melody Maker*, 'Drummer seeking to play for a R&B band':

> They liked my playing enough to ask me to join. If I had an idea that playing with them would also enable me to pull the birds, that was soon forgotten as I thought Ray, Dave and Pete were gay!

So I didn't have high expectations of pulling women. I thought they were very camp and wondered what it was going to lead to.

Clem:

I did some live gigs with The Kinks when Mick had to drop out of a couple of shows. And they proved to me that despite his undoubted talent, Ray Davies was as tight as a duck's arse. Ray ran the group, he was a hard-nosed organiser, and every group needs one, but his brother Dave was totally opposite in nature and happy to let the world drift by. I played with them once in Nottingham when Mick was unavailable and discovered just how tight Ray was. We'd come out of a rehearsal and we all fancied an Indian meal. There were two quite close, one to the left of the theatre and one to the right. Ray sent Dave to check the prices. One was 2/6d, the other 2/-, nothing in it in other words, but Ray insisted we went for the cheaper one. There were four of us and don't forget, I was doing them a favour by stepping in for Mick. Yes, I was being paid but you would have thought, as a nice gesture, they would have paid for mine. No such luck! The bill arrived and Ray worked out how much my share of the meal was. I got on well with all the British bands. The Small Faces I got to know, in particular their drummer Kenney Jones who took over from Keith Moon in The Who when 'Moony' passed away. Because of my connection with The Tornados, Kenney knew more about me than I did him and we used to talk a lot away from the set. I always got on well with the lads in The Hollies too. We did a tour together when their drummer Bobby Elliott was ill and they were a great bunch, and they never fully got the credit they deserved for the quality of their music. Maybe it was because they didn't go for the 'sex, drugs and rock and roll' lifestyle, but they were very talented. Allan Clarke was a great singer and we used to get on really well, we had the same sense of humour. We used to have great fun when having a 'row' behind closed doors and to those outside it sounded as if all hell had broke loose. I lost count of the number of times the theatre manager would come in and ask if he needed to call the police!

As a session drummer I was always in work, whether it was the Top Of The Pops Orchestra or with manufactured bands like Herman's Hermits, charity events.

One job I had was a charity show for Birmingham City Council which ended up with me falling foul of the law again. I was driving around the Bull Ring trying to find my way into the studio, getting exasperated and after a while I gave in. I stopped to phone up the reception girl to ask where the entrance was. No sooner had I stopped, a police car pulled alongside. The copper got out, banged on my window and told me quite aggressively to pull over to the side. I tried to explain to him what was happening and he clearly wasn't interested. That agitated me even more. 'What's this all effin' about?' I asked him, 'Look, I'm lost, I'm trying to find my way into this building.' Straight away he fired back, 'Any more of that I'll book you for abusive language too.' 'Can I get done for thinking as well?' I asked him. 'No,' he replied. 'Right then, I think you're a complete arsehole!'

Back in court, to my surprise, the judge was very lenient, telling the policeman, 'First of all, Mr Cattini was doing the City Council a favour by turning up to appear at the charity show. Secondly, I live around here and I find the Bull Ring a nightmare to drive around too! You should have used some discretion, some common sense!' And I got away with it.

Anyway, then there was the 'Love Affair scandal'. Myself and a handful of other musicians provided the backing for '*Everlasting Love*'. It was a huge seller and there was another hit with the follow up, '*Rainbow Valley*'. The only person who wasn't a session musician on them was singer Steve Ellis, who had one hell of a voice. Then one of the newspapers exposed the sessions as 'a pop music scandal'. I was getting calls from the press night and day about it. It was obvious when the 'band' appeared on *Top Of The Pops*; Maurice Bacon was Love Affair's drummer, and anyone watching would have seen that the movements he was making couldn't possibly have been the drum noise on the record. But Steve, who later formed a band called Widowmaker, had a great voice.

Steve Ellis, one of the finest and most underrated soul singers of the Sixties, appeared as a guest on the BBC Radio Wales 'Wynne Evans Show' in 2017, recalling those heady days of the late 1960s with Love Affair.

Wynne: '*Everlasting Love*' was such an iconic song, did you know straight away it was going to be a massive hit?'

Steve: 'No. Mike Smith the producer told me we were going to go in the studio and do this song. I was only 17, and there was this orchestra in there, not Victor Silvester, modern-like with Clem Cattini, a fantastic drummer and all these session guys from that era, Jim Sullivan, John Paul Jones too. They played me this track and it blew me away. So they said, 'Stick a vocal on it,' and I did it in two takes. When I heard it, I just stood back and thought, 'My God', it was just, you didn't know you had made a hit, you just knew there was something magical about it. The stars were aligned that day! Everything just dropped into place!'

Love Affair followed with more hits – 'Rainbow Valley', 'Bringing On Back the Good Times', 'A Day Without Love' – and accrued a massive following. By 1969 Steve had grown tired of the relentless touring and dissatisfaction with the performances where they were drowned out by the screams of teenage girls in the theatres.

Steve:

> We'd been together since we were kids, we'd grown up on the road. All we did was play live, we played all over Europe, Top Rank tours in the UK. I left at Christmas '69 after a gig at the Mayfair Ballroom in Newcastle, which was a great gig for us. It had got that bad you couldn't hear yourself on stage. I'd had enough. We couldn't hear what we were playing, we were like hamsters in a spinning wheel! It was all a bit surreal. The boys in the band wanted to move into the Prog Rock scene, which wasn't for me and that's when I quit. I put another band together with Zoot Money and committed commercial suicide! We cut an album which Roger Daltrey of The Who produced for us and we toured universities and such places. We played a three-and-a-half month tour of America, which was gruelling. When we returned I told our guitarist Rex Brayley, 'I don't want to do this any more mate.' Playing three-month tours galavanting around the States a couple of times a year because people told you 'You have to go to America, you have to break America.' It was a treadmill. As long as I was making music and playing to people I was happy, but the touring wasn't really for me. A neighbour asked me what I was going to do. I told him, 'I don't know really, I fancy doing

something really different, you know?' He said, 'Why don't you go to work in the docks? My uncle works there, he could get you a start.' I said, 'Really?' It was a bit like the Marlon Brando film *On The Waterfront*. I said to this neighbour, 'Yeah I'll have a bit of that.' So, following an interview with an old foreman, an Irishman, lovely fella, I got this job in the London docks. I worked there, got myself really fit and then decided I'd get another band together – which went pear-shaped when some prat on a forklift dropped two tons of heavy metal blades onto my foot! So that took me out of the game for a while, but eventually I did put a band together with Zoot. It was called *Ellis* and we played all over Europe and the UK. Appeared on *The Old Grey Whistle Test*. Released a couple of albums and had a single '*El Doomo*', which sat at number 50 in the hit parade for weeks! Discontent with the record company grew steadily; we had worked hard to gain a loyal following on the live circuit, but commercial success eluded us and eventually Zoot was disheartened and left.

By the end of the year, Harold Wilson had been elected as Prime Minister, Khrushchev was ousted in Russia, Lyndon Johnson was re-elected President of America, Martin Luther King Jr was awarded the Nobel Peace Prize, Nelson Mandela was imprisoned for life in South Africa and China would test their first atom bomb. The Beatles were at number one with '*I Feel Fine*' and flying to the Antipodes to conquer Australia, and Clem was set to call time officially with The Tornados.

Clem and his brother Laurence

*Right:
Terry Kennedy's
Rock and Rollers.
Back; Ron Prentice,
Terry Kennedy, Clem Cattini.
Front: Ron Baker and
Micky McDonough*
Courtesy www.the-mill.co.uk

*Below: Nora Bristow, who ran the
coffee bar at The 2i's from 1958-61*
Courtesy Paul Daniel

Left: The Dene Aces waiting to go on stage at the Tivoli Gardens, Stockholm
Courtesy Brian Gregg

Below: Clem with Terry Dene and The Dene Aces in 1957
Courtesy www.edwardianteddyboy.com

Clem at Crewe station circa 1958

Clem and Anna's wedding in 1959

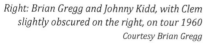

Right: Brian Gregg and Johnny Kidd, with Clem slightly obscured on the right, on tour 1960
Courtesy Brian Gregg

Johnny Kidd and The Pirates, Guild Hall Southampton 1960.
Clem is peering over Johnny's shoulder
Courtesy Brian Gregg

STAR PERFORMERS—Selections register-
ing greatest upward progress this week

This Week	Wk. Ago	Wks. Ago	Wks. Ago	TITLE Artist, Label & Number	Weeks on Chart
1	1	1	5	TELSTAR Tornadoes, London 9561	10
2	4	7	10	GO AWAY LITTLE GIRL △ Steve Lawrence, Columbia 42601	9
3	2	2	4	LIMBO ROCK Chubby Checker, Parkway 849	18
4	3	4	3	BOBBY'S GIRL Marcie Blane, Seville 120	12
5	5	5	1	BIG GIRLS DON'T CRY Four Seasons, Vee Jay 465	12
6	10	14	15	HOTEL HAPPINESS Brook Benton, Mercury 72055	7
7	11	23	37	PEPINO THE ITALIAN MOUSE Lou Monte, Reprise 20106	5
8	6	3	2	RETURN TO SENDER △ Elvis Presley, RCA Victor 8100	12
9	9	16	25	ZIP-A-DEE-DOO-DAH Bob B. Soxx & the Blue Jeans, Philles 107	8
10	14	22	35	TELL HIM Exciters, United Artists 544	6
11	20	27	32	MY DAD Paul Petersen, Colpix 663	8
12	7	9	11	YOU ARE MY SUNSHINE Ray Charles, ABC-Paramount 10375	8

*The US Billboard Hot 100,
week ending 5th January 1963*

*Karl Denver, Gerry Cottrell (Karl Denver's bassist), Heinz, George Bellamy, Clem, Billy Fury,
Alan Caddy. Marty Wilde, Roger LaVern, Kevin Neill (Karl Denver's guitarist)*
Courtesy www.the-bachelors.com

*Right: The Tornados outside The Olympia,
Paris, April 1963. L-R: Clem, Heinz Burt,
Roger LaVern, Alan Caddy, George Bellamy*

Courtesy www.coda-uk.co.uk

The Tornados and Billy Fury, at the Billy Fury Fan Club party in 1963
Courtesy Brian Gregg

Graham Jarvis, Cliff Richard and Clem during a 1970s tour

Clem with The Merseys, Billy Kinsley and Tony Crane, and Chas McDevitt

Clem with his friend Vic Flick, session guitarist who also played the famous riff to The James Bond Theme

Left: Clem with his pals of a Showbiz XI

Below: Clem with his friend former Arsenal full back Pat Rice celebrate winning the FA Cup

Clem looks on as Arsenal goalkeeper Petr Cech plays on his kit with Brian Miller (keyboards) and Anthony Coote (vocals and bass) at the Arsenal training ground

Brian Bennett, Clem, Bruce Welch and Mo Foster

The Rocky Horror Picture Show band

The New Tornados: Dave Graham, Clem, Dave Harvey, Bip Wetherell, with Lynn Alice in front

Above: The prestigious Buddy Rich award presented to Clem in 2012

Right: Clem with Ray Davies and Pat Rice

Anna and Clem with former Arsenal manager Arsene Wenger

Daughters Daniella, Victoria and Giulia

8

A Well Respected Man

My motto was, there's another record to make; let's go and make it. People ask me if I realised I was the busiest session man; I didn't. I thought everybody was as busy as I was. The world of the session musician is unique. I was often working all hours, sometimes three sessions a day in three different studios.

Clem Cattini (2016)

In January '65, as the country was engrossed with the funeral of Winston Churchill and listening to the sombre television commentary of Richard Dimbleby, Clem was working in Abbey Road on a session with The Ivy League boys, Perry Ford, John Carter and Ken Lewis. Accompanying them were Jim Sullivan and Mickey Keen on guitars, former Nero and the Gladiators Mike O'Neill on keyboards and John Paul Jones on bass. The results were *'Funny How Love Can Be'*, *'That's Why I'm Crying'* and *'Tossing and Turning'*, which all became Top Twenty hits.

Over the next two decades Clem's steady style, described as 'technically unflawed, playing with an awesome economy... though he can let rip if he so chooses', proved to be his making as he became ever more in demand for session work.

John Carter and Ken Lewis had been together as a singing and songwriting duo since their school days. Producer Terry Kennedy re-christened them Carter & Lewis and they cut seven singles for Piccadilly, Ember and Oriole between 1961 and 1964. With a close harmony style similar to that of the Everly Brothers, they were soon established as a popular radio team, appearing regularly on

171

Saturday Club and *Easy Beat*.

In 1964 they decided to concentrate on writing and sessions. Perry Ford, real name Brian Pugh, then joined to make them a three-part harmonies group. As The Ivy League they provided backing vocals on Sandie Shaw's '*(There's) Always Something There To Remind Me*', Tom Jones' '*It's Not Unusual*', The Who's '*I Can't Explain*' and '*Anyway, Anyhow, Anywhere*'.

The success of '*Funny How Love Can Be*' prompted the need to form a backing group to go on tour. Mickey Keen, Dave Wintour and Mike O'Neill joined up with Clem to become, what Clem suggested they call themselves, Division Two. Looking back, Clem laughingly says 'It should have been Division One, I don't know why I called it Division Two!'

Disaster struck In July 1965 when Carter, Ford and Lewis were injured in a car crash and Carter and Lewis subsequently decided to pull out. Tony Burrows and Neil Landon came in as replacements.

Throughout 1966 The Ivy League toured the UK and Europe with a band called The Jaybirds, later to become better known as Ten Years After. Carter and Lewis then formed The Ministry Of Sound with Clem and the Division Two team, plus Robin Shaw on bass. A single, titled '*White Collar Worker*'/'*Back Seat Driver*', and an album *Men From The Ministry* were released but gained little interest.

During the summer of 1967, under the name of The Flower Pot Men they recorded a song they wrote to cash in on the flower-power movement, '*Let's Go To San Francisco*'. The single made it to number 4 in the UK charts in September.

Clem:

> When I left The Tornados in 1965 I have to admit I couldn't read a note and I bluffed my way through sessions. It was a case in those days of playing the songs better than what they had been written. It was the early days in pop and nobody knew what to write, and most writers didn't know about pop anyway. We were kept busy, working for Shel Talmy, Mickie Most, Peter Sullivan and Terry Kennedy, criss-crossing London to the Decca, EMI, Regent Sound and Pye studios. The fixers would never tell you which

session it was in case you'd turn around and say you didn't want it. In America, a similar band of session men in Los Angeles were called The Wrecking Crew. Glen Campbell, Hal Blaine and co. were recording the hit records for the Mamas and Papas, Byrds, Beach Boys, Barry Maguire, Elvis... in Detroit they had The Funk Brothers backing up The Four Tops, Temptations, Supremes... Memphis had Booker T. and the M.G.s recording for Otis Redding, Sam and Dave, Wilson Pickett. Why we were in demand was because with us, we all came from a rock and roll background. Most of our peers came from the jazz world. Suddenly you had all these hooligans like myself, Jim Sullivan, Joe Moretti who had come in from the rock and roll groups. In the case of Lulu for instance, she had a good band behind her called The Luvvers and they toured successfully supporting big names like The Hollies, Gene Vincent, played on the same bill as The Beatles and Stones. They were from Glasgow, and were a hardened outfit but like most of the groups at the time, inexperienced in the recording studio. Hence why the record producers preferred to call us guys in to get the job done in quick time. It wasn't a slight on their abilities, more a question of time means money!

The organiser for the sessions was more commonly known as the 'Fixer', the go-between for producers and session musicians. In Clem's case, it was often Charlie Katz, who was a former violinist with his own ensemble The Charlie Katz Novelty Sextet, who were resident on the BBC Light Programme's *Music Box* in the late 1950s and early Sixties.

Clem:

Charlie was a ruthless, hard-nosed character. One particular session with Tom Jones illustrated his uncaring attitude. He'd arranged musicians for the recording of '*Green Green Grass of Home*' at Decca, and afterwards asked the violinists if they were available for the next date. They all said 'Yes' except one, who said he couldn't make it because it was his wedding anniversary. Charlie looked at him; 'I don't think you understand,' he said tersely, 'you WILL be free that day.' In other words, he was telling the violinist if he didn't show up he would be having a long holiday! These guys dictated what, who or where musicians would get work.

He did let the ruthless streak get the better of him one day though, when he was shown up in a very insensitive manner. A recording being done with producer Mike Smith was delayed because a session guitarist hadn't shown up. Mike Smith was furious, venting his anger at Charlie, who told him, 'It won't happen again Mike, when people don't show up for me, they are dead.' Which, sadly, as it happened, was right on the button. God rest his soul, the guitarist had kicked the bucket just the night before!

I have seen punch-ups in the studios with session musicians and producers. One was between two music directors working on an LP with Irish singer Joseph Locke. They were working on different tracks and couldn't decide who went next, and had a fight about it!

Probably the most significant stand-up row I had was with Tony Hatch, the man who wrote the *Neighbours* theme. There had been a mix-up over a Petula Clark session I had to attend to at Pye in Marble Arch. My wife Anna took the message and made a note – 'You have to be there at 2pm.' Ten o'clock the next morning the phone rang and it was Tony Hatch, who was producing the record. 'Where the hell are you?' he asked. 'In bed,' I replied. 'You were supposed to be here at ten!' I dashed down to Marble Arch, set my kit up and he handed me a sheet of music and told me that this is what I was playing. At the time I couldn't read sheet music and Tony grew more and more impatient because I couldn't figure out what and how I should be playing. In the end, I walked out. 'Look Tony, I'm not in the mood for this, I'm late, not sure what you want me to play, I think you'd better get someone else for the session. And by the way,' I said as I marched through the door, 'I've been thrown out of better bands than this one!'

But I knew I had to learn to read the sheet music and I contacted my mate Andy White, who taught me.

Session work could be boring for all of us, and I remember an incident concerning Joe Moretti when he was finding one session particularly tedious. England was the centre of the European pop music business and everyone wanted to make use of our musicians and studios. This day we were working with some French guys and they were just too meticulous. Joe got bored, and I mean really bored. So bored that he killed time by covering himself in Green Shield Stamps! I can still remember hearing a French guy yelp when he went into the booth to speak to Joe and found him looking like an alien. Session men were definitely a breed apart, and had no time for reverence or diffidence, no matter how famous the individual. Like Sir John Barbirolli, the renowned conductor. We were doing some tracks with him and two French horn players who were a father and son team, Jim Buck and Jim Buck junior – or Jim Bucktoo we called him. During a recording, Sir John was not happy. 'The horns are flat,' he said, 'try again.' Then 'No, the horns are now too sharp, still not in tune.' That was it for Jim Senior, who lost his rag. 'Sir John,' he said, 'I can pull on, pull off or I can just f—- off! You decide!'

Jack Lancaster, sax player and session man with British R&B band Blodwyn Pig: 'Some sessions will float along effortlessly and others are filled with tension. I prefer the ones that are filled with good humour. Fortunately they are not so rare.'

Jack, who had taken violin lessons as a child, was inspired after seeing Clem with Johnny Kidd and The Pirates in his hometown Blackpool when '*Shakin' All Over*' was riding high in the charts in 1960. 'They were the first rock band I ever saw live. And I stood in an open doorway outside the football club in Bloomfield Road Blackpool. They wouldn't let me in because I was not old enough to drink!'

In the early Sixties Jack was working regularly in Manchester, 'playing in the backing bands of Wayne Fontana, Dave Berry and others'. In 1969 he formed Blodwyn Pig with former Jethro Tull guitarist Mick Abrahams.

Clem:

American composer Marvin Hamlisch, who composed the theme for the James Bond movie *The Spy Who Loved Me*, '*Nobody Does It Better*' by Carly Simon, was another victim of the session man's totally irreverent view on life. We were doing a recording at the CTS studios in Wembley and after one effort he walked over, very superior, to the guitar player Mitch Dalton. In a real New York drawl, an angry Hamlisch asked him, 'What is this shit you're playing?' Mitch was supposed to be all a tremble that this famous man was upset. He wasn't. Mitch looked up at him, and said, 'Yours'. And we all fell about laughing!

Outdoor concert work was also part of our work and two memories come to mind. The public never seemed to regard musicians as having REAL jobs. Why? I don't know. They think it has to be part time. At one event the typical lady-in-the-tiara came up to the percussionist in the band and asked him, with a real plummy accent, 'What do you do for a living?' 'I'm a percussionist,' he answered. 'No, but what is your real job?' she asked again. 'I'm a percussionist,' he replied once more, 'that is what I do.' Then as she turned to walk away, he asked her abruptly; 'By the way, what does your husband do?' 'Oh, he's in oil,' came the reply. 'Oil! What is he? A frigging sardine?' said our percussionist. End of conversation! But my funniest memory came at an outdoor concert in Cambridge where we were playing film themes and had just finished a rousing rendition of *The Big Country*. Then came a moment's silence... and the longest and loudest passing of wind you had ever heard! The problem was, it made everyone suppress their urge to burst out laughing and that just made it worse! Eventually, no-one could hold back any longer and the whole place erupted! What a session that was!

Clem was omnipresent. Another session in '65 came with Merseybeat legend Ted 'Kingsize' Taylor, who had travelled down from Liverpool to record at the Olympic Studios. Kingsize and the Dominoes had played the Star-Club and other Hamburg clubs for years, but with record success back home evading them Kingsize decided to give it a shot on his own. Ted and the Dominos are known for being the band that gave Cilla Black the opportunity to sing at the famous Cavern Club, which hasn't always been appreciated or acknowledged. 'The Beatles always took the credit for Cilla Black,' says Ted, 'when she actually played first with our band. We were the first people to take her on the road. Everybody says, 'The Beatles gave Cilla Black her chance'. What a load of cock! She would have come to Germany with us, except for the fact that the German connection would only allow English girls over to go to bed with them. If they didn't, you could forget it.'

Clem:

Kingsize was a great singer. Lovely man too. He gave Cilla Black her break when she worked as a hat-check girl in The Cavern, Liverpool. We did a week at The Cavern just after '*Telstar*' in October '62 and I thought she was a cocky so and so. She loved a face and I think she thought we were big stars, I suppose. Then years later I did some sessions with her at EMI and she came up to me and asked 'Who are you then?' I was going to say, 'You obviously don't remember me, I'm Clem,' and then I was tempted to tell her I was the one that told her where to go ...in The Cavern, but I resisted! She always denied working in The Cavern taking the coats. I could never figure that out... I mean, I worked in my old man's caff for God sake! What's wrong about that?

Journalist David Britton interviewed Kingsize Taylor in 1985:

Kingsize Taylor had a powerhouse voice that was lacking in those first generation English rockers. His size and personal magnetism put me in mind of Howlin' Wolf. Ted had an original voice that oozed personality and commitment, who imbued every song he performed with an urgent authority. He was also the first rock 'n' roll singer in that hotbed of beat groups, Liverpool. Later, his band The Dominoes endured a ferocious regime of rehearsals during their Star-Club days in Hamburg that would have taxed The Magic Band under Captain Beefheart.

Here is the undiluted Kingsize, telling his story the way it appeared to him at the time. It's a story like PJ Proby's in which a fantastic vocal talent burned briefly but never quite lived up to its immense potential.

'Our first record was done in 1958 by Landa Records of Crosby, Liverpool. We always made the claim to being the first actual Liverpool rock 'n' roll band, because we had been playing rock 'n' roll since 1956/7. The way it started was when myself and Bobbie Thompson were stood in our local chippie and Bobbie asked me, 'Don't you play guitar?'

I said, 'Yeah, I do.'

'How many chords do you know?'

'Four.' I said.

'Well,' said Bobby. 'I can play three. Should we form a group?' From there it went to anybody who could get hold of an instrument. We would go round on Sunday afternoons to our mate Tommo's house. We often had about 20 people in there. And from them we selected the best for the band.

Our first band, The James Brothers, was the forerunner of rock 'n' roll in Liverpool. We were so influenced by early rock. We really enjoyed what we were doing, nobody had to force us to do anything, and we developed a genuine feel for rock. Other bands took us as an example and began to jump on the bandwagon.

I made this statement that we used to get American records from the sailors using Liverpool docks. I'm talking about 1956/57. Apparently, John Lennon told an American reporter that those people who used to say they got records in from America were talking a load of crap. He didn't know anything about it. He wasn't even on the scene until 1958/59 – and in 1958 he was doing nothing. The Beatles got all their early rock numbers from Kingsize Taylor and the Dominoes, there's no danger about that – because they sat in the front row at Lathom Hall watching us. They couldn't play, because they had turned up without a drummer. They all sat on the front row, and took a line each, *'Dizzy Miss Lizzy'*, *'Slow Down'*. They came to us afterwards, saying, 'I didn't get that...' The next thing is, they're playing that gear. Lennon in particular copied the way I sang those songs.

We didn't write our own material, nobody in the band could. We started at a time when there was no demand for people to write songs. We were playing songs that nobody had heard anyway. It was only later that people felt they had to write their own songs to become individualistic. In our case, we already were; we were the only group playing those hard rock songs. So we didn't have that need, that momentum, to write our own material.

After us came Derry Wilkie and the Seniors. When Derry broke away it became Howie Casey and the Seniors. In place of Derry, they got Freddie Starr, although their live show still included the three of them – a fabulous show. Even in those days, Freddie used to take off Elvis and Eddie Cochran. Freddie was quite influential on the Liverpool scene, because he had been in the film *Violent Playground*. After that they wanted him to do *Oliver!* in America. Some influential showbusiness people came up to see him performing with Howie Casey, and that's how they came to record *'Double Twist'*. They were the first Liverpool band to record for a major company. Later, Freddie used to do a few gigs with us over in Hamburg.

When we went to the Star-Club in Hamburg, we were originally signed by Decca of Germany, who brought out a couple of records by us. Then Phillips of Germany did a couple, and later we were with Ariola, who released *Kingsize Taylor And The Dominoes – Live At The Star-Club* in 1963.

In the Star-Club, a man asked us, 'Are you under contract?' We replied 'Yes.' He asked, 'Would you like to make a record under another name. We'll give you a thousand pounds.' We said, 'You're on.' We went down to Polydor studio after we finished a 7.00pm to 1.00am session at the Star-Club in a mini coach. When we got there, we found the floor of the studio literally covered with buckets filled with beer to help us through the session. We got started right away. We did all tracks on the Shakers album live, one take only for each track – bang bang – and then we walked out and got our money. It was just like a live show, which probably accounts for the tremendous feel on the album.

Because we were already under contract, we had to put the album out under a false name. It was going to be either Noddy and the Red Toecaps, or Boots Wellington and his Rubber Band, or The Shakers. And since The Shakers meant the same in German as it did in English that was the one they used. It was recorded in 1964 and released in England in 1965. The band did another album in Germany. They overdubbed my singing with a German vocalist called Hans Werner. It was never released in England. In fact, I did record a couple of duets with Hans, which they released in Germany.

I would say that this was the best period for the band. We had a very good feel. Sam Hardie on piano, Gibson Kemp was the drummer on most of the records, John Frankland was also on drums, Howie Casey on sax, and a Scotsman, Dave Woods, on sax, and when Howie moved onto baritone sax a Moroccan Frenchman called Muhammad Hari joined us for a time, so that we had three saxes. Sam doubled on organ as well as doing vocals. Bobby Thompson on guitar and vocals. John Frankland did vocals on some numbers. I played guitar and vocals, mainly on the heavy rock songs.

We toured with Little Richard in Germany. The last tour we did in England was the Chuck Berry/Carl Perkins 1964 tour. Gene Vincent joined us at Coventry, halfway through.

We split up at the end of 1964, the beginning of 1965. We did a tour over here where everybody got pissed off. I wanted to go back to Germany, the other members of the band wanted to stay and work over here. We just disintegrated. After that I picked up another band and went back to Germany. Ron Parry was with me on drums. We had a few good musicians, we had a few laughs, but I was getting sick of it by then. Then I had to change that band, and each time I got more and more disheartened. I decided I would leave my reputation there in Germany, at the top. I didn't come down. I could have got loads of work on my own, but without the band it wasn't the same.

By 1965 I'd just about had enough. It got Big Time, the fun had gone out of it. Everything was down to contracts and penalties. It finished me. All the joy had gone out of it. The old band had gone, the musicians you got were all dick-heads. They might have been good musicians, but they had no feel.

I did a couple of records for Studio One in Liverpool, '*I've Been Watching You*', and '*Never In A Hundred Years*'. Bobby Thompson by this time had joined Cliff Bennett and the Rebel Rousers. I was pleased for him. We tended to see the Liverpool bands as muckers.

Cliff Bennett had the one band in the country that really impressed me. Bobby was on his hit, '*One-Way Love*'.

I travelled to London and made some records down there with Clem, Jimmy Page and future Fleetwood Mac guitarist Peter Green. Jimmy played lead guitar on '*Somebody's Always Trying*' and '*Looking For My Baby*', and a couple of other tracks that we did in that session. Clem Cattini on drums, a forty-piece London Symphony Orchestra, and The Ladybirds. Peter Green played the second lead guitar, but it was Jimmy who did that terrific solo on '*Baby*'. We recorded them at the Olympic Studios. I did a couple of others later.

All this recent interest over John Lennon doesn't touch me. I couldn't give a shite what Lennon did, I was doing my own thing. At that time, in Liverpool, I was bigger than Lennon. He used to come and watch me. I didn't go and watch him. I've got more soul in my big toe than people like Tom Jones have in their whole body. Anybody that can sing a record twice in exactly the same way has got no soul. You could go and watch Tom Jones tonight, tomorrow and the day after, and it'd be the same every time. To me, that contains nothing.

If I were recording today I'd still record rock. I still have the feel for rock 'n' roll. It's stood the test of time.

Clem played on many of the biggest hits of 1965 including *'Make It Easy on Yourself'* by The Walker Brothers, three Americans, no relation to each other whatsoever who, having only registered limited success in the States, decided to try their luck in Europe. They were signed to the Philips label by producer Johnny Franz. Bass player Scott Engel, guitarist John Maus and drummer Gary Leeds became a big attraction and achieved more success in the UK with *'My Ship Is Coming In'* and *'The Sun Ain't Gonna Shine Anymore'*. By 1967, just two years after arriving in Britain the 'siblings' had grown tired of each other and went their separate ways and embarked on solo careers.

Another big hit in 1965 was Jonathan King's *'Everyone's Gone To The Moon'*. Inspired by the Space Race, King was precipitating Armstrong and Aldrin's *Apollo 11* flight by four years. In 1965 though this looked a highly unachievable goal, but progress was being made with America's Ed White becoming the first astronaut to walk in space on the Gemini 4 mission, three months after the Russian cosmonaut Alexei Leonov had achieved a similar feat.

White's spacewalk, after propelling himself from his capsule with a jet gun into the dark void of space, lasted just under 30 minutes. Two years later, along with fellow astronauts Gus Grissom and Roger Chaffee, White would perish when a flash fire swept through their *Apollo 1* command module during a launch rehearsal, setting the programme back by 18 months.

Back on the ground, March 20th marked a significant moment in Tamla Motown history when a troupe of Tamla artists arrived to begin a tour of 21 cities in the UK. The line-up included Stevie Wonder, The Supremes, The Miracles and Martha and The Vandellas. Apart from an occasional nod to the American performers, like The Beatles covering The Velvelettes' *'Please Mr Postman'* on their *With The Beatles* album in 1963, little was known about these artists as

Beatlemania continued to dominate the music scene.

The Supremes with '*Where Did Our Love Go?*' and '*Baby Love*' hitting number 1 in 1964 was the first time anyone in Blighty had heard of the Motown sound.

Beginning at Finsbury Park Astoria, London, the show was far from a sell-out and Georgie Fame was added to the bill to help sell tickets as they careered around the country to far flung places including Bournemouth, Liverpool and Wigan, ending in Portsmouth on 12th April 1965.

Midway through the tour, on 28th April 1965, a *Ready Steady Go!* TV special titled 'The Sound of Motown' was hosted by Dusty Springfield. Thanks to Dusty and a growing crop of British fans, by the end of 1966 Motown was a huge part of the British music scene.

If you believed everything you read in the newspapers during 1965, we were on the 'Eve of Destruction', as folk singer Barry McGuire prophesied. Along with a group of Royal Air Force workers called Hedgehoppers Anonymous and their big selling hit '*It's Good News Week*', the end of the world was once again imminent and the placard waving monks of Nepal were heading for the hills again.

McGuire's '*Eve of Destruction*' was one of the darkest records ever released and because of its content was banned by the ever diligent Beeb.

'Protest' was the buzz word those summer months. The songs of P.F. Sloan, Dylan, Joan Baez, Phil Ochs ('*I Ain't Marching Anymore*') highlighted the United States' nightmare with the Vietnam War. Despite the Americans stepping up the bombing of North Vietnam they were losing more and more men every week. President Lyndon Johnson confounded everyone by then announcing he was increasing the monthly draft from 17,000 to 35,000, taking the count to 125,000, news which fuelled the anti-war movement, leading to mass demonstrations and college students burning their draft cards. On November 13th 35,000 marched on Washington to protest against the war.

The demonstrations weren't exclusive to the Vietnam War; on

the West Coast in Watts, Los Angeles, riots erupted following an incident when an African-American was arrested for alleged drunk driving. A roadside argument escalated and the police were accused of extreme brutality, which the community reacted to and six days of battles, looting and arson ensued, leaving 34 people dead and an estimated 40 million dollar bill of damage. The riots inspired Stephen Stills to write '*For What It's Worth*', which became a massive hit for Buffalo Springfield. Add the Civil Rights demonstrations that were ubiquitous right across America, from New York to California, and the country was in a real mess.

There were also fulminations over Bob Dylan, the assigned spokesman for the protest movement, when he shocked everyone at the Newport Folk Festival by forgoing his folk roots and acoustic guitar to go 'electric'. Jaws dropped when Dylan came on stage with a blues band led by guitarist Mike Bloomfield and hammered out new versions of his old songs. Dylan had realised the limitations of the folk scene and struck out on a different route, influenced by The Beatles. The reaction was probably what he expected, cries of 'Judas', boos and heckling was intense. This was Dylan showing he couldn't care less what people thought; he was and never would be a conformist. When he retreated in 1966 and vanished for nigh on two years following a motorcycle accident, fans thought it was more than a coincidence. Was Bob escaping the flak to let things cool down? The electrified albums *Highway 61 Revisited*, *Bringing It All Back Home* and *Blonde On Blonde* were left for his disciples to digest. It was interesting that when he re-emerged in 1968 his first album would be a return to his folk roots with an acoustic set of songs on *John Wesley Harding*. Once more questions were being asked. Was Bob easing himself back in? Teasing his followers? The 'folkies' were temporarily appeased, believing the Messiah was back. A few months later Bob would surprise everyone again, recording *Nashville Skyline*, a country-influenced album, which included a duet with Johnny Cash.

'Protest' was also prevalent in the UK following the announcement of the Queen's Birthday Honours List in, which The Beatles were awarded the MBE for their services to the country on the recommendation of Prime Minister Harold Wilson. The fallout was entirely predictable. Previous recipients of the various awards Her Majesty dished out were generally disgusted, many returning their medals to make the point. Col. Frederick Wagg was so upset that he sent back twelve medals he had earned fighting in both World Wars, resigned from the Labour Party and cancelled his invitation to the party.

'Decorating the Beatles,' he wrote, 'has made a mockery of everything this country stands for. I've heard them sing and play, and I think they're terrible.'

It was probably all very amusing for The Beatles at the time, but four years later, in 1969, John Lennon decided to return his award as an act of protest against the Vietnam War following the My Lai massacre carried out by the US Army in March 1968. His medal was returned with a personal note to the Queen:

> Your Majesty,
>
> I am returning my MBE as a protest against Britain's involvement in the Nigeria-Biafra thing, against our support of America in Vietnam and against '*Cold Turkey*' slipping down the charts.
>
> With love.
> John Lennon of Bag

Copies of the letters, written on notepaper headed Bag Productions, the company Lennon had recently set up with Yoko Ono, were sent to Harold Wilson and the Chancery.

Seized on by the media, Lennon explained: 'Lots of people who complained about us getting the MBE received theirs for heroism in the war. They got them for killing people. We deserved ours for not killing people. In a way it was hypocritical of me to accept it.'

The abuse of the Queen's English was very much a concern in the Sixties, and consternation was deep when the first-ever use of the F-word on television – by theatre critic Kenneth Tynan – resulted in a formal apology by the BBC, four separate House of Commons motions signed by 133 Labour and Tory backbenchers and a letter to the Queen from clean-up campaigner Mary Whitehouse, who urged that Tynan 'ought to have his bottom smacked,'

The next man to use the word on screen, *Daily Telegraph* journalist Peregrine Worsthorne, was denied the editorship of the newspaper because of his slip.

Mrs. Whitehouse was also at the forefront in the condemnation of cigarette advertising on television, which in some ways was a pity because some of the best adverts on the box were those of the cigarettes. 'You're never alone with a Strand', accompanied by *The Lonely Man* theme, a wonderful example.

The Kinks, with whom Clem had played sporadically throughout their early days when standing in for Mick Avory, were in the headlines after an unsavoury incident at the Capitol Theatre in Cardiff. Touring solidly throughout 1965 tensions within the band were never far away, and it boiled over on stage with Dave Davies booting Mick's drums as Mick was about to count a number in.

The Kinks' drummer talked about his career and his association with Clem Cattini and recalled the infamous night in Cardiff during an interview backstage when The Kast Off Kinks, a band of former members John Dalton, Ian Gibbons and Dave Clarke, appeared at the Core Theatre, Corby in 2017.

> The first time I met Clem was at the Pye Studios when I was there with The Kinks. Later on I got to know him better when we played golf at the South Herts Golf Club.
>
> It was by accident I started playing the drums. If my dad hadn't bought me a drum kit I wouldn't have thought of it. I used to go to Scout meetings in Moseley Hill where I lived. They had a dart board, small snooker table and they also played Trad Jazz records there as well. I was told by older blokes that I shouldn't have been there as 'You're supposed to be fifteen.' I was thirteen, but I lived in the same road as the bloke in the Scouts who was forming a band. He had said to me, 'Come along if you want, the guy on drums doesn't want to play. It was only a drum on a chair and a scrubbing brush and stick or something, it was pretty crude. They also had a really good washboard player. So I did go along and quickly thought, 'This is fun,' and I took lessons off a jazz

drummer called Chris Hewitt.

We played the skiffle stuff but because of the lack of transport our gigs were local at places like Cigarette Island in East Molesey and at Eel Pie Island.

At the time I had a job as a delivery driver for a home maintenance store, which lasted for over five years. Later, in 1962, I was working with a kid whose dad was multi-talented; a chimney sweep, a drummer and also an accordion player. The dad came round our house one day to sweep the chimney, saw my drums and said to my mum, 'Ah, you've got a drummer in your house.' She said 'Yeah, my son.' He said, 'Well I can get him some gigs at functions and stuff if he's interested.' So I played with him for a while.

Then one day 'Sweep' rang me and said he'd seen an advertisement in the *Melody Maker* about some guys forming a rhythm and blues band who were seeking a drummer. 'Why don't you go along?' he said. 'They've got a gig at the Marquee, the bloke you want to speak to is Mick Jagger.' So I did go to see what it was all about. 'They're all youngsters,' 'Sweep' told me, 'there's no good me going round, I'm 62.' I met Jagger and the rest of them at the Bricklayer's Arms in Wardour Street. Keith Richards was there, Brian Jones – who was calling himself Elmo Lewis – Ian Stewart on piano and Dick Taylor, who later formed The Pretty Things. They wanted a drummer to do the gig, but really they were looking for a permanent drummer. I told them I'd do the gig but I had a day job and as I had to travel right across London, it was a bit of a drag. I told them I didn't want to waste their time and to get somebody else. And I never heard another dicky bird from them! But who knows what would have happened if I'd have took it on?

I was still living in Moseley Hill when I joined The Kinks. They were another rhythm and blues band back then. That was the scene around London, bands like The Yardbirds, Downliners Sect, Gary Farr and the T-Bones, Pretty Things. The Kinks suited my style, which was a jazzy blues sort of rhythm. The day after I joined I was on *Ready Steady Go!* Then we got managers and I thought to myself, 'This won't last very long.' The fight at Cardiff's Capitol Theatre followed on from a scrap between me and Dave the night before in Torquay. We were having an argument about something and Dave was worse for wear on drink or drugs. He had a fiery nature, used to blow hot and cold and the argument quickly developed into a fight. I had him down, and then as I let him up he whacked me right across my face. He was so off his head he wanted more. I thought 'Sod this,' and as a couple of the boys held him, I ran off down the stairs. Anyway, next night on stage, he put his boot right through my drums, scattering them. I only had the hi-hat left, I picked it up and whacked him right over his head with it. He went down and I thought 'I've got to get out of here'... I thought I'd killed him. So I ran out of the theatre, went down the road and found a cafe where after a while, one of The Kinks' roadies found me. I was upset and worried. I asked the roadie if Dave was alright. He said, 'Unfortunately, yes.' After that I went home for a while, I thought the police were looking for me.

Bassist Pete Quaife: 'Mick was counting in 'Too Much Monkey Business' when Dave kicked his drums over. He smashed his cymbal over Dave's head. Dave passed out, Mick ran off, Ray looked dumbfounded... and I was left still playing my bass to a packed audience! What else was I supposed to do?'

Mick:

We were due to record The Kink Kontroversy album shortly after the Cardiff gig and Clem was called in to cover me in my absence. We had to patch things up though, because an American tour was coming up. Larry Page, our manager, got me and Dave – who had to have six stitches put into his head – together, and we talked about the problem and Larry asked us if we wanted to carry on. So, we put our sensible heads on and we did go to America. Which was a disaster... but that's another story!

Clem stood in for me to play with The Kinks quite regularly in the early days. They all thought how loud he was. Even Dave complained, 'Gor, ain't he loud!' My problem, to begin with, was I was a bit jazzy and as things got louder and louder, and with the drums not mic'd up, I couldn't play loud enough. It was ridiculous. My hands used to bleed!

Last time I saw Clem was when we went to Belgium in 2014, playing with the Swinging Blue Jeans. Clem was at the airport and we had a great chat. He loves meeting the old guys, Pete Oakman, Alan Lovell and all them. We were also at the funeral of singer Danny Rivers when Clem said, 'Who's next to climb in the box?' Danny was from Liverpool but grew up in London. He was discovered by Larry Parnes, recorded for Joe Meek and toured with Johnny Burnette and many other big names. He also appeared on Jack Good's *Wham!* TV show. His voice was well suited to Elvis numbers, and he was particularly good on '*Little Sister*'.

I've had many influences as I've gone along. In the 60s, Clem was a big influence, as was Bobby Graham. I never took much off them though; you think, 'Well that's quite a nice thing,' and you try to emulate them. Bobby Elliott of The Hollies is another one. He was always telling me off for nicking his licks. I used to say to him, 'I'm green to this business, I've got to start somewhere.' We occasionally have a get together to play golf. Micky Burt, who was with Cliff Bennett and Chas and Dave, is another who joins us. It's like a drummers' reunion. Brian Bennett was another influence. Brian's done well writing film scores and jingles for television. He wrote the theme tune to the golf show on television. He also co-wrote Cliff Richard's hit '*Summer Holiday*'. It's a good job he wasn't in The Kinks though, he wouldn't have got a look in even if he could write!

It was great to be part of all The Kinks' hits, but when you look back you sometimes think some of it could have been better recorded. But there wasn't the best recording facilities at the time. Some of it was a bit flat, and there wasn't enough time to spend on it. That's why they used session musicians though, ain't it? So they could get the job done quicker.

Clem:

Obviously I knew the boys. I'd stepped in to replace Mick on the odd occasion when he was ill or unavailable, including a gig in Paris when Mick had tonsillitis and Ray Davies returned from a sabbatical of six weeks, sporting a Mexican moustache. And I could see how there was an underlying friction in the band. Dave must have wound Mick up something terrible for Mick to react like he did at Cardiff. Mick was always a fairly quiet and unassuming lad. Anyway, in Mick's absence, he had disappeared for a month or so, Mitch Mitchell, who had followed me into The Tornados, was actually lined up to replace him if he didn't return.

I recorded most of the *Kontroversy* album and also tracks for the *Kwyet Kinks* EP, which included '*A Well Respected Man*', a great Ray Davies composition. Ray was developing his songwriting style and gradually moving away from the three-chord rock numbers. Lennon and McCartney might have been the flavours of the month, but Ray was right up there with them. It was when The Kinks returned from America after they had heard The Byrds' '*Mr. Tambourine Man*', the 12-string jangling sound they achieved, inspired Ray to write '*See My Friends*', a massive hit in '65. That started the trend of what you might call 'kitchen sink' songs, to borrow an expression from the film world. '*Dedicated Follower of Fashion*', '*Dead End Street*', '*Sunny Afternoon*', '*Days*', '*Waterloo Sunset*' and The Kinks' albums *Face To Face*, *Village Green*, every bit as evocative and brilliant as what The Beatles were doing.

9

Top of The Pops

'Swinging London' was the centre of the universe in 1966. Providing the soundtrack were a number of seminal albums by the most influential bands of them all, The Beatles, The Rolling Stones and The Kinks. *Revolver*, *Aftermath* and *Face To Face* pushed the barriers of rock and roll to otherwise unimagined limits, the days of 'Moon and June' long deemed passé. '*Tomorrow Never Knows*', Lennon sang on *Revolver*. *What a drag it is getting old*, sang Jagger on '*Mother's Little Helper*'. Ray Davies' '*Dedicated Follower Of Fashion*' summarised the whole summer of fancy and fantasy. And in the background there was the England football team about to win the World Cup at Wembley. What a glorious and wonderful time it was to be young! Surely there's never been a summer like '66.

England v West Germany was a game that every football-mad fan wanted to be at, including Arsenal-mad Clem, who had to forgo the chance due to work commitments at EMI:

> I missed the most historic game in English football due to working on a session at Abbey Road in the morning, but I did manage to get home to watch the Final on the television. It was ironic in a way because at that stage the 'Fixers' wouldn't usually bother ringing me for a session on a Saturday if Arsenal were home. They used to check the fixture list first! They had probably checked the papers beforehand and saw that Arsenal weren't down for a game and assumed I wasn't interested in the World Cup Final! Another game I remember for other reasons was the Arsenal v Liverpool Cup Final in '71, the one when Charlie George scored the winner. John Lennon phoned me the week before asking if there was any

chance I could get him a ticket. I said to him, 'What! You should be getting me a ticket!' It must have been for someone he knew, because John was never a football fan as I recall.

The number one record at the time of the famous World Cup victory was Chris Farlowe's '*Out Of Time*', which the ubiquitous Clem played on. He was also on another massive hit this year, '*Sorrow*' by The Merseys, a duo comprised of Tony Crane and Billy Kinsley, who were an abridged version of The Merseybeats who had since gone the way of many of the other Sixties Liverpool bands with the hits drying up as the pop world was forever changing.

Clem:

> '*Sorrow*' was a great song produced by Mike Smith and an arrangement by Keith Mansfield. We did two takes, the first one was with the band backing Tony and Billy and then Mike put some orchestration on the back of it. These were the days when I was working around on average 21 sessions a week. My record was 24 during 7 days, but by the end of the week I was absolutely shattered. It was too much and I said I'd never do it again. My hands were sore, my brain addled.

'*Sorrow*' became one of the biggest hits of 1966, during a year that saw The Who, Small Faces, Kinks and Stones all driving ahead along with of course, The Beatles. '*Substitute*', '*All Or Nothing*', '*Sunny Afternoon*', '*Paint It Black*' expanding the boundaries of pop. Jimi Hendrix then appeared on the scene in 1966 to light up the London club scene further with his virtuosity and flamboyance. The impact Hendrix had can never be overestimated. When Eric Clapton, Jeff Beck and Pete Townshend saw him they were frightened to death. Hendrix might just as well have come from another planet.

The London scene was exotic, exciting, bewitching. In the clubs around Soho and the West End, John Mayall's Bluesbreakers, Cream, Georgie Fame and the Blue Flames, Fleetwood Mac, Zoot Money's Big Roll Band and Geno Washington's Ram Jam Band were at the forefront of what was being heralded as a 'British Blues Boom'.

Colin Allen, drummer with Zoot Money, recalls working non-stop throughout those years in the London clubs:

> We would work at the Marquee from around 7 in the evening and then go over the road to the Flamingo for an all-night session where Georgie Fame and the Blue Flames were resident. That's besides playing at the 100 Club, the Cromwellian and other gigs around the country. I was more into jazz than the blues, couldn't get all those songs about 'Woke up this morning, found my baby gone' etc, and Zoot's Big Roll Band was more soul-orientated, which suited me fine. I preferred Ray Charles, Nat King Cole to Muddy Waters and Howlin' Wolf.

For all that, Colin's next stop on his journey was to join up with John Mayall's Bluebreakers!

> That came about when John Mayall phoned me up out of the blue. John used to always carry a shoulder bag with him, and inside was a tape recorder. He used to go to gigs, tape a band and then listen to them later and decide if any of the members would suit his own band. This he did with me. 'I've heard you play, I think you'd fit in with the Bluesbreakers,' he told me over the phone. Straight away I thought, 'Oh, no, not all that blues stuff!' but then he said he's cutting an album, my mate Mick Taylor was in the group and they were off for a tour of the States shortly. My mind went, 'Bingo!' 'Yeah, sure, John,' I said, 'when do we rehearse?' He then surprised me by saying, 'We don't rehearse, we just turn up!' So this I did for the album *Blues From Laurel Canyon*. It was a great experience really. With Zoot we used to rehearse all the time when not playing gigs. With John Mayall, you played off the cuff. He would say to Mick Taylor on guitar, 'Play a shuffle in C' to get us going. I used to watch Mick and follow him! The *Canyon* album was recorded in three days! Mixed on the fourth and that was it. No hanging around and taking months over recording an album.

The Merseys' Billy Kinsley recalled the making of '*Sorrow*' and the memorable year of '66 for Bill Harry's *Mersey Beat* newspaper:

> Tony and I had returned to Liverpool to look for musicians to form a backing band, which is what Kit Lambert and Chris Stamp our new managers wanted us to do. They had done a great job

looking after the affairs of The Who and saw us as a kind of Walker Brothers, or something along those lines. We went to the Blue Angel in Seel Street and The Masterminds were playing. Joey Molland, the future Badfinger guitarist, Chris Finley and George Cassidy were in the line-up. They played well, all had a good image and stage presence, so they were invited to join our backing band. They all said 'Yes' straight away. A drummer we liked was Kenny Goodlass, who had been in The Escorts, and he joined as well. Our first gig was a few days later and we went down a storm as The Merseys. 'Sorrow' was discovered on the 'B' side of the McCoys' 'Fever'. It was a Neil Young-type of vocal and country and western sounding. We loved it. I rearranged the harmonies and decided to add a vocal line that was sung after the main line and that was it, we knew we had a winner. We'd got hold of Jimmy Page, Jack Bruce and Clem Cattini to play on it in a small studio in Denmark Street. We changed it again and then got a bigger band, with John Paul Jones replacing Jack who couldn't make the second session, and did the song live at CBS Studios in New Bond Street, London. The Beatles, Frank Sinatra and The Troggs stopped us getting to number one, but 'Paperback Writer', 'Strangers In The Night' and 'Wild Thing' were all classic records and we realised that at the time. 'Sorrow' has since become a Sixties classic itself and mentioned as a favourite by many artists. David Bowie later recorded a version for his *Pin Ups* album.

Our next record was Pete Townshend's 'So Sad About Us', a Kit Lambert over-produced, overdone, egomaniacal catastrophe! Kit believed he was the new Phil Spector, and he clearly wasn't.

The Merseys toured many times with The Who; at least four major tours, as well as one-nighters before that as The Merseybeats. We were still based on Merseyside, but spent more and more time in London and became great friends with The Who and got to hang out with them.

Traveling by road was pretty tiring. I remember how excited we all were when the M1 was finally linked to the M6. Traveling by rail was getting much better, so we started to go by train to recording sessions as we'd be much fresher relaxing and taking it easy. I recall I first flew from Speke to Heathrow for our second recording session as we'd blown our voices on our debut in the studio and didn't want to blow it again!

Sorrow was what Clem was feeling when he heard about the tragic fatal car crash near Radcliffe, Lancashire involving his old buddy Johnny Kidd on October 7th 1966. The accident occurred while Kidd and Pirates bassist Nick Simper were travelling home from setting up a gig in Blackpool. Johnny was sitting in the front seat alongside the driver Wilf Isherwood. Simper, who later played with Deep Purple, received head, neck and arms injuries and said he didn't know what happened. 'Johnny turned round to talk to me, and the next minute, the car veered right across the road and straight into an on-coming car.' The driver of the other car, 17-year-old Helen Read sadly also died. Emergency services were quickly on the scene, but Johnny was dead on arrival at Bolton Royal Infirmary.

Clem was shattered by the news and paid a fine tribute to his friend: 'Johnny was tremendously important to British Rock and Roll. Cliff Richard, Johnny and Billy Fury were the pioneers of rock in this country. They put it on its feet and laid the foundation for what came afterwards.'

Around this time Clem was working with an up-and-coming songwriter called Graham Gouldman from Manchester. Graham had given some of his best work to The Hollies and Herman's Hermits: *'Stop! Stop! Stop!'* (retitled *'Bus Stop'*), *'Look Through Any Window'*, *'No Milk Today'*. In '66 he was trying to make it on his own, and recording his material with hired session men, which included Clem, John Paul Jones and Phil Dennys.

Graham called the group High Society and released a Seekers-styled song titled *'People Passing By'*. The record passed everybody by as it happened, and he tried again with the same musicians under the name of The Manchester Mob. They revived two classic rock songs rolled into one with *'Bony Maronie'*/*'At The Hop'*, which was released on Parlophone in January 1967. Later it was recalled as 'a fantastic record packed with energy, but rather unfashionable at a time when the hippie fad was coming in big.' With hindsight, the record was arguably too early rather than too late, as a year later, in the early months of 1968, a Rock and Roll revival was underway in Britain with The Move releasing the Duane Eddy-inspired *'Fire*

Brigade' and The Beatles doing their bit with a nod to Fats Domino with '*Lady Madonna'*. There was even an outfit, albeit short-lived, led by future Mott the Hoople singer Ian Hunter, doing the rounds as At Last The 1958 Rock And Roll Show. Record companies, keen to cash in, released a number of old classics which re-appeared in the charts, years after their initial release. The likes of Dion, Elvis, Duane Eddy and Bill Haley were suddenly all the rage. Much to their delight, no doubt!

Clem:

> Following on from this excursion with Graham Gouldman I accepted the job with the TOTP Orchestra when they moved down from Manchester to London to record the shows. The Musicians Union had banned pop stars from miming to their records, which meant that artists either had to pre-record their numbers especially or perform live with the Top Of The Pops Orchestra. The ban also saw the end of TV shows like *Thank Your Lucky Stars*.

Leader of the TOTP Orchestra was classically-trained musician Johnny Pearson, who had appeared on *Top Of The Pops* in early 1965 as the pianist with Sounds Orchestral, whose '*Cast Your Fate To The Wind*' reached no. 5 in the charts. Johnny joined the staff of the show in 1967, the same year as Clem and the scantily-clad Pan's People dance troupe were introduced.

The move to London was initially to be for six months at the BBC TV Centre Studio 2, but was relocated to the larger studio at Lime Grove Studios. In November 1969, with the introduction of colour, the show returned to the BBC TV Centre where it stayed until 1991 when it moved to Elstree Studios.

You would have thought that the professionalism of the orchestra guys would have been well appreciated by the 'stars', but it was not always so... as was later reported further down the line.

> The assembly of jobbing musicians, mostly those more accustomed to easy-listening arrangements for crooners like Matt Monro and Des O'Connor, had to suffer as disorganised pop stars

often arrived at the studio on the day with no band parts at all. Pearson and the orchestra frequently had to improvise backing tracks. Inevitably the session men, almost all middle-aged, often struggled with the enormous range of rock and pop tunes with which they were presented.

Another problem for Pearson was that, on the conductor's rostrum, he had to contend with the extensive and rigidly-enforced provisions of the union's rule book. In rehearsal, if a tea break was due, the orchestra would break off in the middle of a song and walk out, leaving American funk and soul superstars scratching their heads.

Being a session man may have lacked the glamour and all the trimmings of being a 'rock star' on the road touring and lapping up the adulation, but in reality they were often more secure and happy with what they were doing, and getting a regular wage. Returning from a tour of the States with The Hollies in 1966, bass player Eric Haydock had had enough. '*I Can't Let Go*' was The Hollies latest top ten hit, and if the rest of the boys in the band felt they 'couldn't' let go', Eric did.

The touring was getting to me but also I was starting to think of settling down a bit with my girlfriend and on coming back from that tour I went along to see our management to see about getting some money to put down on a house we were wanting to buy in Hazelgrove, Stockport. The Hollies had been touring consistently for around three or four years, all over the world, we had numerous hit records, million sellers, yet when I asked our manager about getting hold of some cash, he said 'what cash?' I had thought it was ominous when I pulled up outside the office in London in my modest mini and saw his bright yellow flash looking E Type Jaguar parked up! 'What's going on here?' I thought to myself. Anyway, he said, 'we haven't got any cash'. 'Where's it all gone then?' I asked him. He said 'well, there's loads of bills to pay don't forget, and there's five of you in the band'. So, all that hard work for all those years, working non-stop and we were still skint! I told the rest of the boys I'd had enough. They thought I would cool down after a bit but I was adamant. 'You all might want to work for nothing, but I don't!' I told them. It's a familiar and typical story of the music business though. One big effing rip-off! With some gigs and a recording session to fulfill the management asked Jack Bruce to replace me but he turned it down. They got Bernie Calvert, who is a lovely lad, eventually but meantime I had a phone call from the Kinks. It was a Friday night and they asked me if I would be interested in joining them to replace Pete Quaife who had his own issues. Must be something with us bass players! The Kinks had a gig in Southport which wasn't far to travel for me but I told them I was still officially contracted with the Hollies and I'd have to turn them down. As soon as I put the phone down, I thought to myself, 'what have I done?' Or words to that effect! I should have joined them. I got on great with them all, Mick, Ray and Dave. Their manager told me that for some reason I had a calming effect on the Davies brothers who were always fighting and I'd be great for the band. Biggest regret of my life!'

Eric formed his own band, Haydock's Rockhouse – an eight-piece including a horn section, Hammond organ, and they went out very successfully for over two years before that became untenable. 'Rockhouse was a great band, I loved it, but really it was too big. Too costly to run, and it was too unwieldy, but it was great at the time,' Eric reflected.

Derek Quinn, guitarist with Freddie and the Dreamers, also had similar issues to Eric's which came to a head after a tour of the States:

> We were offered 90 grand to do a six-week 30-odd city tour of the States with support from a couple of bands, one of which were The Beau Brummels. We thought right away, 'Wow, we'll have some of that.' We completed the tour, appeared on *The Ed Sullivan Show*, had a lot of fun but it was still a slog, travelling everywhere by coach for hours and days on end... but at the end of it, we were getting paid 90 grand!
>
> But it was a similar story to Eric's. I went to see our management afterwards to try and extract some money, money I thought was due, and I was told the same. There isn't any! 'What's happened to the 90K?' I asked. Well, it turned out that out of that sum the support bands had to be paid, the hire of the tour bus, which was

over 3 grand a week, taxes, fees for the musician union on the West Coast of America, and then again on the East Coast! The fuel, air fares, hotels and then also the fees of the agents and the venues. I felt as if I owed them money! I think I realised then that basically while it was and had been great fun, I wasn't going to make any money of this career. I finished, it was around '69/70 time, and I went into partnership with the similarly-minded Karl Green of Herman's Hermits, running our own agency.

Revolution was in the air in 1967. The 'Baby Boomers' were rallying against the Vietnam War, the establishment, conformity. Tired of it all, the 'Flower Power' and 'Hippie' legend came to fruition. Thus, we had 'The Summer of Love', perhaps described best in *It's Steel Rock 'n' Roll To Me*, published in 2005:

> Flower Power was born in 1967 on the back of lyrical chickweed, propagated by The Beatles' masterpiece *Sgt. Pepper's Lonely Hearts Club Band*, cultivated by Donovan's *A Gift From A Flower To A Garden* and pollinated by American West Coast bands Jefferson Airplane, Grateful Dead and The Electric Prunes. Songwriters churned out an endless stream of horticultural anthems and the counter-culture that epitomised the hippie era emerged. Hippy culture came to represent an antidote to American and communist bloc global aggression, particularly in Vietnam, whence horrific images of war appeared on television screens throughout the western world. Together with reports documenting the Ku Klux Klan's malevolence towards the Civil Rights Movement sweeping through the southern states of America, the nightly news bulletins gave rise to the sixties anti-war movement with the mantra; 'Make Love, Not War'.

> Festivals became popular following the success of Monterey, near San Francisco, which saw Jimi Hendrix, the Mamas and the Papas, Canned Heat and other top line acts appearing. In Britain a show entitled 'Barbecue '67' was held at the Tulip Bulb Auction Hall, Spalding, Lincolnshire in May featuring The Jimi Hendrix Experience topping the bill alongside Cream, The Move, Pink Floyd, Geno Washington and Zoot Money.

> There was also the 'Festival of Flower Children' in the gardens of Woburn, Bedfordshire featuring Jimi Hendrix yet again, plus The Small Faces, Marmalade, Tyrannosaurus Rex amongst a host of

other acts.

Progression, you could call it. The days of the Larry Parnes/ Arthur Howes 'package tours' were numbered.

One of the last featured The Hollies, Tremeloes, Spencer Davis Group and Paul Jones on the treadmill of Granada cinemas in '67. This tour would also be the last for Graham Nash of The Hollies. A year after bassist Eric Haydock had left, Graham had grown disillusioned too. Not only with the hectic touring schedule, but also the direction the group was going in.

Eric Haydock:

> When Nashy left the Hollies, they were at the crossroads really. The songwriting which was shared between the front three, Nash, Allan Clarke and Tony Hicks, had dried up. You do get to the stage like in the studio, you'd be looking at each other for ideas, what can we do next? Graham was a prolific writer though, and coming out with stuff like '*Marakesh Express*', '*Our House*', '*Teach Your Children*' which he later recorded with Crosby, Stills and Nash and achieved great success. When he took these songs to the boys in The Hollies the response was 'We don't want to play all that hippy shit.' That's what caused the split. We had become friends with the Mamas and the Papas when in the States, and Graham had seen the way ahead for him. He took up with the fat girl, Mama Cass... you had to be a brave man to take that on!... but that was Graham... if he could get a toe in, he'd do it! I still believe that if The Hollies had recorded Graham's stuff it would have been them as the superstars, not Crosby, Stills and Nash but there you go.

The year began with Tom Jones at the top of the charts with '*Green Green Grass of Home*', the first of many number one records that Clem was featured on this year. Tom Jones was being railroaded down the entertainer/balladeer route after being advised by his manager Gordon Mills and producer Peter Sullivan 'to leave all the psychedelic rubbish to The Beatles.' 'Tom was a rocker and was reluctant,' said Mills, 'I said to him, 'Why try and compete with them?'.

Amidst all the hit records Clem was involved in there were as many that never made it past the odd airing on a pirate radio station. A Twickenham band called The Kool were one such outfit. A single, '*Look At Me, Look At Me*', featuring session musicians The Ivy League's Division Two, was released on the CBS label and, and sadly, nobody did look at them.

'*Tiger*' by the jazz-orientated Julie Driscoll and The Brian Auger Trinity never made it either.

Ensconced in the studio Clem looked on as the psychedelia era gripped. Abbey Road was all but the exclusive residence of The Beatles, as they produced the epochal *Sgt. Pepper* album, singles '*Strawberry Fields Forever*'/'*Penny Lane*' and the anthemic '*All You Need Is Love*'. On June 25th 1967 the Beatles represented the UK on the *Our World* TV special, performing '*All You Need Is Love*' via global satellite to an estimated 400 million viewers. Amongst those invited to the screening were their old Liverpool friends The Swinging Blue Jeans. Bass player Les Braid had a special memory:

> I was talking to John Lennon in the toilet before they went on. I asked him if he was nervous, with the whole world watching. He stunned me when he replied, 'Well I'd feel a whole lot better if I had wrote the second verse.' If you watch the video, John sings the first verse without looking at the music stand and then the second verse he's singing what he'd wrote that morning on the paper he has on the stand. Which was amazing.

Also in Abbey Road was Pink Floyd, who were putting together their equally groundbreaking debut album *The Piper At The Gates of Dawn*. Amazing pieces they were, but whilst they took months to record, Clem was doing his regular stint of three sessions a day and taking a leap into the 'Flower Power' scene with '*Let's Go To San Francisco*'.

> Well, everyone was going mad over this thing they called psychedelia, and Scott McKenzie's '*San Francisco*' resonated with all the youngsters, particularly in America, where the student rebellion against the draft and the Vietnam War was paramount. Suddenly the West Coast was where everyone wanted to be, apparently. Eric Burdon and The Animals released '*San Franciscan*

Nights', which was another huge hit. The music press were filling their pages with stories about love-ins, Haight-Ashbury, Monterey, bands with exotic names like Jefferson Airplane, Grateful Dead, The Doors. It all sounded glamorous, and the music, it has to be said, captured the imagination. Over here, John Carter and Ken Lewis came up with an idea to gatecrash the party and wrote a song called '*Let's Go To San Francisco*'. It was almost a spoof really, and as the Flower Power thing was all the rage we called ourselves The Flower Pot Men. And it was one of the biggest hits of the summer.

Another huge hit during this summer of love was Keith West and '*Excerpt from a Teenage Opera*'.

Clem:

> I was the drummer on that session too which showed up just why there is a humour gap between us and the Germans. Mark Wirtz, a German, was the musical director and at the end of the recording guitarist Jim Sullivan made the mistake of going into a vibrant guitar solo in what was supposed to be a sad, morose finish. We all cracked up laughing – Herr Wirtz did not! As Jim finished, this Teutonic voice boomed over the loudspeaker, 'Gentlemen,' said Wirtz, 'No more please.'

Teenage Opera was Mark Wirtz's attempt at a 'Rock Opera', which if it had been completed would have pre-empted Pete Townshend's *Tommy* by some three years. Keith West was the vocalist with the band Tomorrow, which also featured future Yes guitarist Steve Howe. *Teenage Opera* was described later in *Mojo* August 1996 as a 'Paisley pop curio which would have nestled neatly alongside The Kinks' *Village Green Preservation Society*.'

Keith West:

> Steve Howe had worked with Mark Wirtz on a backing track and asked me to write some lyrics for it. He played me the music and we talked about building the song around a character and he thought of the name 'Grocer Jack', which I cringed at. At the time I was writing a lot of story songs often based on characters I had come across. I thought, Let's make it really sad, the character dies,

so why don't we get a big chorus of kids on it? This was the '60s and anything could be tried.

'Teenage Opera' was released in August 1967 and reached number two in the charts, being kept off the top spot by Engelbert Humperdinck's 'Last Waltz'. The 'opera' project was abandoned shortly afterwards and Keith West returned to carry on playing with Tomorrow.

Mark Wirtz, who produced some of the era's most notable records including his very own 'A Touch of Velvet, A Sting of Brass' recalled:

> EMI gave us the worst studio time, 10 o'clock in the morning. Abbey Road was a cool studio but my god it didn't come along with energy. Some people say Keith West's success led to Tomorrow's break up. Keith sang 'Grocer Jack' because he was one of the people on the project. When it came to the demo at least it seemed most natural for him to sing it. We wrote it together and he was a vocal artist. It came out so well we decided to put it out like that. It certainly didn't conflict with Tomorrow at the time. Keith often said it ruined his career making 'Grocer Jack'. Well, it made his career as well because nobody had really heard of Tomorrow much in those days. But the thing was that when Tomorrow went on tour people wanted to hear 'Grocer Jack'. As a trio! When you think of it, it's kind of ludicrous. You could do it today with synthesisers and technology but not then. So Keith West forever blames *Teenage Opera* for ruining what would have been his career. I could say the same thing. Ultimately I too became known for *Teenage Opera*.

The following year, in May 1968, Clem would work with producer Mark Wirtz again, with two members of the defunct band Tomorrow, John 'Twink' Alder and bassist John 'Junior' Wood, plus his session friend, piano player Nicky Hopkins. They recorded a single for Parlophone titled '10,000 Words In A Cardboard Box' under the name Aquarian Age, which received a very favourable review; 'A perfect slice of psychedelic pop with prominent orchestration that adds to the impact of the song. It doesn't always have to be about fuzz guitars!'

One of the most popular films to hit the cinema screens in 1967 was the Warren Beatty/ Faye Dunaway gangster movie *Bonnie and Clyde*. The story of the infamous American bank robbers during the Depression era of the 1930s. The soundtrack was '*Foggy Mountain Breakdown*' by Lester Flatt and Earl Scruggs. It was never released as a single to cash in, and songwriters Mitch Murray and Pete Callander took the opportunity to write what became a classic, '*The Ballad of Bonnie and Clyde*', which was recorded by Georgie Fame.

Mitch Murray explained in *1,000 UK Number One Hits* by Jon Kutner and Spencer Leigh how they were inspired to write the song after seeing the movie:

> We both decided that they had blown the music. They should have had a hit song and so we thought we'd write one. At first we considered giving it to Joe Brown or Lonnie Donegan, but they didn't seem quite right for the song. Then the managing director of CBS told Peter that they had signed Georgie Fame and were looking for a big hit. We added a special jazzy bit for Georgie – 'Bonnie and Clyde got to be Public Enemy Number One' – as we thought that would sell it to him, but he wasn't very keen on the song. We did a demo with machine guns and skidding cars and we were asked to go to the session with our sound effects. The producer Mike Smith had his problems and Clem Cattini had to re-record his part, as Smith explained: 'The sound effects were wonderful but we discovered an electrical fault and we had clicks all through the rhythm track. I had to go back into the studio and, using George's vocal track and the front line from the brass, the musicians had to put down a new rhythm track, which is not easy. To this day, Georgie doesn't quite believe they did it, but we ended up with an outstanding record.

Clem remembers the session well:

> Mike had put the tapes in the boot of his car and there was a petrol leak and somehow this affected the tapes which had the rhythm section on. Mike phoned me and asked me if I was busy. I said I wasn't and he asked me if I could go down to the studio at midnight! Don't think Georgie was aware of that but whatever, it was his biggest hit for years!

Engelbert Humperdinck came to prominence after being taken under the wing of Tom Jones's manager, Gordon Mills. Clem, who played on a number of his records including his breakthrough 'Release Me' and 'The Last Waltz', recalled:

> Engelbert had no equal in the superstitious stakes. I knew him when he was struggling to make an impact in the early Sixties under his real name of Gerry Dorsey. Years passed and I believe he had a tough time of it. Then Gordon Mills heard him, liked him, and offered to manage him. He changed the name to Engelbert Humperdinck, and 'Release Me' became a million seller. A few years later I was at the Talk of the Town in London when I saw him. 'Gerry,' I shouted, and he turned round really stunned and horrified. He came straight over and I thought he was going to land one on me! 'Don't call me that! My name is Engelbert!' he rasped. He later explained to me that he had had no luck with the name of Gerry Dorsey and that he only associated it with ill fortune. From now on it had to be Engelbert. That is showbiz for you!

Clem also played a part in Gene Pitney's 'Something's Gotten Hold Of My Heart':

> I was on the demo that was sent to him in America and he loved it. The problem was that the record he made over there didn't have the same feel, and Pitney asked for the rhythm section to be sent over to him for the master take. It worked, and he was delighted.

Pitney had the chance to thank Clem for his contribution when he came over the following year in 1968. 'Arthur Howes Presents the Gene Pitney Show' saw Gene touring the country with a supporting cast of The Status Quo, Amen Corner, Simon Dupree & The Big Sound, Don Partridge and The Mike Cotton Sound.

Simon Dupree:

> Gene Pitney was a real likeable guy, one of life's true gentlemen. He travelled on the tour coach with the rest of us, played cards with us, listened to our bad jokes and told a few. When the tour coach stopped for lunch, he wasn't averse to paying for the whole

party. At the end of the tour he paid each member of the Mike Cotton Sound who backed him on stage a £50 bonus. He had no need to do this as they'd already been paid by the agency. £50 was a lot of money in 1968. On the last night of the tour Status Quo gave him a hard time. They covered him with 'crazy foam' just as he was about to go on stage. Being the professional he was, he changed his suit, arrived on stage on time, and still gave his usual good performance. He took all this with good humour.

Clem's roll of honour continued to rise, with credits on umpteen Top Twenty hit records:

For all the stuff that was being released that year, there was still room for the balladeers and odd quirky records. And I played on most of them! Engelbert Humperdinck's *'Release Me'*, Tom Jones and *'Funny Familiar Forgotten Feelings'*, *'If The Whole World Stopped Lovin''* by Val Doonican. People don't remember them when they're doing a retrospective of '67, doesn't quite sit with the Pink Floyd, Grateful Dead and co., does it?

One of the more unusual sessions was that of one of the great guitar heroes of the time, Jeff Beck. The former Yardbird cut a record that you would scarcely have believed possible, coming from an acclaimed superhero blues guitarist. Produced by Mickie Most, *'Hi Ho Silver Lining'* was a singalong and future karaoke staple, completely out of character for Beck, who since described it as 'Like having a pink toilet seat hung around your neck for the rest of your life.'

In Martin Power's biography *Hot Wired Guitar: The Life of Jeff Beck*, he writes,

'Hi Ho Silver Lining' is probably nowhere near as bad as Beck would have it, though it was a disastrous choice for establishing his credentials as a major player in the new 'serious' rock market. Essentially three minutes of perfect pop fluff.

In collaboration with Mickie Most, it was the producer who insisted that Jeff sing the vocal. Jeff wanted to get a new singer for his Jeff Beck Group, and had former Shotgun Express and Steampacket vocalist Rod Stewart in mind. Beck told *Guitarist*;

'Mickie said no, I don't want that silly poof singing on this record, you're the star.' That's what he said!

In August 1967 the Establishment recorded a victory over the Pirates – not Johnny Kidd's old band – but the pirate radio ships. Latching onto the murder of Reg Calvert, one of the protagonists of pirate radio, the government condemned all who were connected by labelling the DJs and owners of the stations as criminals. Calvert had been shot following an argument with a former army captain in a mansion in Suffolk. Calvert was a colourful character, an entrepreneur and manager of The Fortunes and Pinkerton's Assorted Colours as well as being part owner of Radio City. DJ Dave Lee Travis claims the first bad press for the pirates followed the murder of Reg. The tabloids made hay, proclaiming that all who were involved with the pirate stations were corrupt. It was the turning point in the government's war with the pirates. Reg's killer was arrested and charged with murder, but his plea of self-defence was accepted.

With the demise of the pirate stations the BBC re-organised themselves and modernised the Light Programme, Home Service, and Third Network into Radio One, Two and Three. Radio One was launched on Saturday, September 30th 1967 with The Tony Blackburn Show, the first record played on the new station being 'Flowers In The Rain' by The Move. Looking back, the first ten records makes interesting reading. After 'Flowers' came 'Massachusetts' by The Bee Gees, 'Even The Bad Times Are Good' by The Tremeloes, 'Fakin' It' by Simon & Garfunkel, 'The Day I Met Marie' by Cliff Richard and The Shadows, 'You Can't Hurry Love' by The Supremes, Engelbert's 'The Last Waltz', 'Baby, Now That I've Found You' by The Foundations, 'Good Times' by Eric Burdon and the Animals and 'I Feel Love Comin' On' by Felice Taylor.

Two of the most unlikely hits of 1968 and featuring Clem once more was 'Cinderella Rockefella' from 'Israel's answer to Sonny and Cher', Esther and Abi Ofarim, and Leapy Lee with 'Little Arrows'. 'Rockafella' was recorded at the Philips studios and composed by

Mason Williams of *'Classical Gas'* fame, another huge hit this year. Esther had some form, having represented Switzerland in the Eurovision Song Contest in 1963. The couple had been married in 1959, and following the success of *'Cinderella'* embarked on a world tour in 1969 which, alas, sadly proved to be one trip too many. The one-hit wonders divorced.

Leapy Lee was yet another one-hit wonder with *'Little Arrows'*, a novelty type number in the vein of *'Happy-Go-Lucky Me'* by Paul Evans. Leapy may have appeared to have burst on the scene in '68, but in fact he'd been around and on the verge of great things for over a decade. He cut his debut single, *'It's All Happening'*, in 1962. *'Arrows'* was only kept off the top spot by The Beatles' *'Hey Jude'*. His career went off the rails in 1972 when he was sentenced to two years in prison following a bar fight with Alan Lake, husband of actress/singer Diana Dors. On his release he settled in Saudi Arabia before relocating to Majorca, Spain in 1983 to open his own pub.

1968 was proving to be a busy year for Clem. He was also involved in a Donovan session which produced his top ten hit *'Hurdy Gurdy Man'*. The song had been given to Donovan by his producer Mickie Most in an effort to boost and toughen up his sound. Since enjoying hits with *'Catch The Wind'*, *'Mellow Yellow'* and *'Jennifer Juniper'* Donovan's record sales were slowly decreasing amidst the emergence of the psychedelia and heavy rock sounds of the late Sixties. Jeff Beck, who played on the sessions for the accompanying *Hurdy Gurdy* album, says: 'He wasn't making it very big with the airy-fairy butterfly stuff he was singing, and Mickie thought it would be bizarre to have a wild rock band behind him.'

John Paul Jones and Alan Parker were also on the session. Shortly after this Jones and Page decided to put a band together that would become the template for Heavy Rock – Led Zeppelin. For the drums, they wanted Clem and asked their manager Peter Grant to contact him. Grant had been taking control of the affairs of The Yardbirds during their latter days when Page was the guitar star of the group following on from Eric Clapton and Jeff Beck. Clem had also been depping for Jim McCarty during this period too. The Yardbirds had finally imploded, and Grant and Page, along with Page's session mate Jones, were moving in a heavier direction, looking for a 'power trio' to play behind a lead singer, which would be Robert Plant. Not unlike, as Clem suggested 'the re-shuffled Pirates line-up of a decade before.'

Clem:

> The thing was, I was very busy doing sessions at the time. It was one session after another. If anyone needed a drummer at short notice, they always used to call me. I had been on the road for nine years, and suddenly I was at home, getting into my own bed at night. Peter Grant phoned and asked me to go to lunch with him to talk about a project. We never had that lunch. Not for any reason. I was just too busy. He called again, but again we didn't have that lunch. A year later, when Led Zeppelin's first album was in the charts, I saw Peter again and asked him if that was the project he wanted to talk about. It was, but there's no point regretting anything. I can't look back and change things. It wasn't a conscious decision, just circumstances. But there again, was I the sort of person that could go all around the world in that scene? I don't know. I could never imagine me throwing a television out of a hotel window for a start off! And I wouldn't have liked having my hair that long! The funny thing is, I had played with Jimmy Page on dozens of sessions, and I worked with John Paul Jones in Lulu's backing band for two years. I'd even done a session for singer Robert Plant's first band. But I couldn't really see myself with Zeppelin. They were probably better off with John Bonham.

A debut album Clem appeared on this year, along with his old mate Jim Sullivan, was that of acoustic progressive folk band Amazing Blondel, titled *Amazing Blondel and A Few Faces*. Blondel were Eddie Baird, John Gladwin and Terry Wincott. Sometimes categorised as psychedelic folk or as medieval folk rock, their music was more a re-invention of Renaissance music, based around the use of period instruments such as lutes and recorders. But they still needed a drummer!

A strange session Clem did was with Paul McCartney at EMI:

An instrumental version he was doing on the *Magical Mystery Tour* album I think. '*I Am The Walrus*' was on it anyway. Paul called the album 'Percy Thrillington'. It never got released though, because Paul didn't want people to know about it. Don't know why. I was later talking to a guy who worked at EMI during the '60s about The Beatles, and he told me that I would be surprised at the number of tracks Paul played drums on their albums. One track was '*Back In The USSR*' on the *White Album*.

Keyboards player Bip Wetherell:

> If you listen to '*Back In The USSR*', which was Paul on drums, it was awful. Ringo was a great drummer, but he only did just enough. Apparently Ringo wasn't in the studio at the time so Paul just got on with it, which must have pissed Ringo off. But it was Paul McCartney and he could do what he wanted.

Clem agrees: 'I'm glad you said that. Ringo did what was necessary, that's right.'

Whatever the contributions were of the various members of the band, The Beatles' influence on everyone was perhaps best summed up by music journalist Ray Connolly: 'The Beatles were way ahead, they were like a locomotive pulling everyone along behind them.'

And the next leg of their journey came with the doomed Apple adventure. Advised that they were basically skint and in debt, which on the face of things seemed ridiculous, they were told a way to get around the debts accrued was to create a business of their own, or two... so Apple came to be, offering services and studio time for free to anyone who had a shred of talent but were stymied by the record companies. Boutiques and offices were opened in Savile Row, London; anything went. And unfortunately when the Apple empire crumbled everything did go... a free-for-all ensued as fans descended on the Apple headquarters like locusts. What followed was the beginning of the end, as The Beatles fought over who to hire to sort out the mess. Paul McCartney wanted his father-in-law Lee Eastman to take control. The other three wanted American businessman Allen Klein. The impasse was the catalyst for the inevitable demise of the world's greatest-ever rock band.

Clem was called upon to work with Ralph McTell when the folk singer recorded his debut album *Eight Frames A Second* with producer Gus Dudgeon and Tony Visconti at Pye. Ralph, who later had a huge hit with *'Streets of London'*, recalled the session in an interview for *Mojo*:

> I saw myself in the tradition of guitar singer/songwriters, *à la* Bert Jansch, and here I was surrounded by session musicians about to record my first album and invited to 'strum' along. I think Tony Visconti explained to Gus my sensitivities and a mic was set up for my guitar and I became an integral part of the arrangements. Among the famous names on that session were Clem Cattini and Jack Emblow on piano accordion. Tony Visconti was new to the job as well, and as nervous as I was. I asked Gus what the guitarist was doing there and he told me, 'He's going to play guitar.'
>
> 'Well what will I do then?' I asked
>
> 'You can strum along as well,' said Gus
>
> I nearly walked out right then. I thought of myself as a guitar player who just happened to write and sing songs. Had no one noticed? I was crushed and depressed. It was only much later that I realised I had been signed as a singer/songwriter and my guitar playing was a secondary consideration.
>
> I guess like all those new to the job Tony may have tried too hard to impress, and threw in the metaphorical kitchen sink in the form of a cymbalum (a kind of grand piano version of a hammer dulcimer), which stood out amongst all the regular instruments needed for the job. It was played by a Hungarian gentleman who had a very strong accent. He was very reverential to its national identity, and a little bewildered by what Tony wanted him to do. He even proceeded to give us a recital of pieces to show us what the instrument should sound like. It was a special moment on the session. Tony had to explain that it was just the 'sound' he was after. The title track *'Eight Frames A Second'* was done in a couple of takes. I found it very difficult to work to a music chart as I couldn't read music and the repeated takes were trying. However, most of the songs were recorded that day and my solo efforts on another. I was very happy with *'The Mermaid and the Seagull'* and even thought the addition of waves and seagulls was nice.

I rattled off '*Hesitation Blues*' in one take and also '*Blind Blake's Rag*'. I was just amazed by the way the songs sounded with the other musicians, but I had never worked like this before and although everyone was encouraging and supportive in the studio I thought I would have been happier and sung better had I been on my own, which after all is what I was used to.

As Neil Armstrong and Buzz Aldrin were making their giant step for mankind when walking on the Moon in July 1969, Clem too was finally making his own giant step, across to America, seven years after the aborted Larry Parnes and Tornados proposed tour of 1962 to play in Lulu's backing band.

Clem:

I have to say it was an experience going to America in 1969. I met several Mafiosi and had to turn down an invitation from Frank Sinatra. I got over there despite the objections from Charlie Katz, the guy for whom I was committed to doing a considerable amount of work. I rang him after Lulu had rang me. She was on her way to Miami where she was due to collect an award from NARM (North American Music Manufacturers). She was in New York and was having problems with the musicians who were working with her for the concert which was to be in Miami. To be honest, I think she felt very alone and a little afraid in the States and wanted someone she knew and could trust to help her. She asked me to come over – not a whole band or anything like that. Just me. Katz was adamant. 'No way,' he said, 'I can't let you out of the things you are committed to and you won't be going.' I had to ring Lulu's management team, headed by Gordon Mills to say I couldn't go. They were strong and very influential – just how influential I was to find out. They were called 'The Taffia' in show business and I realised why! Within half hour Charlie rang me back. 'It's OK,' he said. 'You are going to America.' I later found out that Mills's office had rung him and made him aware of how much work they put his way. If he wanted that to continue, I was to go to the States. Job done. Not the end of the adventure, though. I was allowed in, by an agreement with the American Musicians Union, on a one-entry visa. Bear that in mind. While travelling from New York to Miami to meet up with Lulu, the stewardess was chatting to me and was fascinated by the music business. I arranged for her and her husband to have tickets for Lulu's show and she then invited me to lunch with her and her husband in the Bahamas. Yes please! So we took off from Fort Lauderdale and landed at Bimini. In front of us was a huge guy at passport control. 'Passport,' he asked. 'I'm British,' I said, 'surely I don't need one?' He acknowledged that, but then said, 'How are you going to get back into America?' My heart sank. The passport was at the hotel and if they made me send for it when we got back to the States, my visa would have been invalid and, so, no show with Lulu. The pilot then said not to worry and to just follow him when we got back to Fort Lauderdale. 'Just don't say a word!' he instructed. I didn't. When we landed back in Florida he just said to the passport guy, 'American citizens,' and we were allowed straight through. Close call though. Not perhaps as close a call I had while coming to terms with American expressions. I was a smoker at the time and I did get some strange looks when I said in company, 'Anyone fancy a fag?' Of course, over there 'fag' means gay and I did cause quite a stir.

One regret from the tour was that we had to reject an invite from the legendary Sinatra. At the convention, he asked that Lulu and her entourage be guests at his private table for a show at The Fontainebleau. Unfortunately we had to turn it down, because Lulu was singing at The Diplomat at the same time. But I did have an interesting rendezvous with Italian-Americans while in Miami. One huge guy in a dark suit noticed my surname. 'You Italian?' he asked. I explained that both my parents were, and yes, I felt very Italian. 'My great grandfather came from Italy,' he said. Pleasant enough chat, and I thought no more of it. He did ask me what hotel I was staying in mind, which I thought was a bit odd. Then I got back to my room and there were four bottles of spirits there, vodka, whiskey, bourbon and gin. All good stuff – and with a note. 'Great to meet a fellow Italian,' it said. Later I found out he was in the Mafia!

Lulu was a wonderful lady and she got on great with my wife Anna. Over the years she became a great family friend. She even came on holiday with us – and I have been a guest at both her weddings. Of course I knew both her and Maurice Gibb of The Bee Gees, and I'm afraid to say that the union was never going to last. I had worked with The Bee Gees on their first album, and on several tracks like '*The New York Mining Disaster 1941*'. Maurice and Lulu met when they were both on *Top Of The Pops* and the romance blossomed. But Maurice was a big drinker and I am sure that is what drove them apart. She couldn't put up with it, and I was used as a kind of go-between. Often I had just got off to sleep after a live gig and the phone would go at around 3am. It was Maurice pleading with me to contact Lulu because she had walked out on him again after another row. Lulu herself would be in a right state. It was forever on-off. Don't get me wrong, without a drink Maurice was a great guy, and his two brothers Robin and Barry were great to socialise with and to work with. But it was no great surprise to me when Maurice and Lulu split. It was an ill-fated marriage. A funny incident I had with Lulu though was when we talking in a corridor of a venue we were playing up north, and Rod Stewart came walking through. We were having a conversation and he came and stepped right in between us. 'Excuse me,' I said, 'that's a bit rude, isn't it?' He looked at me, said something smart in reply, and I grabbed him by the throat and pinned him up against the wall! Lulu looked on and was alarmed – 'don't hit him!' she said!

1969 had been a good year for Clem, work-wise if not financially! He was still on a fixed-rate as a session man, but Peter Sarstedt's '*Where Do You Go To (My Lovely)*', Thunderclap Newman's '*Something In The Air*' and The Family Dogg's '*A Way Of Life*' were all added to his portfolio. 'Another band I worked with around this time was Jethro Tull. Clive Bunker was the band drummer, but I played sessions on some tracks for the album *This Was*, which was recorded at EMI.'

As the 1970s beckoned he would continue to be in demand by a whole roster of artists, some mainstream and some quite unlikely, in the field of what was labelled 'prog rock'. Albums by Robin Trower, Beggars Opera, Ugly Custard, Hungry Wolf, Rumplestiltskin and Edwards Hand would all bear Clem's trademark. As Clem would later state, 'I'm not ashamed or embarrassed to admit I played on anything, some of the albums were just a bunch of us session men having fun. Whether it was 'heavy rock', 'prog rock', call it what you will, or working on records by Clive Dunn, Benny Hill, or The Wombles, basically, in the end, it was all just work.'

10

Progress in the 1970s

'The Top Of The Pops Orchestra were called the mushrooms, because we were always kept in the dark!' – Clem

'If you can remember the 1960s, you weren't really there.'

One of the great quotes of the 20th century, but whoever it was came out with that belter you would have to say the sentiment is at best, grandiloquent, if not pretentious. Many have claimed to have made the quote; Pete Townshend, Grace Slick, Timothy Leary... you might as well throw Harold Wilson into the mix as well... but it's all baloney. The inference of course is that if you weren't as high as a kite half the time, you missed out. You didn't get it, you couldn't have been there. But did you really have to be stoned out of your mind to enjoy *'Telstar'*, The Tornados, the so-called Summer of Love, the magnificence of The Beatles' *Sgt. Pepper*, Pink Floyd's *Saucerful of Secrets* or Engelbert Humperdinck?

By 1970, the Psychedelic phase was passing over, the flowers were in the bin, peace and love seemed as elusive as ever, the Vietnam War was still making the headlines. The enthusiasm for the space race was wilting just like the flowers since the *Apollo 11* Moon landing of July '69. There was a revival of interest with the disastrous *Apollo 13* mission, but it was like another era was over. The Beatles, who everyone had followed and taken inspiration from, brought the curtain down on the '60s when they announced their disbandment in 1970.

The Sixties had been a decade like no other, and is remembered by many as the most exciting ever in the music business. Everything went, from rock, country, folk, ballads, psychedelia, blues...Topol, The Piltdown Men, Acker Bilk.

For all that, though, the Sixties ended on a grim note when a fan was knifed to death in front of the stage by Hells Angels at The Rolling Stones' 1969 Altamont concert in San Francisco. The show, organised by The Stones, it was said, because they had missed out on the Woodstock Festival the previous August, was hoped to have been staged in San Francisco's Golden Gate Park, scene of Love-ins, Human Be-ins, the birthplace of Flower Power, but the idea was knocked on the head by San Francisco City Hall so Altamont, a speedway venue fifty miles to the north of the city, was chosen instead.

It should have been the grand finale to their 1969 US tour, aimed at restoring The Stones' credibility following a few barren years and the drug busts of Messrs Richards and Jagger and the death of guitarist Brian Jones. Instead, Altamont degenerated into a festival of mayhem that marked, as one observer called it, 'the brutal end of the 1960s.'

The omens hadn't been encouraging when Hells Angels, hired as security guards, started beating fans over their heads with pool cues during Santana's opening set. When Jefferson Airplane singer Marty Balin was then knocked out by an Angel, it was clear there wasn't a good vibe. The Flying Burrito Brothers and Crosby, Stills, Nash and Young kept the feel-good factor going with their country rock, before the Stones eventually appeared late into the night – earlier than expected, as The Grateful Dead had pulled out because of the violence. The Stones' performance was constantly interrupted by the Angels fighting, and the chaos that ensued made the arena look like a war zone with Mick Jagger asking for calm and 'love thy neighbour'. 'C'mon people...' Michael wailed desperately.... as an Angel battered another one over the head! 'Hey man! It's Only Rock and Roll! Keep cool, C'mon...'

Credibility restored or not, the Stones' myth as the bad boys of rock was only enhanced by the event. As they entered the Seventies they were back at the forefront as the self-proclaimed 'Greatest

Rock and Roll Band in The World', the virtuosity of guitarist Mick Taylor, who had replaced the late Brian Jones, taking the band to another level. Their albums *Let It Bleed*, *Sticky Fingers* and *Exile On Main Street* had Taylor's stamp all over them.

Whilst the dust was settling on the car crash of Altamont, John Lennon was telling Jan Wenner of *Rolling Stone* that 'The dream is over', prompting the *Melody Maker* of January 10th to declare: 'Let's hope in 1970 we see the break up of both The Beatles and The Stones. Let's face it – they've had a good innings, and even they must now admit their whole concept is now pure dullsville.'

Maybe the *MM* was yearning for another jazz revival.

While those in the music environment wondered what the 1970s would bring, Clem was finding himself busier than ever. As far as Clem was concerned, he didn't care what the music was called... Rock, Prog Rock, Country Rock, Glam Rock, Folk Rock, Blackpool Rock.... Clem played on everything! Even novelty items 'Grandad', 'Ernie', 'Two Little Boys', 'Whispering Grass' by Windsor Davies and Don Estelle. All number one records that proved the longhairs didn't have it all their own way in the charts.

Clem virtually lived in the studios working on numerous projects. During 1970 he was high in the charts playing on Edison Lighthouse's 'Love Grows' and White Plains with 'My Baby Loves Lovin'. Clem was also involved on an instrumental version of Jane Birkin and Serge Gainsbourg's 1969 huge hit 'Je T'aime... Moi Non Plus' which had been banned by the BBC because of its suggestive lyrical content and heavy breathing. Decca's A&R Tony Hall recognised the potential of an instrumental version, and put together a group of session men; Clem, guitarist Chris Spedding and former Third Ear Band and Gun guitarist/piano player Tim Mycroft. A non-sexy version of 'Je T'aime' was recorded entitled 'Love At First Sight' and became a Top 20 hit. It was after the session when Hall played the tape to Paul McCartney, who casually remarked 'Sounds nice' ...and there lies the origin of the name given to the group!

In between the session work, with this plethora of musicians jazz flutist Bob Downes recruited Clem and an ensemble that read like a Who's Who for the recording of his album *Electric City* in 1970: Dave Brooks, tenor saxophone; Don Faye, baritone saxophone; Nigel Carter, trumpet; Kenny Wheeler, trumpet; Bud Parks, trumpet, flugelhorn; Harold Beckett, trumpet, flugelhorn; Ian Carr, trumpet, flugelhorn; Ray Russell, guitar; Chris Spedding, guitar; Herbie Flowers, bass guitar; Daryl Runswick, bass guitar; Harry Miller, bass guitar; Dennis Smith, drums; Alan Rushton, drums; Clem Cattini, drums; Robin Jones, congas, timbales.

In *The Rough Guide to Jazz*, in which Bob is down as a Concert, Alto and Bass Flute, Chinese, Japanese and South American Bamboo Flute and Tenor and Alto and Soprano Sax player, *Electric City* is described as 'quite a mixed bag':

> A batch of vocal tunes sports the album's most overtly rock-oriented, groove-based arrangements, and vocals by Downes himself. To say that Downes' vocal gifts are not on par with his head-turning instrumental talents would be putting it kindly, but there are plenty of other sides to this outing. Such tunes as '*Crush Hour*' and '*Dawn Until Dawn*' bear heads that show the influence of '60s post-bop jazz, interwoven with modal improv sections bordering on free-blowing freakouts. It's here that the sax and flute skills of Downes really shine, as he turns in solos that are alternately blistering and searchingly poignant. Then there are odd detours like '*West II*', a Caribbean-flavored tune that echoes Sonny Rollins' '*St. Thomas*', and the melodic (mostly) balladic '*In Your Eyes*', which sounds like it could have come off King Crimson's contemporaneous *Lizard* album. There's an appealingly rough-around-the-edges quality to it all that gives the feeling of barriers being broken down and new worlds discovered.
>
> Songs such as the opening '*No Time Like The Present*' might have invited speculation that Polygram perceived Downes' eclectic music as something of a Trojan horse into the lucrative rock market, but this material's jazz element confounds any accusations of selling out. '*Gonna Take A Journey*', for example, begins as a free-blowing session, culminating in a heavy jazz-rock jam underpinned by assorted guitars and drums and an ensemble riff over top.
>
> Whilst the vocal tracks may not be to everyone's taste, Downes nevertheless manages to impart a feeling of fervent, almost naïve

honesty and a considerable amount of tenderness, as in the ballad '*In Your Eyes*'.

The ensemble arrangements are excellent and the solos, mainly taken by Downes and the guitarists (particularly Spedding and Russell), are positively gripping. Downes is a virtuoso flautist, as evidenced by tracks like the bluesy '*Keep Off The Grass*', but he also demonstrates some fiery free-blowing saxophone work on numbers like '*Crush Hour*'. This is an essential piece of psychedelic jazz history.

Which, if nothing else, also goes to prove the versatility that Clem Cattini possessed! Add jazz/fusion to his CV!

The scribes would have you believe that 1970 was a historic and heavyweight year for Rock 'n' Roll.

Sadly there were casualties, as we lost Jimi Hendrix and Janis Joplin in 1970. The Doors' singer Jim Morrison would join them a year later, creating a curious statistic when it was realised that all three of the rock stars, Hendrix, Joplin and Morrison, plus Brian Jones, who had tragically passed away in 1969, were all the same age – 27.

As Lennon professed, it was time to move on. New genres – 'Progressive Rock' or 'Underground', 'Country Rock' and 'Glam Rock' – were the flavours. The Edgar Broughton Band, Yes, Slade, Atomic Rooster, Family, Blodwyn Pig, and Quintessence gave the children of the Sixties a sense of maturity.

The baby-boomers, now reaching their twenties, could have been forgiven for thinking that the charts were now becoming irrelevant, but the next generation of teenagers, dubbed 'teenyboppers', were coming through and lapping up the glitz and sequins of Slade, Bowie, The Sweet, T. Rex and The Bay City Rollers. Some light relief, you might say, from the elongated Hammond organ marathons of Rick Wakeman, Keith Emerson and Hugh Banton of Van Der Graaf Generator.

Slade emerged as a major attraction. Loud stomping music, all glitter and sparkle, they hit the jackpot with '*Merry Christmas Everybody*', which has been played to death every Christmas since, much to Noddy Holder and the boys' delight!

Frank Lea, bass player Jim Lea's brother, followed the Wolverhampton band everywhere, and indeed stepped in to play drums during Don Powell's absence following a road accident in 1972. 'Don had been involved in a fatal car crash and I filled in at short notice to play a couple of gigs on the Isle of Man. It was the first time I'd ever been on stage! I just played virtually the same beat through everything!'

Slade are remembered, apart from their awful spelling and a great catalogue of hits which included '*Mama Weer All Crazee Now*', '*Look Wot You Dun*' etc, for the outlandish gear they used to wear on stage, but Frank Lea revealed it was only when they were on *Top Of The Pops* that they used to dress up:

> That was only for the cameras. All the bands were trying to outdo each other with their dress. Guitarist Dave Hill was the most flamboyant. During one show Dave went into the toilet dressed in what can only be described as tin foil, just as Humble Pie singer Steve Marriott was shaking hands with the vicar. Steve came out flabbergasted! 'This bloke just came in,' Steve yelled in disbelief, 'he looks like he's made of metal! He's dressed like a nun, complete with a nun's habit. And wearing huge boots!' 'Blimey!' I said, 'it's the Tin Man out of the Wizard of Oz!'

The curiously-named Edwards Hand was another obscure outfit that Clem Cattini was asked to help out on some sessions. Welshman Rod Edwards (keyboards and vocals) and Englishman Roger Hand (acoustic guitar and vocals) were formerly known as The Piccadilly Line, but to their credit realised they were off track and went forth with their new name, releasing a self-titled album which was produced by the esteemed George Martin at Abbey Road. Not one for throwing accolades around, George nonetheless described their music as 'exceptional'. Their second album *Stranded*, featuring James Litherland on electric guitar, Clem on drums and bassist John Wetton, better known for his time with Family and King Crimson, received glowing reviews:

Stranded opens with the funky, progressive '*US Flag*', a splendid song suite that displays a strong, rootsy American influence. A superb blend of styles, West Coast-influenced rock tracks alongside all out progressive anglophile pop symphonies that at times utilise the kind of everything including the kitchen sink tactics employed by Brian Wilson.

Unfortunately though, despite having a welcome hand from these seasoned musicians, *Stranded* went down the plughole and was left just where the title indicated!

From Edwards Hand, Clem moved on to Hungry Wolf, an ensemble comprising a brass section of John Edwards, Cliff Hardy and Ken Gouldie on trombones, Tony Fisher, Bobby Haughey and Derek Watkins trumpets. Herbie Flowers on bass, Alan Hawkshaw on keyboards, Alan Parker on guitar and Peter Lee Stirling on vocals.

A self-titled album (which was the fashion), *Hungry Wolf* was released on the Philips label and described as 'primarily an instrumental pop rock affair with swirling freaking organs and various wood instruments accompanying guitarist Alan Parker. The mixed session of jazz, pop, psychedelic, in short a condensed set of rare grooves with some particularly successful vocal parts, is notable on '*Revolution*' and '*Waiting For The Morning Sun*'.'

Hungry Wolf then morphed into Rumplestiltskin, the name taken from the Brothers Grimm fairytale.

Clem in 2015:

> Alan Hawkshaw, Alan Parker, Herbie, Peter and I were playing live in the studio. We were making music together. You were making a record. Now you are making a product. Union and BBC rules were among the frustrations in the early days. When I started there was a union rule stating that you must have the singer in there with the band when you were recording. It was stupid. I did something with Decca which took 93 takes because the singer kept making mistakes. The band were doing their job right. Then sometimes you'd get people substituting for the singer. It was a stupid rule, and I was glad when it was scrapped. The BBC's ban on playing records with session men was also an annoyance. I

played on Rumpelstiltskin and we were session musicians and had to use pseudonyms; I was down as Rupert Bear, because if the BBC knew I was a session man and all the guys on the album were session men, they wouldn't play it. So we had to come up with silly names so they wouldn't know who we were.

Rumplestiltskin was described as 'a classic example of a band that very few even knew existed. Another band whose record company's handling of them was tragic.'

Producer Shel Talmy had this to say:

I produced Rumpelstiltskin, which was a put-together band of very good session guys, and we almost made it. We had a whole concept. We were going to do a comic strip and all kinds of stuff. It was really a fun thing. And good songs, great music, 'cause these guys really could play. That album went on Bell Records, who just totally screwed the whole thing up. It was really unfortunate. We made two albums that I was very pleased with; that, I think, should have made it. Remember that Led Zeppelin were quality session players that made it big. Rumplestiltskin were on the right path with the wrong record company.

A record store manager (unnamed) recalled he had access to just about any recordings, and when he saw the comic book cover of *Rumplestiltskin* he was curious, and Shel Talmy's name as producer sealed the deal.

One listen to this absolute gem of a record and I was hooked! Every cut is really, really great, big chunks of guitar with monster hooks, bass-lines that shake the ground and slabs of hot, hot Hammond organ with a commanding soulful voice soaring through it all unscathed. Really solid unique heavy meaty tracks! This album was seriously great! Take the first track, '*Make Me Make You*' – classic hooks, transitions and totally hip and cool passages – at a little past six minutes it sounds as though Keith Emerson dropped in for a bit. This track alone demands repeat listenings, if you like it you'll love the rest. The culinary lyrical recipe of '*Pate de Foie Gras*'; 'You take some livers from a goose, two tablespoons of goose fat too, three eggs cooked and cook them real hard, salt and pepper 'til it's best for you, paprika is a must but only just, an eighth of a spoon is sure to do' – to anti-militaristic '*Squadron Leader Johnson*' and everything is coloured in the heavy psychedelic hues.

It's a shame this band didn't make it into the big time. This was basically a project made up from the top UK session players at the time. Unsure if they even played gigs, as all five of them went under pseudonyms for the purposes of the album.

Being session players, the music is of course, very well performed. A really funky organ and rhythm section, dirty distorted sounding guitar and a really excellent soulful vocal on top. The bass playing in particular here is truly amazing! Really great catchy tunes throughout with plenty of improvisation without being pretentious at all. A must-have for any fans of early '70s prog or funk.

Shel Talmy employed Rumple to back American artist Tim Rose, who was known for his compositions '*Morning Dew*' and '*Hey Joe*', which Hendrix made famous, on his album *Love – A Kind Of Hate Story*. Tim preferred to be known as a folk singer, but this review of his album was less than favourable: 'There is little for the purist folk fan here, Rose's own compositions are suffocated by ill-advised readings of The Bee Gees' '*I've Gotta Get A Message To You*', Rare Bird's '*Sympathy*' and Peter Sarstedt's '*Where Do You Go To (My Lovely)*'.

Seems like the punters agreed, as the album failed to make any impact.

Ugly Custard was next on the menu for Clem, with Alan Parker, Herbie Flowers and Roger Coulam again adding the ingredients: 'An impressive crew of studio/session musicians embarking on what could have been the umpteenth boring exploitation album. Luckily, it turns out to be surprisingly good. Side one of this all-instrumental LP is made up of covers of songs like '*Scarboro' Fair*', '*My Babe*' and Stephen Stills' '*Hung Upside Down*', while side two includes Parker originals. Strangely enough, side one is actually better, pairing imaginative arranging with expert playing.'

1970 won't honestly be remembered for Bob Downes, Edwards

Hand, Rumplestiltskin or Ugly Custard, but for the inevitable demise of The Beatles, Jimi Hendrix and Janis Joplin within weeks of each other.

Rumours had been rife for a long time about the break up of The Beatles, and John Lennon had done little to encourage their fans during a revealing interview with the *New Musical Express* in which he said that life as a Beatle was never as fab in the days of Beatlemania as most people believed. Nor was life as a Beatle today all that pleasant, and The Beatles splitting-up was a possibility:

> It just depends how much we all want to record together. I don't know if I want to record together again. I go off and on it. In the old days, when we needed an album, Paul and I would get together and produce enough songs for it. Nowadays, there's three of us writing prolifically and trying to fit it all into one album. Or we have to think of a double album every time, which takes six months. That's the hang-up we have. It's not a personal, 'The Beatles are fighting' thing, so much as an actual, physical problem... None of us want to be background musicians most of the time. We didn't spend ten years making it to have the freedom of recording studios to be able to have two tracks on an album. It's nothing new, the way things are. It's human. I'm more interested in my songs, Paul's more interested in his, and George is more interested in his, that's always been. It's just that usually in the past, George lost out because Paul and I are tougher. We've always said we had fights, it's no news that we argue.

In *Melody Maker*, Lennon discussed further:

> In the beginning, it was a constant fight between Brian (Epstein) and Paul on one side, and me and George on the other. Brian put us in neat suits and shirts, and Paul was right behind him. I didn't dig that, and I used to try to get George to rebel with me. I'd say, 'Look, we don't need these suits. Let's chuck them out of the window.' My little rebellion was to have my tie loose, with the top button of my shirt undone, but Paul would always come up to me and put it straight. I saw a film the other night, the first television film we ever did... and there we were in suits and everything ...it just wasn't us, and watching that film I knew that that was where

we started to sell out. We had to do a lot of selling out then. Taking the MBE was a sellout for me.

Lennon revealed he had stalled on accepting the MBE when The Beatles first received notice of the award; 'I chucked the letter in with all the fan-mail... It was hypocritical to take the MBE, but I'm glad, really, that I did, because it meant that four years later I could use it to make a gesture.'

If you remember the 1970s, to paraphrase that earlier pearl of wisdom, you will remember the news in January that Britain's currency was gearing up for change, with the 'half crown', the 2/6d coin, now no longer legal tender. Lovers of LSD - pounds, shillings and pence, not the hallucinatory mind expanding drug - were in for another shock, when the ten bob note (50p) joined the half crown in the bin. Ted Heath's Conservative government were teasing us through the monetary quagmire to eventual decimalisation in February 1971.

The natives weren't happy, though. When it was announced the day we were switching over to metric was to be called 'D-Day', old soldiers were up in arms. Historian A.J.P. Taylor called it 'a monstrous offence against one of the most glorious days in our history.'

It had been decided to reduce 240 pennies to 100 (new pence), 12 pennies to a shilling (the bob) was to become 10. The tanner (sixpence) and threepenny bit followed the half crown and ten bob note into the bin. Confusion reigned.

The singer/songwriter phase and harmony-based groups were well established, and featuring regularly on a new television rock show *The Old Grey Whistle Test*. Joining the gang was a trio with two formidable members of one of the highest-profile bands of the Sixties, Hank Marvin and Bruce Welch of The Shadows, together with Australian guitarist John Farrar.

Bruce Welch:

All five of us, Cliff and The Shadows, had around ten years together as a group and by 1968 I think we'd all had enough. I had. I thought we'd done everything we could have done. Hit records, albums, movies, tours, even the dreaded pantomimes. Brian Bennett felt the same and left as well. We'd played with all the American greats like Jerry Lee Lewis, Gene Vincent, Roy Orbison, The Everly Brothers. They were great characters, and there's a true story, well known, about Jerry Lee sharing top billing at the Harlem Apollo in New York with Chuck Berry. Jerry Lee was from Louisiana where there was racial tension and segregation. He alternated on nights with Chuck at The Apollo, and this night when Chuck was headlining Jerry Lee set fire to his piano after a rousing performance which culminated with *Great Balls Of Fire*. As he walked off he passed Chuck and snarled, 'Follow that, n****r!' There was no love lost there!

Clem tells another story of similar vintage concerning Jerry Lee and Chuck:

There was one doing the rounds that they were both on the same show and Jerry Lee was designated the opening slot. 'There's absolutely no way I'm going on before that n****r!' he screamed. The producer panicked, offered Jerry another 5 grand and Jerry 'reluctantly' backed down and agreed to go on first. He then went back to the dressing room. Chuck Berry was sitting there: 'Did you get us an extra 5K Jerry?' It was all a big con!

Bruce:

After a sabbath Hank and I, looking for a change of direction, which coincidently was the title of an album Brian Bennett recorded, formed a vocal group with Australian John Farrar to become Marvin, Welch and Farrar. John had been a member of a band called The Strangers who supported The Shadows on the tour 'down under'. As well as being a good guitarist, John was also a great singer. We thought we could emulate Crosby, Pie and Mash as we called them, and all those other groups like The Byrds and The Eagles, but people wouldn't accept us. Wherever we played they would shout for *'Apache'* or *'Wonderful Land'* and it was disheartening. We tried to grow and expand from the instrumental stuff, but that's the way it was. We couldn't escape our past. We supported Cilla Black on one of her TV shows in 1970, providing harmonies to Cilla singing The Beatles' *'Norwegian Wood'*.

I later produced her 1980 album *Especially For You*, which was recorded at Abbey Road. Cilla, in my opinion, wasn't a great singer, and compared to Dusty Springfield there was no comparison. Dusty was a truly great singer, the best we've had in Britain, great performer and personality. The Shadows first came across her on one of our early tours with Cliff. She was a member of The Lana Sisters back then before she teamed up with her brother Tom and Mike Hurst to become The Springfields and then as a solo singer.

We cut a couple of albums as Marvin, Welch and Farrar with our old friend Clem Cattini on drums. Clem was great to work with, and they were good albums but they didn't really sell. Maybe they'll be recognised as one of the 'great lost albums of the 70s' someday! We lasted around two years and then we all got back together for the first of the Shadows reunions.

1971 began with Dave Edmunds at the top of the charts with '*I Hear You Knocking*', a re-run of Smiley Lewis and Fats Domino's 1955 hit. Taking over from Dave at the summit was actor Clive Dunn, otherwise known as Corporal Jones in television's *Dad's Army*, with the sentimental '*Grandad*', which provided Clem with another notch on his belt of number one hits. '*Grandad*' was composed by Herbie Flowers and Kenny Pickett of The Creation. 'Possibly the cheesiest song ever,' is how one critic called it, but all the same it was a firm favourite on radio and with disc jockey Tony Blackburn and his dog Arnold.

The story behind Flowers writing the saccharine ditty was that after meeting Dunn at a party the actor, learning Herbie was a composer, challenged him to write him a novelty song. Herbie accepted the challenge and claimed he was completely stuck for a hook until a friend called to visit and rang his doorbell: 'One of those models popular at that time which had two small tubular bells which played a high-low two note 'Ding-Dong.' That was the Eureka! moment. I had my 'Gran-dad' hook!' Comedian Benny Hill provided Clem with another novelty record to add to his comprehensive list of hit records he'd played on. '*Ernie (The Fastest Milkman In The West)*' was 1971's Christmas Number one. It was also later revealed to be one of former Prime Minister David Cameron's favourite eight records when he appeared on *Desert Island Discs* in May 2006.

'*Ernie*' was inspired by Hill's early career as a milkman in Eastleigh, Hampshire. The song tells of the fictional exploits of Ernie Price, a milkman who drives a horse-drawn milk cart. It relates to his war with the bread delivery man (two-ton Ted from Teddington) and their efforts to win the heart of Sue, a widow who lives on her own. When Ted sees Ernie's cart outside Sue's house all afternoon, he becomes enraged and violently kicks Price's horse, Trigger. The two men resort to a duel, using the wares they carry on their respective carts, and Ernie is killed by a rock cake underneath his heart, followed by a stale pork pie in his eye. Sue and Ted then marry, but Ernie's ghost returns to haunt them on their wedding night.

A sad tale, whichever way you look at it.

Bands heading to Wales for a gig in '71 would have constantly found themselves running around in circles thanks to a Welsh Language Society campaign. Hit-makers St. Cecilia, in demand following the success of the Jonathan King produced '*Leap Up and Down (Wave Your Knickers In the Air)*' were just one group caught up in the chaos, as guitarist John Proctor recalled:

> We were on a mini tour of Wales and spent a lot of time driving around with absolutely no idea where we were going – thanks to the Welsh Nationalists painting out the English road signs and turning the signposts around. In some cases they had removed them altogether!

Eight members of the Welsh Nationalists were rounded up and appeared at Swansea Assizes Court, charged with plotting to steal and destroy English road signs. An attempt by the accused to have the hearing heard in Welsh fell on deaf ears. Two Welsh women supporters in the public gallery of the courtroom were thrown out for reading aloud from pamphlets and chanting 'Justice for the Welsh Language!' They were subsequently jailed for three months for refusing to agree not to interrupt the case.

Meantime, The New Seekers tried to harmonise everybody with their heart-rendering '*I'd Like to Teach the World to Sing (In Perfect*

Harmony)', which included Clem Cattini on backing vocals as well as drums. 'Well, I couldn't help but hum along,' a modest Clem admitted.

The song, which went to number one in 1971, was also the theme to a television commercial for a particular well-known soft drink.

One of the hottest bands to emerge this year was T. Rex, fronted by Marc Bolan. Formerly darlings of the Flower Power set as Tyrannosaurus Rex, three of their singles, *'Telegram Sam', 'Get It On'* and *'Hot Love'* were recorded with Clem Cattini's stamp on them. Where Clem found time to do all this beggars belief, but in March he was to be found working at Kingsway Studios with David Bowie, Herbie Flowers and Alan Parker on a Peter Noone session.

Mickie Most, producer of the Herman's Hermits hits, had been given the demo of a song Bowie had written called *'Oh! You Pretty Thing'*, and told Hermit Noone, 'I think I've just found your first solo single'. On first hearing, apparently, an excited Noone declared 'That's It! It's perfect!' Bowie, soon to become a mega-star with the success of *'Ziggy Stardust'*, had hoped his friend Leon Russell would be interested in the song but admitted, despite reservations, 'Herman's done it quite well to be honest'. Talking to *Melody Maker*, Herman (Noone) revealed he'd changed a line in the song from 'the earth is a bitch' to the more radio-friendly 'the earth is a beast,' and 'We wanted the same feel that was on the demo and Mickie Most said, 'Let's get Bowie over here.' Then David comes in, says, 'I can't play it all the way through. I get tired. I'm not a real piano player!'

Clem's memory?

> Bowie kept messing it up, he was so bad on piano. They had to get somebody else in to do it. So all these geniuses they keep talking about! And David Bowie would never admit that Alan Parker played guitar on his record. Asked why, he said it wouldn't do his reputation any good!

Herman:

> We tried to record it from the demo, which was just David on the piano, but he couldn't get it. We had Herbie Flowers, the world's

greatest bass player, and the best people in the studio, the best drummer in Clem and everything, but nobody could play the part that David Bowie played because David played it in F sharp. He could only play on black keys. And for normal piano players, that's unusual and difficult. We wanted to record the song in F and nobody could do it. So Mickie says, 'Let's record one section and then we'll cut the tape and repeat it three times.' David says, 'That sounds like a good idea.' So he plays it perfectly once, everybody loves it, it's a great version, then we repeat it. It was one of the first bits-and-pieces type of recordings. David played it great once and we worked around that. We just put the vocals on it and Mickie put some violins on it that night, I don't know why, we didn't need them. But he said, 'If you don't like it we'll get rid of it.' But of course they never got rid of anything if they spent money on it.

Whatever the problems and arguments over the recording of the song, they made the Most of it and Peter Noone appeared on *Top Of The Pops* to promote it with Bowie miming on the piano and Clem in the background with the Orchestra.

'*Oh! You Pretty Thing*' made it to number 12 in the charts and would later appear on Bowie's album *Hunky Dory*.

Noone's version failed to impress the *NME* though, with Charles Shaar Murray stating: 'It's one of rock and roll's most outstanding examples of a singer failing to achieve any degree of empathy whatsoever with the mood and content of a lyric.'

Next in Clem's canon was a record which prog rock fans found excruciating, but nonetheless went all the way to the top of the charts. A singalong novelty, '*Chirpy Chirpy Cheep Cheep*' by a band playing it safe by calling themselves Middle of the Road.

There may have been a snobbish attitude to the Scottish band many regarded as manufactured but, in fact, they had been on the road since 1964 and had encompassed a varying and interesting career.

'Middle' began life as The Electrons, then later changed their name to The Douglas Boys to back Glasgow singer Jan Douglas. Sally Carr then joined the group in 1967 to replace Jan as lead singer and they became Part Three, then Part Four, and they could have been excused for not knowing if they were coming or going by this point, as with Latin American numbers featuring heavily in their live act their management then encouraged them to reflect this in their name, so Part Four became Los Caracas. A bio explains their next move:

> In 1968 they appeared on television's *Opportunity Knocks*, winning many of the heats, but despite their popular appeal no interest was shown from recording companies. The band had plans to move to Argentina, but delayed their decision to play on a cruise ship to the Caribbean. A new name was necessary, and all agreed on Middle of the Road. En route to South America the band hit a hitch whilst in transit in Italy. Left stranded and penniless, they worked the local restaurants. The group was heard by an RCA A&R executive, who invited them to Rome for a recording test. Things went well and they recorded three songs *'Yellow River', 'I Can't Tell The Bottom From The Top'* and *'Jesus Christ Superstar'.* Italian producer Giacomo Tosti found *'Chirpy Chirpy Cheep Cheep',* which was written and recorded by Lally Stott. When the band first heard it they expressed reserve, but Sally Carr soon convinced them it was a good idea. Copious supplies of Bourbon were available in the studio when the song was recorded, but on its release it went to Number one in many countries including the UK. *'Chirpy'* stayed in the UK hit parade for 35 weeks and sold 8 million records worldwide, elevating Middle of the Road to the third most popular recording artists in the Billboard Charts in 1971.

Discotheques were bouncing to the sounds of *'Chirpy'* and Chicory Tip's *'Son Of My Father',* but for many the charts were rapidly becoming bland and, indeed, Middle of the Road. Still, the record companies weren't complaining, as sales were soaring. Music journalist David Hepworth claims that 1971 in his opinion was the 'greatest year ever for rock'. Which, you have to say, is a matter of opinion.

Disc jockeys were now as famous as the guys who were making the music. John Peel, Dave Lee Travis and Tommy Vance were as much in the news as The Stones, David Bowie and Marc Bolan, which wasn't going down too well with some. Deep Purple singer Ian Gillan called Radio Luxembourg DJ Tony Prince and his companions 'parasites on the backs of musicians.'

In the fashion world, temperatures were rising with the arrival of the delectable hot pants, much beloved by the male half of the population. With long legs and just a hint of cheek to tease, testosterone levels soared. What followed next had the opposite effect – the maxi skirt! Invented to dampen masculine ardour by covering up the flesh, the maxi had the same effect as that of being caught in bed with your girlfriend by your mother.

They may have been perceived as elegant or conversely hideous, but the next fashion item to take a grip of the nation came with platform shoes. Stilettos were out. Footwear with six or seven inch soles that resembled blocks of 4x2 wood were an ugly addition in the fashion world. Ghastly things. Long hair, which may have been a hangover from the Sixties, bell-bottom trousers, cheesecloth shirts, tank top t-shirts, were all embraced by the maturing men of the Sixties, but an alternative counterculture emerged with the shaven head hairstyle, braces to hold the pants up and boots that were given the soubriquet of 'Bovver' – the Doc Marten. And that was just the girls! The uniform for those who had an abhorrence of flower power, Atomic Rooster, peace and love, Campari. It was welcome to the 'skinheads'; you could say the precursor to the punk phenomenon that was just a few years down the line.

Still working away, whatever the fashion, Clem was enlisted by Virgin Records owner Richard Branson to help out on a re-recording of an album by German Krautrock outfit Slapp Happy. The ensemble from Wumme, a town on the river of the same name in Northern Germany, were formed in 1972 as Faust by British experimental composer Anthony Moore, whose credentials would later include collaborations on Pink Floyd albums and playing in a band called The Dum Dums.

Slapp Happy's album *Casablanca Moon* had been recorded in Germany for Polydor, who rejected it. Relocating to England,

Branson agreed with Polydor that the original recording had indeed been Slapp Happy and he employed a 'huge cast of guest musicians' under the direction of violinist Graham Preskett to try again at his Manor Studio in Oxfordshire. By all accounts, it worked. Released on Richard Branson's Virgin label, the re-recording, now self-titled *Slapp Happy*, was transformed and would later gain recognition in *Galactic Ramble*; 'a peregrination through British rock, folk and jazz.. from merely a good album into an all-time counterculture classic... with its over-the-top arrangements, peculiar melodic progressions, irresistible hooks and Dagmar Krause's arch singing, the finished product is like a stoned cabaret performance from the Weimar Republic. For one album at least, Slapp Happy were the most brilliant, inventive, wigged-out pop songwriters in the world.'

Which altogether makes *Sgt. Pepper* sound like an album of nursery rhymes, but despite them thinking it was 'Getting Better', the album never sold and, with a little help from their friends, Slapp later merged with English avant garde outfit Henry Cow, formed by Fred Frith and Tim Hodgkinson at Cambridge University in November 1974.

The Manor, which was sold in 1995, gained a feature in *The Independent*:

> Opened in 1971, the Manor was converted by 21-year-old Richard Branson to become Britain's first residential recording studio, lifting album-making out of cramped city studios and placed in the countryside. In the early 1970s Sandy Denny, John Cale, the Bonzo Dog Doo-Dah Band, Faust and Tangerine Dream. XTC, Black Sabbath, INXS, Rush, Radiohead and countless others all recorded there. It was an unknown teenage multi-instrumentalist who fixed the Manor's place in the rock annals and helped to secure Branson's Virgin business empire. Mike Oldfield, who arrived at the Manor in 1972 to start work on *Tubular Bells*, recalled; 'There was a wonderful atmosphere, it was new, exciting. There was nothing that professional, nothing successful, at that time. Just a great feeling that something important was starting to take root.'

Branson:

Before the Manor, rock musicians would go in just like classical musicians, three-hour sessions, then go home – very un-rock'n'roll! They liked to record through the night and sleep through the day.

Though decidedly laid-back, the Manor was not immune from rock excess. Branson:

I opened the door one day to find a guy with a gun looking for Keith Richards, because he thought Keith had gone off with his wife, I had to argue with this man that neither Keith Richards nor this man's wife were at the Manor. As I was arguing with him, I saw a naked Keith Richards and this man's naked wife running across the lawn behind him.

'These days,' Oldfield says, 'anybody with a decent PC or Mac in their bedroom can achieve professional recording results. I do miss the big tape recorders and mixing desks.'

Headlines in 1972 would include the discovery of a Japanese soldier by the name of Shoichi Yokoi who had been wandering about for 28 years in the Guam jungle. His first words back in civilisation were 'Is the war over, sport?'

A state of emergency was declared by Ted Heath's government over a miners' strike which was set to escalate and incorporate the power workers, dustbinmen, candlestick makers.

Another major news story was that of a Uruguayan aircraft transporting a rugby union team crashing at around 14,000ft in the Andes mountain range, near the Argentina/Chile border. Sixteen of the survivors had to resort to cannibalism in order to survive.

The United States last manned Moon mission, *Apollo 17*, was launched and Commander Eugene Cernan was able to claim the distinction of being the last man to walk on the Moon. The event was the inspiration behind Elton John's worldwide hit '*Rocket Man*'. Elton was on a crest of a wave, with four top ten hits, '*Rocket Man*', '*Daniel*', '*Honky Cat*' and '*Crocodile Rock*', but none of them achieved the goal of a number one, all put in the shade by an outfit from Coventry called Lieutenant Pigeon with '*Mouldy Old Dough*'. On *Top Of The*

Pops, Clem Cattini, sitting with the Orchestra, would have witnessed first-hand the dexterity of 'a smiling granny called Hilda Woodward on piano'. A follow-up, '*Desperate Dan*', reached the top twenty, but the novelty soon began to wear thin and the Pigeons were duly sent back to Coventry.

The Vietnam War continued, though America had begun the process of withdrawal of troops and only 133,000 remained when the Christmas bombing of North Vietnam caused widespread and worldwide condemnation. It was the turning point.

In March 1973 a peace agreement was signed by the United States and South Vietnam and communist North Vietnam. Although honoured to a degree, the agreement was violated by both North and South as the struggle for control in South Vietnam continued. In April 1975 the capture of Saigon, the capital of South Vietnam, by the People's Army of Vietnam and the Việt Cộng marked the end of the war and the start of a transition period to the formal reunification of Vietnam. The flag of the Socialist Republic of Vietnam was raised over the presidential palace and Saigon was renamed Hồ Chí Minh City, after the late North Vietnamese President.

The last two American servicemen to die in Vietnam were Charles McMahon and Darwin Judge.

The capture of Saigon was preceded by the evacuation of almost all the American civilian and military personnel, along with tens of thousands of South Vietnamese civilians who had been associated with the southern regime. The evacuation was the largest helicopter evacuation in history.

Clem's reputation stretched right over the ocean, to the land of Uncle Sam. American legend Lou Reed, having left The Velvet Underground to start out on a solo career, decided that for his debut album he would go to London and engage the top session men.

Clem was booked, along with guitarist Steve Howe, keyboardist Rick Wakeman and guitarist Caleb Quaye. The self-titled album, *Lou Reed*, was recorded for RCA and produced by Richard Robinson at Morgan Studios, where Rod Stewart recorded *Every Picture Tells a Story*.

Despite the expectation and presence of such esteemed musicians, the material was deemed lacklustre and uninspiring by the music press:

> *Lou Reed* is a truly rare thing: He's singing his songs, yet it doesn't sound like he's totally present. Even the goofiest half-baked Reed tracks such as *'The Original Wrapper'* fill a listener with his presence: He's the only guy who could have made that. To record *'Ocean'*, despite Clem Cattini being an excellent musician, the result was awkward, even crude. This debut solo album isn't awful, but it doesn't suggest in any way that Reed will go on to become one of the most striking, distinctive figures in rock music.

Clem's memory:

> All I remember was having to play Timpani for hours on a thing called *The Sea* [which actually was *The Ocean*!]. We finished it and Lou Reed was raving about the swell of the sea, the sound of pounding waves I was making on the drums. 'That was great man, I could see that you were getting into it, thinking of, like the ocean.' To be honest, I didn't know what he was talking about. I wasn't thinking anything! All I was thinking of was, 'Let's get this done so I can get home for supper!

Andy Greene of *Rolling Stone* was disappointed with the effort:

> Anticipation for Lou Reed's debut solo LP had been high. As the leader of The Velvet Underground, he'd written some of the most brilliantly twisted songs of the previous decade. And now, after a long hibernation, he was beginning the next phase of his career. Unfortunately, he didn't arrive at the London recording sessions with many new songs, and wound up simply regurgitating old Velvet tunes like *'I Can't Stand It'*, *'Ride into the Sun'* and *'Lisa Says'*. Producer Richard Robinson teamed him up with Yes members Rick Wakeman and Steve Howe, and their radically different musical styles simply didn't mesh.

The resulting album was limp and wildly disappointing, and it stalled out a pathetic Number 189 on the Billboard 200. 'There's just too many things wrong with the album,' Reed admitted shortly after it came out. 'I'm aware of all the things that are missing and all the things that shouldn't have been there.'

Reed's solo career seemed dead on arrival, until he redeemed himself with *'Walk on the Wild Side'*, which was released that November.

Reed's compatriots from the US, Ike and Tina Turner, were likewise looking to record in London following their re-emergence as chart stars with *'Nutbush City Limits'* in 1973. *'Nutbush'* was their first success of note since *'River Deep, Mountain High'* in 1966. A follow-up album was required to cement their return from relative obscurity, in the UK if not the States. Ike Turner was producing, and set about hiring a group of session musicians which included Marc Bolan and Clem Cattini.

Clem's recall is:

> First of all, he paid me in American dollars, but it was the frosty tension between Ike and Tina. They were obviously on the verge of splitting up. Tina spent most of the time sitting in a corner, very quiet. Never said a word. There had been talk for a while about Ike's abuse of Tina. He was intimidating. Came across as a monster, not very nice at all. After the sessions I was asked by Ike if I'd be interested in joining his band. I wasn't really and was even less so when the engineer told me 'He'll end up breaking your kneecaps!' It was only a short while later that they did split up. Proved to be the best thing that Tina could have done.

One of the biggest selling albums of 1974 was Paul McCartney and Wings' *Band On The Run*, edged out of the top spot by a compilation of The Carpenters' hits. The iconic cover of the album, depicting a 'band' of convicts, has been the cause of much discussion ever since. Who were the 'convicts'? Why were they chosen?

In 2017 Kenny Lynch, one of the bandits, recalled the photo session and how those involved were selected:

> At the time, I was working in Glasgow when Paul phoned me. I'd been there all week and the girl on the reception had kept telling me, 'This geezer's been on the phone again for you, says he's Paul

McCartney.' 'Piss off,' I said to her. 'No,' she said, 'he says it's him'. So next time I took the call. It *was* Paul! 'Christ, you're harder to get hold of than Salman Rushdie!' he said.

'What do you want Paul?'

'I want you for a photograph I'm doing for my *Band On The Run* album cover, how long are you in Glasgow?'

'Well I'm here until Saturday, but I'll be back on Sunday.'

'Right, get down to Osterley Park, West London when you get back.'

'Who's taking the photograph?' I asked him.

'Why?' Paul asked, 'What does that matter?'

Knowing Paul, it would probably have been David Bailey or something. It'd take all day, hanging around, freezing the bollocks off you. 'Who is it first?' I asked.

'I've got Clive Arrowsmith.'

'Right, gotcha, I'll be there.' I knew Clive Arrowsmith would get the job done without much fuss. I turned up and John Conteh, World Light Heavyweight boxing champion, television chat show host Michael Parkinson, gourmet Clement Freud, actors Christopher Lee and James Coburn, plus ex-Moody Blues guitarist Denny Laine and Paul and Linda from Wings were all there, and we had to make out we were escaped convicts. We were all friends who used to drink and hang out in the clubs, Tramps, the Ad-Lib, Speakeasy.

According to Paul, we were the only ones whose numbers he had in his phonebook and were in the UK at the time. Clive took a batch of photographs with us all against a stable wall, and the job was done in half hour. He showed us the polaroid snapshots and they were really good. No messing about. David Bailey would have taken all effin' day!

Challenging *Band On The Run* for best-selling album of the year was an unlikely one produced by Mike Batt – the Wombles!

Mike had created the group based on the popular children's television show, and asked Clem Cattini, Chris Spedding, Les Hurdle, Ray Cooper, Rex Morris, Eddie Mordue and Jack Rothstein to play on the songs, with Mike himself covering the vocals.

The first album, *Wombling Songs,* according to Batt 'was really just background music for the television series.' It spent 17 weeks in the UK album charts. The second album, *Remember You're A Womble,* saw Batt experimenting with songs in a variety of musical styles which included pop, rock, classical and surf rock in the style of The Beach Boys. 'It's really the first proper album for The Wombles as a group.'

The album cover depicted Batt and the session musicians dressed in full-size Womble costumes. The album spent 31 weeks in the UK album chart.

Two more albums followed; *Superwombling* and *Keep On Wombling.*

Clem was insouciant to accolades:

> I never went into pop music hungry for fame but I won't lie – it was great while I was in the limelight when '*Telstar*' was such a hit. To be recognised for the part I played in such a successful record – Margaret Thatcher once wrote to me to say it was her favourite song – is a tremendous accolade. I feel I am justified in feeling very proud about that. But by becoming a 'musical navvy', by adopting the 'have-drums-will-travel' approach, I was able to meet and work with some fantastic people and also be part of tours that took me round the world. The words of Joe Meek were always in my ears. 'All you need,' he used to say, 'is enthusiasm.' My reply to that was you can't feed a family on enthusiasm! No, the profile did not bother me. I just wanted to work and those tours gave me many happy memories.

> One tour that stands out is the Cliff Richard tour during the mid-70s, when we went to Hong Kong, Australia and New Zealand. By then, Cliff had become a born-again Christian. What brought that about only he can answer. What I will say is that he did live life to the full in his early days as a rock star. He had a fling with the wife of Jet Harris, the bass guitarist with The Shadows, who were his backing band. I think he maybe reached a stage where he was so wealthy, had so much cash behind him that there was like a void in his life. It happened with The Beatles when they became involved in the Hare Krishna philosophy. Cliff, I think, was searching for something because the wealth he had accumulated had left him

with so much time on his hands.

With me, I didn't have the luxury. As part of an Italian family and as someone who married an Italian girl, I was brought up, naturally, as a Catholic. But it wasn't something about which I was fanatical. In fact, whenever I was asked about my religion I used to answer, C of E. That's Church of Egypt. I don't go too often because it's too far to travel!

But to Cliff, it was a really serious matter – as I witnessed on tour. I was contacted by his management about going on tour which, as well as the Far East, also included Europe as well as many venues in Britain. I had played drums on 'Devil Woman', the record that sparked a renaissance after a few years in the pop wilderness. Because he had long split with The Shadows, he wanted me and I was joined by Mo Foster, Terry Britten and Graham Todd. We were all session musicians, all for hire if you like, and Cliff knew he could trust us and rely on us on stage. One thing I remember about 'Devil Woman' was that when he recorded it he didn't realise the song was about a prostitute. When he did realise, he dropped it from his set list on tour. Cliff never travelled with us. It was him and us. We travelled separately, but trust me that was no bad thing. There was no resentment or anything like that, because we could live as near as you could to a normal a life while on tour because, quite simply, no-one recognised us. We could look round various cities that we went to, we could eat without being bothered and sit and have a drink together. Of course, it wasn't all glamour. Many people seem to have the idea that touring with a rock band or major stars like Cliff was all sex and drugs and rock and roll. Nothing could be further from the truth. So many times it was airplane, airport, coach, hotel, eat, sleep. Then play, then on to the next destination. What I will say about Cliff though, is that he insisted that three days in the week he would be free. That gave you a decent bit of leisure time. It was during times like that that me and the rest of the band would think about stupid awards to give each other, and the most famous was the Brown Nose Award regarding Cliff. In other words, who could do the most creeping – and I won it hands down just as we were leaving Australia.

We were already at the airport and there had been an almighty downpour which had left water laying everywhere. As Cliff's limo arrived, I saw him get out and in front of him was this huge puddle. Quick as a flash, I took off my rain mac and put it over the puddle so he would not get his feet wet. That was it. That clinched the Brown Nose Award for me! No-one else came near.

One problem that I have never had is an ego that needs to be bolstered all the time. Some of the well-known names have, but in reality they are just the same as the rest of us and they have the same basic needs. Like Jaco Pastorius. He was the world-famous guitarist with an American jazz/funk group called Weather Report, and it so happened that during one of Cliff's tours he was checking into the Amsterdam Hilton the same time as us. Mo Foster idolised him and couldn't resist the chance to go and meet him in person. He went up to him at reception and said, 'Mr. Pastorius, I just wanted to say I have been a huge fan of yours for years and just wanted to say hello.' You know what the reply was? 'Thanks. Do you know where I can get my underpants washed?' Talk about normality!

To be fair, Cliff was never elitist or anything like that. He would never have looked down on us, or treat us as inferior. He would come and eat with us and hang out with us. And I believe his religious beliefs were sincere. Exactly what branch of Christianity Cliff followed I honestly don't know. But Graham Todd, the keyboards player in the band, was a Scientologist and that caused some problems. It seemed that the basis of Scientology was 'Whatever I want to do – I will do.' So there were times when we would be walking across the tarmac to a plane and he would be smoking! I told him to put it out in case he blew us to high heaven, but he refused. He wanted to do it, and he did.

I had my revenge on Graham Todd and his 'I will do what I want when I want' attitude when we were at a dinner in Australia and he stood up to make a speech. I saw my chance and decided to put a huge chocolate gateau on his chair without him seeing me. He sat down and 'splat' – all over the seat of his pants. 'It was something I wanted to do,' I said. He was not happy... but he had no answer.

We used to call these tours with Cliff 'finger-pointing tours'. He would give services in a church or at a gig and everyone would be pointing towards heaven. But he did have one success. On one of them was John Perry, or Champagne Perry as we called him. Why? Because we had to either pour him into bed or pour him out again in the morning. If it would go up his nose he would sniff it – if he could drink it, he would. And he always wore clogs. One morning, Cliff was in church and we all felt obliged to go while he held his service. At the end of it he would always say, 'Now if anyone wants to join me in Jesus, can they come forward now.' We all sat still, needless to say – and then suddenly there was this 'clip clop' sounds coming up the aisle. It was Champagne. He had been converted.

I only ever talked religion once with Cliff. It was after a gig and he had earlier that evening been telling his audience that he felt sorry for atheists. 'Their lives must be so empty, because they have nothing to believe in.' Back at the hotel he asked me what I thought. I decided to give him an honest answer. 'How do you know they are not as happy not believing in God as you are believing in God?' He didn't really look happy to answer that question, to be honest. Did it affect my relationship with him? Put it this way. I wasn't asked to tour with him again! But in all seriousness, that must have been a coincidence. I have met up with him on many occasions since and each time he has greeted me with a huge hug. And I won't hear a word against him when it comes to his knighthood. He was given it for the most noble of reasons – his work for charity, which I can tell you was considerable. The others from the pop world? A joke! SIR Mick Jagger – why? What has he done apart from earn millions. SIR Elton John – again – why? Neither of them come near Cliff in terms of the contribution they have made.

'Beggars can't be choosers' may have sounded like a put-down for the Glasgow band Beggars Opera, formed in Glasgow in 1969. Signed to Vertigo Records, they had released four albums with little success or recognition. By 1975 they were giving it one more go and hoped that the inspirational recruitment of Clem on drums might just give them the break they needed. The review didn't bode well:

The desperation implied in the title is borne out in the music... The glory days of Prog Rock a few years behind them, Beggars Opera issue a dull album of mainstream rock in an attempt to get gigs and a steady income. In fact, the only tracks to rise above the mediocre are the hard rocking opener '*I'm A Roadie*' and the long spacey closing ballad '*Death*'.

'Kiss of...' for the band as well, by the sound of it.

Re-issued in 2008, time hadn't made it any more palatable for the discernible rock fan and News Editor Tim Jones in *Record Collector*: 'The album is overtly disco-funk, the title track is stodgy soft rock, '*Hungry Man*' is a period amalgam of styles from pub rock to proto-synthpop, and '*Bar Room Pearl*' is anything but.

Tim didn't care for it, I think it's fair to say.

Clem's credits continued to roll; J.J. Barrie's '*No Charge*', Hot Chocolate's '*So You Win Again*'. The Brotherhood Of Man with '*Save Your Kisses For Me*', '*Angelo*' and '*Figaro*'. The list is endless. '*Welcome Home*' by Peters and Lee, Billy Connolly's '*D.I.V.O.R.C.E.*'.

'That was a session that didn't take long,' remembers Clem. 'We had that number down in no time, a couple of takes and Billy said, 'Right, c'mon, let's go to the pub.' He had great respect for musicians being one himself, and he was just as funny off the stage as he was on it.'

Chicory Tip's '*Son Of My Father*' was another massive hit which bore Clem's imprint. Tip guitarist Keith Hubbard (2018):

> Those records were made with session musicians. Clem is a fantastic drummer. Everyone I have spoken to has nothing but a good word to say about him. There was a number of line ups of Chicory Tip over the years for the All Star Shows. My time was 1975/76, when we recorded '*Good Grief Christina*', '*What's Your Name*' and '*Cigarettes, Women and Wine*', which was the final single and refused airplay on the BBC because of the content of the lyric!

During 2017 Clem was recalling his time with the TOTP Orchestra to The Tornados' 1980s keyboard player Bip Wetherell.

Bip: 'Was it the Musicians Union who forced the move to London, because the show had to become live? So you had to be all members of the Musicians Union?'

Clem: 'Well, thing is, no, because it wasn't allowed, they changed the law because you had to be a member of the Union. But then they said, by law, you don't have to be, but the way they got round it was, they turned it around and said 'You're not allowed to work with a non-Union member. I remember I did a TV show with Dana ('*All Kinds Of Everything*'), and they wanted to record the show for an album, which they did, and then the Union said 'You can't, because Clem Cattini is not in the Union.' But I was in the Union! Caused a lot of hassle at the time. I rang them up and the girl in the office checked all the names of the artists on the album sleeve and they had spelt my name with a K! And there was no name in the Musicians Union with a Kattini! I said, 'I've been in the Union since I was 17!'

Grunts and moans about the Orchestra were wearisome, with artists of all genres lining up to complain. Even Cliff Richard had his doubts. 'They had no feel for the tracks,' he complained. 'You could tell they didn't even like rock and roll.'

Clem:

> There were benefits. I met real stars and was able to work with real stars. Many of them were nothing like their public image. People think they are all Big-time Charlies, but in reality it is the people around them who are worse. Their entourages, especially the Americans, were the problem. The Jackson Five brought their own musicians with them and their drummer was insistent that he be playing on *Top Of The Pops*. 'You don't have the feel to play with them,' he said. What I don't know is what he meant. What I do know is that he was out of his head on something, with slurred speech and a real obnoxious manner. The song the band was playing was '*Rockin' Robin*' which, by any stretch of the imagination, was not the most difficult piece of music. Anyway, a young Michael Jackson came over and sorted out the problem. The American drummer was sent out of the studio and Michael – only in his early teens at the time, but acting very mature – came over and said, 'Sorry about that, I am sure it will be fine with you on the drums.' When we finished playing he made a point of coming over to me, and said, 'That was just great, just fine. It was very, very good.' He needn't have bothered but he did, and that made me feel really chuffed – and impressed by this well-mannered kid. Stevie Wonder was the same. Stevie is so talented that he can play any instrument. 'Can I show you what I want?' he said. I did as he asked and he was delighted. 'Great sound man, great sound.' Again, quite a compliment. The Stones apart – they

were always aloof – I got on great with many of the British bands.

At times in my stint on *Top Of The Pops* I would have to sit back and pinch myself. Here was I – the son of a cafe owner from Borough – mixing with the good and the great of the pop music world. On a weekly basis I would be talking to David Bowie and Jeff Beck, and whenever Tom Jones came in the studio we would talk about the times that Joe Meek rejected him because he wasn't good enough! I was able to mix with hugely-talented people like The Four Seasons and Frankie Valli, and stars of the Merseybeat explosion like The Searchers, Swinging Blue Jeans.

Through those *Top of the Pops* years I also met the likes of Gerry and The Pacemakers, Freddie and The Dreamers. Gerry and his band I got on well with, but I couldn't tell you much about Freddie Garrity. He was as mad as a balloon! He was always fidgeting, always on the move. I worked with Freddie and The Dreamers on a television show for Southern Television. I travelled down to Portsmouth every week. I'd worked with them a number of times when with The Tornados, and all that jumping around he did on stage... to be honest, I couldn't stand Freddie Garrity.

Dreamers' guitarist Derek Quinn revealed with self-deprecating humour the reason why the band performed like buffoons on stage with silly 'dances' during an interview with Francis McMahon on Tameside Radio in 2018: 'We knew we weren't brilliant musicians, and we thought that if we did these silly routines, making a visual effect would disguise our inadequacies as musicians!'

Clem:

The most impressive guy I had the pleasure to work with was Roy Orbison. What a lovely guy. Not many people realised that Roy was an albino and that, as well as dying his hair jet black, the reason he always wore those trademark dark glasses was because of the glare that would harm his eyes. I was privileged to work with him for a month at the Talk of the Town in 1968 – and that was when he stood up for me in a row with one of the diners! Roy loved rock and roll, the louder the better. That love was not shared by one of the audience who, after a really rousing number, came up to me and shouted, 'Shut the **** up!'

Roy wouldn't stand for it and in that distinct Texan drawl told him, 'I asked Clem to play loud. In fact, I'm going to ask him to play louder! Now YOU sit down!' We didn't hear another word from the guy! After that I was constantly being asked by Roy to play louder. I was coming off with bleeding fingers I was hitting the drums so hard, and he'd still want me to play louder! Roy and I got on well. I was with him in Belgium when he got the tragic news about his kids being killed in a fire back in the States. That was terrible. I never saw him again. He passed away in 1988.

Among the others I got on well with was Cliff Bennett, John Leyton and Jet Harris. John, for all his great looks and charisma on stage, is essentially very shy. When he finished he lived a bit like a recluse in a flat in Victoria, and I had to go round to persuade him to start performing again. He was reluctant at first, but now he realises just how popular he was and still is. Jet – he owed his pop career to me! I lent him the money to buy an amplifier back in the early Sixties so that he could join The Shadows, or The Drifters as they were back then. As well as a great bass guitarist, he was also an accomplished double bass player. He had to fight his demons, that is, the booze. He left pop music and became a bus conductor, but later came back as part of the popular revival shows which were a huge hit.

Eric Haydock of The Hollies was a huge fan of Jet Harris:

Jet had an expensive six-string bass, cost £199 which was a lot of money back then – you could buy a terrace house for £250. But Jet couldn't cope with it and he switched to a Jaguar Bass and tuned it down. I bought a six-string, which took six months to get here from California. They didn't fly them here then, they came by boat around the Cape Horn. When it arrived it didn't have a case! I carried it around in a cardboard box for six months! Then I discovered that new strings would cost £30! A hell of a lot of money back then. They weren't mass-produced, and like many of us did I boiled the strings in a pan to clean them up when they were getting dirty. You'd get another 100 miles out of them!

Clem:

A complex but lovely lady was Dusty Springfield. Her real name was Mary O'Brien. She was gay, which at the time you couldn't allow anyone to know because it was a taboo. It could have cost her a career in pop music because of the narrow-minded attitudes of the time. She was in a group called The Springfields, and to make it more complicated, her brother Tom, who was also in the group, was also gay. As anyone who was gay at the time, they had to live their lives in secret.

Sort of thing we had to put up with on *Top Of The Pops* was one when we were rehearsing with ABBA for their appearance and performance of their Eurovision-winning song '*Waterloo*'. The producer, a big guy, came down and asked, 'What the hell's going on here?'

We said, 'We're rehearsing.'

'Rehearsing? What for, this is a picture show. If people want to hear their record they go out and buy it. They want to see the pictures.'

The music was, as far as he was concerned, secondary. The Orchestra got slaughtered, there was a lot of stuff in the papers about how bad the Orchestra was.

Tina Charles went as far to say, 'It was a nightmare. You had to use the terrible band that they had – they should have been pensioned off years ago – and you had the kind of musicians who had no feel, all they were doing was reading the notes. And they couldn't give a shit. They were in the pub from one to three, and they'd come back in and read the notes. Once I had to do '*Dance Little Lady*' and it was twice the speed, and I couldn't stop, because I thought: Well, if I stop I'll be classed as being an awkward artist.'

What Tina Charles forgets is, I played on her records! That's what we had to put up with. The band that was playing on her track was the one that played in the studio. We got terrible stick. I played on a Gladys Knight and The Pips track and the Orchestra was so bad that Al Jackson, Gladys' drummer, great American drummer with Booker T. and the M.G.s, said to me afterwards 'Ah great man, great feel', and he wanted to borrow my snare drum after the show for a gig! That was a great compliment. We became great friends, and it was so sad when he died, he was shot by intruders in his home in Memphis in 1975.

Bip Wetherell:

From a technical point of view the sound man, who's in the *Top of the Pops* studio all day long trying to get a sound out of a set of drums, trying to get a sound out of the brass section because they've got to play '*Everlasting Love*', and next it's Ralph McTell and '*Streets of London*', he's on a hiding to nothing. In a recording studio they had all day and all night time to get the track perfect. The TOTP Orchestra would have seven tracks to learn to play in a day. George Michael, for instance, employed eleven saxophone players to come to the studio to record '*Careless Whisper*' before he decided it was number 8 who got the five minute riff at the start. That's how anal some of these guys are.

Clem:

> There was an incident, funny enough, when I did a tour with Frankie Valli and The Four Seasons. Next day I was on drums for the TOTP Orchestra and the Seasons' guitar player said to me that night when we playing a gig, 'You know, it amazed me today. You had to play five different kinds of music, five different styles.' I said 'Yeah'. But that's the way they did it those days. In America, it wouldn't happen. There'd be a specialist for the country music, a specialist for the jazz, specialist for pop music... the guitar player couldn't believe it.

> We recorded the show on the Wednesday, we'd turn up not knowing who was on, what we would be playing, because it had to be kept a secret before the show went on the telly on the Thursday. It was a closely-kept secret. I had a row, a go at who I called the poison dwarf, Lynsey de Paul. Every time she came on *Top Of The Pops* she did nothing but moan about the orchestra. I said to her, 'You spend a week in the studio doing one track, we come here and have to do five or six tracks in one and a half hours!

Johnny Pearson would have to explain to stars like Elton John that they had just 20 minutes to run through their number with the Orchestra, which was corralled in a corner of the studio and hardly ever seen on camera. When Simon and Garfunkel arrived to sing their hit '*Bridge Over Troubled Water*' and saw the thinly-populated string section, they refused to perform and returned to their hotel.

Clem:

> Art Garfunkel was weird, we backed him on '*Bright Eyes*', the song

from the *Watership Down* film. When he arrived at the studio the first thing he asked was, 'Have the boys got any gear?' I told him we didn't do coke or whatever he was on and he screwed up his face and walked off. Looked totally perplexed. That was a great record though, even if he never communicated with us much.

I had two nice compliments; one was from a guy called Alan Florence, one of the top sound men at Pye Studios. He was the engineer on the Status Quo stuff when I was on the session for *'Pictures of Matchstick Men'*. He said, 'When I walked into the studio and saw you in the corner, I knew there wouldn't be any problems getting the sound right.' Which was a great compliment. There was another, Steve Smith, a top American drummer. There was this night we used to have every year at a hotel in Watford when all the drummers would meet up. You had all these kids up on stage, and every time I got up they would ask 'Can you play *'Shakin' All Over'*?' That was the first thing they wanted me to play. When I finished and went to sit with Steve, he said 'Do you know, that's the first time tonight that it sounded like a band up there?' And I thought, 'What a nice compliment.'

I remember a time I got the hump about the insults we were getting when the Bay City Rollers and the band Kenny were on *TOTP*, two bands who I actually played on their records. I went over to them and started shouting. They were taking the mickey out of the band. I said, 'You can take the piss out of the band, but remember I played on your records!' It's easy to criticise but unfortunately in that period of time, it got to the stage when session musicians were regarded as 'They can't play', 'Don't have the feel' and all that. I was lucky in that respect because that's what got me into sessions, because I was a rock and roller. I wasn't a Big Band player. And I had the feel for it, so I've been told.

There was an article at the time in one of the papers stating that the reason we didn't go on the road as the Bay City Rollers was that we were pot-bellied, middle aged musicians! What! Well, I was 30 and I wasn't pot-bellied!

The Scottish band left little impression on Clem, who played on *'Bye Bye Baby'* and *'Give A Little Love'*, two number one hits. 'That's showbiz for you, working with hugely-talented people one day, the next with totally mediocre manufactured groups like the dreadful

Bay City Rollers. I played on the majority of their records, the fee was the same and the money was as good as anyone else's, and I can assure you that the guy you saw on television never played drums in his life!'

The Rollers had started out in Edinburgh as The Saxons. Numerous changes and a change of name and management later led them to getting a record deal with Bell. They decided they wanted a more glamorous name, and came up with the idea of looking at a map of America for inspiration. Bay City stared at them from the page, and the Bay City Rollers were born. Attired in tartan clothes, half-mast trousers that somehow got away with it in the fashion stakes, and after their first hit record everybody was wearing tartan! Songwriters Bill Martin and Phil Coulter were asked to come up with a song for the band and they met them in the studio.

Bill:

> The first hurdle was when I realised that they could hardly tune their guitars! I thought then that the only chance we've got is to use session musicians to lay the tracks. But the Rollers didn't want that. They wanted to write their own hits, to play – they'd have been better at blowing their noses! They just weren't capable. There was no way!

So whether they liked it or not, the old guard of Clem, Herbie Flowers and Alan Parker were called in to do the job. And the Rollers rode their luck and achieved fame, capturing the imagination of a teenybopper market on the back of the session men.

More enjoyable sessions came in 1975 with one half of the rock and roll legends The Everly Brothers, Phil Everly, for his solo album *Mystic Line*, and Greek singer Demis Roussos on his 1976 album *Happy To Be*. Demis had come to prominence with the chart-topping 'Forever and Ever' in 1973. Sadly he passed away in 2015 following ill-health at the age of just 68.

By the advent of the punk revolution Clem was losing interest:

> Making music was changing, and I'd had enough of working

with the musicians in the Top Of The Pops Orchestra. There was a violinist called Charlie Gilchrist who was always drunk. Two guys in the orchestra had to hold him up, unbelievable. Johnny Pearson, who we used to call 'Mighty Mouse', was always warning and threatening some of these guys. But he never carried the threat through. The brass boys were forever coming back late, pissed, and Pearson should have fired them. But the following week, they were all back there again. They shouldn't have been. It was the same crew basically every week. You were booked on three-month contracts, sometimes though the BBC wouldn't need you because they were using film or miming acts. We wouldn't have anything to play. We still got paid for it all the same though! I grew tired of it around the time the punk thing started. The punk stuff didn't do much for me, we weren't required anyway and when they were on I used to go out for a pint! Then the 'New Wave' era, with studios using drum machines and synthesisers, became the fashion and I have to admit, I'd had enough.

Not before he was asked by his old friends The Kinks to help out on their new album *Misfits* in 1978, though. Guitarist Dave Davies: 'Clem Cattini did a great job playing drums on this. I love it – and *'Love Life'* its one of my favourite tracks.'

'The Kinks return to their rock territory with *Misfits*,' is how the press greeted the album, though not too enamoured with the recording was bassist John Gosling, who recalled in *Record Collector* of Februry 2008:

> It's not easy working with a megalomaniac. I got tired of being used and abused just to satisfy Ray Davies' unreasonable and selfish demands. We were doing 12 hour shifts on a single song, and it was hardly a Kinks album with all the extra people involved and the amount of tweaking employed to make much of it listenable.

However, the influential US mag *Rolling Stone* was slightly more enthusiastic, calling the album 'nearly a masterpiece'.

Dave Davies also got Clem involved on two albums he was producing for folk/rock singer Claire Hamill, *Stage Door Johnnies* and *Abracadabra*. Claire later spent some time with Wishbone Ash, and worked with Jon and Vangelis.

The 1980s saw Clem moving into a different direction, as drummer in the house band at Caesar's Palace, Dunstable – a venue that had built up a great reputation for attracting BIG star names. Contemplating semi-retirement – or so he thought – when a surprise phone call from a stranger brought about another twist in Clem's career.

The caller was a guy called Bip Wetherell.

11

On the Road Again

'Then, come the turn of the '80s, I really had had enough. The music changed, it was all mechanical, drum machines, synthesisers creating music. Musicians weren't required. There wasn't much work or respect for the 'old school' session men, and I completely lost interest.' – Clem.

This was an opinion shared by Jeff Beck, who commented that the '80s was 'Just push-button music' and confirmed in the *Melody Maker* in January 1980) that 'The sound of the 1980s is the synthesiser. The guitar/bass/drums combo won't disappear of course, but Kraftwerk, The Human League, Gary Numan etc are the visible vanguard'.

Clem was once again pondering his future. Just turned 40, he had virtually seen and done it all, but there was still a number of twists in his career to come before he settled for the carpet slippers.

For all that, it was heartwarming for the Sixties generation to see Pink Floyd at the top of the singles chart with '*Another Brick In The Wall*' as we entered a new decade. Of the old guard, The Rolling Stones were still churning out albums and the occasional hit like '*Emotional Rescue*', the evergreen Cliff Richard with '*Carrie*', and David Bowie with '*Ashes To Ashes*', which sadly could have been the epitaph for John Lennon, who in December 1980 was shot dead by a deranged fan outside his apartment in the Dakota Building, New York. It was one of those moments like the JFK assassination in 1963 and the demise of Elvis in 1977, when everyone can remember where they were when they heard the news. Bob Dylan was still around, going off in a different direction, steering towards spiritual and gospel with his albums *Shot Of Love, Slow Train Coming* and *Saved,* which left many of his disciples confused to say the least.

Music, as usual, provided a distraction from all that was happening in the world, and in particular here in Britain, where historian Dominic Sandbrook was to comment:

> The advent of the 1980s saw Britain as a country struggling to hold back the tide of change. Headlines dominated by one battle after another. Margaret Thatcher's government inviting confrontation from the coalminers when closing twenty pits and effectively increasing the dole queues by 20,000 men. The closures caused a schism within the National Union of Mineworkers, turning miners from the doomed pits against those of the 'productive pits' who refused to support the strikes led by NUM leader Arthur Scargill. All-out war ensued as picket lines, supported by striking steelworkers from around the country, themselves under threat with the steel industry struggling to survive, were crossed. It was time to stand together, as Thatcher called the miners 'the enemy within'.

Sandbrook called it 'the tensions of collective loyalty against individual aspirations that caused a fault line throughout Great Britain.'

The miners' strike lasted a full year, the longest in British history, before they caved in. Coalminers, steelworkers and shipbuilders were all destined for the dole queue, and the despair in communities led to unrest and riots around the country, cities going up in flames; looting and vandalism spread like wildfire.

Much of the 'heavy' industry in the country was deemed to be outdated, unproductive. A hard fact of life, but technology was taking over.

The Falklands War dominated 1982. Waves of patriotism was witnessed as a Task Force headed south to fight and regain the islands from the Argentines, who had laid claim to the outpost in the South Atlantic. Images of the conflict which filled our television screens for the next three months which were reminiscent of the

Vietnam War of the Sixties. A harsh reminder of what war was all about for the Baby Boomers, whose forefathers had experienced World War II. Victory in the Falklands came at a heavy cost, with 14 ships and 900 lives lost. Prime Minister Margaret Thatcher revelled in the victory, milking the moment, portraying herself as a 1980s version of Winston Churchill – a great war leader. It was arguably convenient too, as a distraction from the strife caused by the strikes which were consuming the country.

In the home, the emergence of the Video Tape Recorder was the death knell for theatres and cinemas as struggling families found it was cheaper to hire a film from a 'video shop' than going to the pictures for a night out. Likewise, radio became unfashionable, as listeners deserted to embrace the new era. One of the biggest hits of the decade summed it all up; 'Video Killed The Radio Star' by The Buggles, a duo consisting of singer/bassist Trevor Horn and keyboardist Geoffrey Downes.

The early 1980s also saw the demise of the vinyl record with the introduction of the Compact Disc. Seemed a great idea at the time, small, compact (as it says on the tin), but over time has become much maligned, the quality often bemoaned as being too tinny, 'clean'. Coinciding with this, and on the back of the video tape, MTV was introduced in America. Thus started the video to accompany the new releases by artists of all genres. Everything was changing... they call it evolution.

A feature in *The Guardian* described how Paris and New York had been the focal points throughout the 1970s, but looking forward:

> ..as we embraced the '80s London was to become the creative powerhouse as Britain rode out a recession and its youth culture leapt back into the world spotlight. One band defined a new direction for music and shifted its driving rhythm from the guitar to the bass and drum. Spandau Ballet, one of four British groups (with Duran Duran, Culture Club and Wham!) led dozens of stylish young clubland acts into the charts. They spread the new sounds and styles of London around the globe so that designers of its street fashion, too, became the toast of world capitals. The

soundtrack was hard-edged European, synth-led, but bass-heavy: German sounds such as Kraftwerk. Spandau bassist Martin Kemp expressed; 'I'm not really a musician. I belong in a club dressed as sharp as a razor. That's the thrill, just being there, excited by where you are and the people sharing the night with you.'

Spandau Ballet sounded defiantly unrock-like by playing the new synthesised electro-pop and singing about being 'beautiful and clean and so very, very young'. Guitarist Gary Kemp:

> We were making the most contemporary statement in fashion and music. London was a horrible place. The record industry had stalled, sales were declining, the charts were bland. Memories of the Swinging Sixties and the buzz the mods brought to Soho consumed me. I badly wanted a new swinging London. There had to be a way...

The national press labelled the fad and its followers the 'New Dandies', 'Romantic Rebels', until the music weekly *Sounds* came up with the 'New Romantics'.

The *Daily Telegraph* waded into the debate, describing discos as 'a dehumanising threat to civilisation.'

New Romantics may well have been the vogue, but by comparison Clem Cattini would have probably called himself an 'Old Romantic' as he enjoyed his latest role in the house band at one of the country's leading nightclubs.

Clem:

> I received a call to see if I was interested in becoming drummer at a place in Dunstable, Bedfordshire with an ambitious name of Caesar's Palace. Now everyone knows of the famous venue of same name in Las Vegas where Elvis, Tom Jones, Sinatra and all the huge names in the business were or had been resident. Vegas! The ultimate in showbiz razzamatazz and glamour. So, what was this Caesar's Palace in an unobtrusive place like Dunstable all about? There was no desert or Strip as far as I knew of in this town near Luton. It pricked my curiosity, and I set out to find more. It was run by a chap called George Savva. Cabaret had become massive in the 1970s with nightclubs like Batley, the

Bailey's Empire, hugely successful venues where you could enjoy artists of the calibre of Shirley Bassey, The Four Tops, Gene Pitney, Freddie Starr, Tom Jones even... along with the customary chicken or scampi in the basket. It was a new direction for me, which I accepted. It wasn't my first venture though; I had been thrown in at the deep end some years before when I was working with Lulu in Glasgow. First of all, the bass player was nearly electrocuted. He was holding his bass when he touched the music stand, which had bare wires hanging down which nobody saw. There was a flash and I knew what had happened straight away. I kicked the stand away and turned the power off. What a start that was! Then next thing, I went out for a snack with the MD John Coleman. John fancied a dish of mussels, which must have been off. Half hour before the show he was ill. He'd turned grey, was sick as a dog and rushed to hospital! The producer said, 'You'll have to be the MD!' 'What!' I said, 'I don't know what to do.' The musicians looked at me. Then I said, 'Ok, look I'll count you in and take it from there.'

Bass player Dave Harvey was a fixture throughout the decade playing alongside Clem:

My connection with Clem started in 1980, when I was the House Bassist at Bailey's in Watford. We would have new artists to back each week, and when Grace Kennedy was booked in the guitarist came to tell me they were bringing just the MD and Clem Cattini on drums, who was a name I had seen on many albums and heard about. I went to the stage and got my music, looking around for Clem who I had never seen before, then he came and shook my hand and the rehearsal started. He kept calling over to me, telling me 'Well done' and 'Nice feel,' also 'Well read,' and made me feel 10ft tall. We had a great week, and after that he put my name forward for sessions and any work he could involve me in. It was like being given the 'Gold Seal', which I have always been so grateful for. I went on to play with Clem on The Kids From Fame Tour and on many sessions and so many albums by so many artists and scores of live concerts and shows. The Tornados connection took place after the club Caesar's Palace closed down where Clem and I played in the House Band.

Clem:

The Telstar tour was the first we did in the 80s. It was hard as well really, because you ask anybody about The Tornados and nobody remembers them. But you mention *'Telstar'* and they go, 'Oh yeah, that was the Tremeloes wasn't it?' That was a problem at the time. It was also the best band we'd had, with Bip on keyboards, Dave Harvey on bass and Lynn Alice singing, until it all started falling apart with health problems.

Clem helped organise a benefit concert for Lynn, who was suffering with cancer, at the Beck Theatre, Hayes, inviting many of his old friends along to participate, including Cliff Bennett, Brian Poole, Craig Douglas, Mike Berry, Billie Davis and Jess Conrad. One who wasn't invited and was upset about it was David 'Screaming Lord' Sutch. Clem had known Sutch since the Joe Meek days, but as he said, 'If I'd invited everyone, it would have been a very long night.' Clem did acknowledge Sutch was very upset, and worried for a long time if the perceived snub tipped him over the edge. He later took his own life in 1999. Clem does have fond memories of Screaming Lord Sutch, laughing as he related a story during an interview on Radio Oxford in 2015: 'We were on tour and playing at a theatre in Hatfield. David used to light things with a match during his act, which was a voodoo-type sort of carry on. This night, he set fire to one of his props and it all went wrong. He burnt the place down!'

Clem had been head-hunted for 'The Kids From Fame Tour', which was an American television series based on the 1980 film of the same name. A mixture of drama and music, *Fame* followed the lives of students at the fictional New York City High School for the Performing Arts. The popularity of the series in the UK led to several hit records and live concert tours by the cast.

Clem:

I was working with Grace Kennedy at the time, a British singer and television presenter who was born at Montego Bay, Jamaica. Grace first came into the public eye after winning the TV talent show *Opportunity Knocks*, and was subsequently signed up by the BBC to present her own Saturday night prime time entertainment show, *The Grace Kennedy Show*, which ran for six series from

1981–83. I was doing a lot of television work, *The Tommy Cooper Show*, Benny Hill. The job for the *Fame* tour came through the 'Fixer' after an American MD had asked him to get someone for the British shows. I turned it down initially, didn't really fancy a long tour or gig again, but I was kind of pushed into it. I'm glad I did it though now, it was a great experience and I loved it. We broke all box office records playing five nights at the Albert Hall, which was recorded and released as an album. The orchestra was quite a big band, with drums, percussion, two guitars, bass, two trombones and sax players, two keyboards and all the equipment that goes with it. It was actually Deep Purple's gear we used for the tour which was great, as their roadies were employed to hump it around everywhere. The roadie who looked after my gear was fantastic. He'd set my drums up, tune them, everything was measured out, I didn't have to do a thing but turn up and play. And I have to say, those guys don't ever get any credit.

After the Albert Hall we played in Southampton for three sell-out shows, a UK tour and then left for a trip to Israel, which was another experience. A guy I really liked was Gene Anthony Ray who played Leroy, the black guy who emerged as a real star from the television series. He had the teenage girls queuing up to meet him by the thousands. He was a sex god to them. Only one problem, if the truth was known – he was gay! Leroy had a partner with him the whole time we were on the road, but it was all kept very quiet. And without going into individuals, there were a good few of the cast who liked their coke. And I am not talking about a soft drink! In fact, the word was that when we played Manchester the city was cleaned out of the stuff. Israel was interesting to say the least. Although us in the band were English, the cast was American and there were obvious security issues to be dealt with. What they did was take over an entire floor of the Hilton in Tel Aviv. Everyone connected with the show was given a pass, and at each end of the floor were armed security men. They had an intimidating presence. No pass, no entry – it was simple as that. It was also on that tour that Leroy showed what a real gent and real star he was. It was announced to the whole group that the following day the 'principals' would be going on a tour to Bethlehem. Leroy said immediately, 'What do you mean 'principals?'' When we were all told it meant the cast and not the band, Leroy came back straightaway, 'No way. We are one group and either we all go or no one goes. No debate'.

But it wasn't always the happiest of tours. Remember Debbie Allen? In the television show she was the one whose catchphrase was 'You want fame – well fame costs. And this is where you start paying!' Trust me... she was the same in real life. There was one night in Brighton when the show was supposed to start at 7.30pm. We were all on stage, warmed up ready to go. Then the director came out with his instructions and looking very flustered. 'Play!' he said. 'Play what?' we said. 'Anything! Anything at all. There is a row down there and they are not coming out yet.' Apparently Debbie had fallen out with the guy who played Bruno and no-one was backing down. So we played. And played. And played. '*My Old Man's A Dustman*', '*Oh We Do Like To Be Beside The Seaside*'... anything that would fill time while Debbie and Bruno resolved their differences. Eventually they did – at about 10.30pm! I think we finished about 1.00am the following morning.

In 1983 Clem's old friend from the '60s and Tornados days, Billy Fury, passed away following a heart attack. Billy had been dogged with ill-health ever since a child. After his success in the Sixties his career went into decline like so many others in the wake of the 'Beat' boom. He re-appeared in the '70s, starring in the rock and roll film *That'll Be The Day*, where he more or less played himself. The film was a huge success.

A real comeback seemed on the cards in the early 1980s, when he was tempted into the studio again to record the tracks for the album *The One And Only Billy Fury*, which was issued after his death.

Stuart Coleman, producer of *The One And Only Billy Fury*:

The final sessions were a sad state of affairs because Billy wasn't a well man. He was frail, and he had so many health problems over the years but his voice was immaculate, and he was in wonderful form. When we cut '*Devil Or Angel*', he said: 'I didn't think I could sing like that any more.' If you listen to the first middle eight, he sounds exactly as he did when he was 18 and he was amazed that he could do that... He was getting erratic towards the end. I was booking studio time and he wouldn't turn up, partly because his confidence in his own ability was ebbing. He said to me: 'I'm becoming a cabbage. I might as well go out in a blaze of glory.' He was 42 and he knew he'd never collect his pension.

Clem:

> I went to Billy's funeral, which was held at the St John's Wood church in London. There were a lot of old friends there: Marty Wilde, Jess Conrad, Eden Kane, Tony Read, Hal Carter, Mick Green. Larry Parnes, who I hadn't seen since the early Sixties, was also there. He had dementia and looked terrible. Didn't know anyone. Sadly Larry died too, not long after Billy.

An album re-released on cassette in 1984 featuring Clem and some old session friends was *No Introduction Necessary*, originally recorded as far back as 1968 as a vehicle to give singer Keith De Groot a boost in his career. Journalist Dave Thompson told the story of the album and Keith's career:

> Keith De Groot had been on the fringes of the London music scene since the early '60s at the time, recording with legendary producer Joe Meek and releasing three singles under the pseudonym 'Gerry Temple'. He also worked as a session singer and worked briefly with Chris Farlowe. By 1967, however, Keith was out of a gig and feeling depressed, and his friend, record producer Reg Tracey, offered to bankroll sessions for a debut album in hopes of re-launching his career.

> DeGroot called on a couple of old friends to help with the project: Glyn Johns (who engineered and co-produced) and Nicky Hopkins (who played piano and wrote the arrangements). The sessions took place at Olympic Studios in London.

> Johns and Hopkins brought in their session pals John Paul Jones (bass), Clem Cattini (drums), Big Jim Sullivan (guitar), and Albert Lee (guitar). Sullivan and Lee were not available for the second session, so Jimmy Page, on break between Yardbirds tours, filled in.

> Everyone agreed to work for minimum wage except for Jimmy Page, who did the session in exchange for the publishing rights to the two original compositions on the album.

> The original stars of the show were the twin guitars of Albert

Lee and Big Jim Sullivan. Keyboards were the province of Nicky Hopkins; Chris Hughes came in on saxophone; the drum slot was filled by Clem Cattini; and the atmosphere in the studio was one of barely-restrained delight. Watching from the control booth, Tracey and engineer Glyn Johns swiftly realized that there was little to be gained from trying to marshal the sessions in any conventional manner. Rather, it was far more productive to simply point the musicians at a song, then let them get on with it. The album consisted mostly of cover versions of songs by Jerry Lee Lewis, Buddy Holly and other rock & roll artists of the era, as well as several original cuts composed by Keith De Groot and Nicky Hopkins.

Nine songs had been completed when disaster struck: a session was booked, but neither Lee nor Sullivan were going to be able to make it. Casting around for suggestions, Tracey quickly settled on Page, calling him in for the last round of recordings, a total of five songs. The sessions complete, Tracey, however, had to re-evaluate the results. Though he turned in a fine performance, De Groot had been utterly sidelined by the sheer weight of talent arrayed behind him. Indeed, as Tracey listened to the tapes, it swiftly became clear that what had started life as an unknown singer's solo album had instead been transformed into the ultimate rock & roll party album, as performed by some of the ultimate rock & roll party animals.

A deal with the British record label Spark was duly arranged and the album, beguilingly titled *No Introduction Necessary*, was released in late 1968. Perhaps unsurprisingly, it did little, although all of the featured players were famous enough on the session circuit, to the average man in the street their names meant nothing. A year or so later, and *No Introduction Necessary* may have been able to take advantage of the Led Zeppelin boom. But by then, it had already been deleted. It would not see the light of day again for close to another two decades.

It has since been issued dozens of times under a variety of titles: *Rock 'n' Roll Highway, Lovin' Up A Storm* and *Burn Up* just three examples.

1986 saw Clem reunited with old shipmates Brian Gregg and Alan Caddy for a one-off reunion gig at the twentieth anniversary Johnny

Kidd Tribute show at London's Rock 'n' Roll Club, based at the rear of the Olde Cherry Tree Inn in Southgate. Although the greatest honour of the evening went to Dave Sampson who sang vocals, and which led to his appearance at the '87 Weymouth Rock Festival alongside Gene Vincent's famous Blue Caps, The Pirates seemed never to have been away.

Clem:

> I then reformed The Tornados around 1988 after a phone call I received from keyboard player Bip Wetherell requesting if his band could use the name, and if I was interested in teaming up. So it was that another chapter began!

Bip:

> I was in a local band at the time playing Tornados and '60s stuff. I suggested to the guitarist Dave Dean the idea of trying to get Clem, an original member, to join us to make it authentic. I managed to find a contact for Clem and it was a short while after I flew down to Torquay in my helicopter with Dave to meet Clem, who was playing in a show with his current band. When we arrived Clem said, 'I've never been up in a helicopter'. So I took him for a whirl and then we came down, the band's singer Lynn said, 'I've never been in a helicopter either.' So I took Lynn up for a quick whirl round the resort. Later, before heading off home back to Corby, I told Dave I would have to put in a flight plan and pay a £25 landing fee before we could leave. When I went to pay it I was told that'll be £100. 'I thought it was only £25!' I replied. 'You've landed four times sir, that's £100.' So, it cost me £100 for the pleasure of meeting that lot in Torquay!

Clem:

> Bip took on the challenge of booking gigs and organising Sixties tours, and it was great fun meeting up with many old friends from the day still out there performing. Some weren't so great though, if I have to be honest. Ricky Valance was one, a 'star' we played with a good few times during the 1980s. Joe Moretti, who played guitar on 'Tell Laura I Love Her', was with us at the time and after

playing the hit Ricky Valance went up to Joe and screamed at him that the solo wasn't right! I mean! Joe was a fantastic player! I told Ricky Valance to remember that the musicians always have the last laugh. I told the guys in the band that next time we back him we'll play an upper third. Course, he came on and was screaming trying to reach the notes because we were playing so high! Made him look a right idiot.

Bip:

Ricky Valance wasn't the brightest. I asked him if he was the guy who got killed in the air crash with Buddy Holly. He said 'No, that wasn't me.' He couldn't see I was taking the piss. We played one gig when he came into the dressing room before the show and told us, 'I'm not going on first, I'm the star of the show boyo! I don't open the show. I've got a number one record.' He did have, in the Christian charts! He'd turned all religious and found God or something. Anyway, we said 'Great!' We could go on, do our bit and get off home! Another gig was when we were playing the Hammersmith Odeon on the Golden Oldies Show and he fell off the stage after taking a bow at the end of the performance. He fell head-first into the orchestra pit and the compere, comedian Mike Lee Taylor, quipped, 'That's the best I've ever seen him go down!"

Clem:

The best one was when we were on a radio show the day that John Lennon died. When Elvis had died the radio played his records all day long and they did the same with John, played The Beatles and Lennon's records all day. I said to the DJ 'Thank goodness Ricky Valance is still alive!' Later on, he came up to me and thanked me for the mention!

The Tornados were featured in a March 1991 issue of *The Stage*:

Happy Birthday to The Tornados, again touring with Golden Oldies with original drummer Clem Cattini, who is apparently going through a fortune in drumsticks. 'The fans just have to have a souvenir and it's usually my drumsticks,' explains Clem, who reformed the band last year after receiving the first royalties from the '60s hits. Lead singer of the new line-up is Lynn Alice, who has a different problem with souvenirs. Apparently she finds the punters are more interested in her tights and usually loses three pairs an evening. Meanwhile the mobbing goes on. At a recent 'Mums In The Gulf' benefit concert in Port Talbot, the group had to wait an hour before they could get out of the dressing rooms. Police protection is being arranged for future gigs.

A memorable and somewhat amazing encounter for Bip was the day he got talking to a guy who was at one of The Tornado's shows...
Bip:

> The guy obviously knew Clem, and I asked him if he was or had been in the business. He said, 'Yeah,' and I asked him what he was doing now and he said, 'Oh, I've got my own milk round!' 'What did you do then?' I asked him. 'I was a drummer.' It was a bit like drawing teeth, and I asked him who he played with. 'Jimi Hendrix,' he said! It was Mitch Mitchell. And all he wanted to talk about was his milk round!

Clem:

> Mitch later appeared in the 2009 film *Telstar* about Joe Meek, the film in which James Corden played me and I appeared as John Leyton's chauffeur!

Other stars of the 1960s Bip and Clem worked with included Freddie and The Dreamers, a band that Bip, who was also a nightclub owner, had more reason to remember than most...

> I booked The Dreamers for my club in the 1980s and paid the agent the fee, because Fred didn't know who I was. The agent wanted £1,500. I sent the cheque off, The Dreamers arrived in the afternoon, sorted their gear out etc, and then Freddie Garrity turned up and asked 'Who's the boss?' I told him I was, and he asked me for his money. I told him I'd paid the agent. He said as far as he was concerned I hadn't paid anybody. And if I didn't pay him there'd be no show. I had to go to the cash office and get £1,500 quick before the idiot would go on. It took me about a month to get my money back. I suppose he'd probably been ripped off so

many times in his career, I don't know, but I was upset about the whole thing.

Bip and Clem recalled the time they both felt the same dismay about the ever-changing record business, during a lunch following a gig at The Core Theatre, Corby in 2017.

Bip:

> The day I stopped being a DJ was when I went to the shop where I always bought my records and the guy said to me, 'You have to have this, its brilliant.' I asked him what it was and he put it on for me to listen. It was '*Agadoo*' by Black Lace. I said, 'I can't do this anymore.'

Clem:

> That was awful, but the one that finished me, my favourite hate record, was '*I Will Survive*' by Gloria Gaynor. Used to drive me nuts, that and '*YMCA*' by The Village People!

Bip:

> I opened up a karaoke bar in my club and gave out tickets for the punters to write down what song they would like to sing. They kept on coming up with '*I Will Survive*'! and I started ripping them up and putting them in the bin.

Clem:

> I did a wedding up north and this guy came up and asked me to play '*You'll Never Walk Alone*'. I was the band leader, I said 'No.' Well he kept on coming back, and I kept telling him, 'No, I don't like it and I won't play it, I'm the band leader!' Sorry Gerry.

Bip:

> I was working with Gerry and the Pacemakers one time and I said to Gerry, 'I have to tell you, '*Don't Let The Sun Catch You Crying*' is one of my big favourites. Is that the one that made you a lot of money?' 'No,' he said, 'my daughter came in one day years

later and said, 'Dad, they're playing your record 'Ferry Cross the Mersey'. I asked her why, and she told me it was the 'B' side of 'Relax' by Frankie Goes to Hollywood. That record sold millions! Thank you Holly Johnson!

One of the biggest thrills of Bip's life, and Clem's too probably, was meeting and being photographed with American astronaut Buzz Aldrin on the QE2 in 1997.

Bip:

> Flying is a passion I've had all my life, and growing up in the '60s when the Space Race was in full flow, like most people I was engrossed with it. The Moon landings, the Apollo missions, it was fantastic. So discovering that the second man on the moon, Buzz Aldrin, was on board the QE2 when we The New Tornados were working, that was such a thrill. And to meet him and talk about flying, I told him I had a helicopter, don't know if that impressed him or not, but I thought, what the hell, it was an amazing experience.

Clem had a surprise call from Ashley Hutchings and Richard Thompson, both founder members of folk rock group Fairport Convention, to play on a session for an album they were producing called *Twangin' 'n' a-Traddin'*. Clem remembers:

> That came about when I was working in Manchester. Ash asked me if I was available to play on this album they were doing. I told him I was working in Manchester and he replied, 'Well that's handy, that's where we are recording it.' Strange one to do for them really. They got a guitar player in, good player he was, Colin Pryce-Jones, a Buddy Holly-lookalike who played with Shadows tribute band The Rapiers. Unfortunately, when he turned up though, his gear didn't work! I felt sorry for him, he'd travelled a long way to get to the studio and then his gear let him down, so they had to get another guitar player in. We did 'Telstar' and a few other rock things, it was clearly something Ash had desired to do, a nostalgic trip to his teenage years, an instrumental album featuring the hits of The Ventures, The Shadows, Bill Black and The Tornados.

Twangin' 'n' a-Traddin' received favourable reviews, including this:

After a lifetime of inspiration, innovation and creativity, Ashley fuses rock 'n' pop instrumentals with traditional arrangements, folk tunes and some of his original songs. Richard Thompson, Clem Cattini and Colin Green help with a variety of styles for an album that fans will probably find curious and intriguing. In simple terms, *Twangin' 'n' a-Traddin'* pays homage to the long-gone age of pop music during the late 50s and early 60s when the Top Twenty of the day would always feature a number of instrumental hits. 'When I started to learn my instrument all those years ago,' says Hutchings, 'it was the sound of Johnny and the Hurricanes and Bill Black's Combo which I longed to emulate, not The Spinners or The Kingston Trio.' The approach is also evident in the choice of musicians who play on the album. Hutchings' regular sidekicks including Richard Thompson, Simon Nicol, Phil Beer and Simon Care are joined by genuinely legendary session men of the '60s, notably guitarist Colin Green, best known as a member of Georgie Fame's Blue Flames, and drummer Clem Cattini, who played on so many of Joe Meek's classic productions. These included The Tornados' '*Telstar*', which even topped the American pop charts, the first British single to do so, some three years before the British Invasion. Hutchings' Big Beat Combo, with the great Clem Cattini on drums and the completely unexpected penny whistle of Richard Thompson, radically but eloquently rearranged '*Telstar*' along with other classic hits – The Shadows' '*F.B.I.*', The Ventures' '*Walk Don't Run*' and a rebel-rousing Duane Eddy medley.

Simon Nicol:

As a participant in those sessions, I have to say that Ashley created a bit of a monster in tackling the project with so little preparation (at least as far as the foot soldiers could see) and it's remarkable so many minutes of pretty good performance emerged in such a short space of time. Basically it was heads-down from the start, and very little socialising or chit-chat happened: we moved from one piece to the next and it was a bit of a blur. It was a pleasure though! Clem won't recall me, but I consider having had the chance to play with one of the great originals of British music culture was a treat as well as a bit of an honour.

In 1990 Clem received an offer to work on *The Rocky Horror Show*, which was described as a 'musical and humorous tribute to the science fiction and horror B movies of the late 1940s through to the early 1970s.' The story told of a newly-engaged couple getting caught in a storm and coming to the home of a mad transvestite scientist, Dr Frank N. Furter, unveiling his new creation, 'a sort of Frankenstein-style monster in the form of an artificially made, fully grown, physically perfect muscle man named Rocky Horror, complete with blond hair and a tan.'

The band which toured the United Kingdom throughout the decade included Dave Brown as Musical Director and on piano; Chris Parren, synthesisers; Geoff Driscoll, tenor saxophone; Clem Cattini, drums; Derek Griffiths, electric/acoustic guitars, and Alan Ross on bass guitar.

Clem proved to be as ubiquitous as ever, as bass player Roger 'Sniffs' Nicholas revealed:

> I was playing a gig with the Cupid's Inspiration boys Terry Rice-Milton and Alan Warner in Ponders End, London, and who should 'happen along' but Clem himself! He was persuaded to get behind the 'skins' and we did a song together to mark the occasion, as it were. I was really pleased to say that I had shared the stage with him, because he is a true legend. The definitive session drummer, 'cos he would go the extra mile when all other session 'musos' had left! The Tornados were something else, of course! Clem drummed on the Cupids hits: '*Yesterday Has Gone*' and '*My World*', and most of their LP tracks.

It was during the 1990s when Alan Lovell, singer/guitarist with The Swinging Blue Jeans, met Clem on 'The Solid Gold Rock 'n' Roll' tours:

> They used session guys to back the artists, and I was backing PJ Proby, John Leyton, Mike Berry and Jess Conrad. The drummer was a guy called Matt Poole, who happened to be a friend of Clem's and it was Matt who introduced me to him. When Matt was unavailable Clem would sit in for him. We exchanged phone numbers and kept in touch.

I was backing Tommy Bruce at the Annual Chippenham Eddie Cochran Memorial Festival when I met Robert Plant. The Led Zeppelin singer said to me he was there 'to just enjoy the rock and roll music.' I'd met Robert before, and he came over to say hello. During our conversation I happened to mention I'd been talking to Clem just previously. He asked, 'Clem? Do you mean Clem Cattini?'

I said, 'Yeah, he's backstage drinking coffee with his wife Anna. He's been on, did you see him?'

He said, 'No, see him? I want him to play on my new album!'

I asked him if he had a pass, he said no, so I told him I'd go and get Clem and he said, 'Would you?'

I found Clem and told him, 'I've just been talking to Robert Plant.'

'Good grief,' Clem replied, 'I played on his first two singles.'

'Well, he wants to meet you.'

'No, I can't do that,' Clem said, 'he won't want to see me, that was about 30 years ago.'

'Well he does,' I said, 'he wants you to play on his new album.'

I eventually coaxed Clem to join us, and when Robert saw him he flung his arm right round him, unbelievable, and they must have talked for over forty minutes or more.

Another star I had the privilege of working with Clem for was Norman Wisdom. We did a tour with Norman and he was fantastic. We were invited to play for the Queen at St. James's Palace and entertain a party of military veterans, old soldiers, Wrens - they were all there. It was something the Queen did as a thank you for these guys putting themselves on the line in defence of the country. Norman topped the bill.

We also played a night at the De Montfort Hall, Leicester with Norman, which was memorable. We used to start the show off, and then pretend that we'd made a cock up, Norman would then make an entrance from the side of the stage, and say 'Ooh sorry... am I not on yet?' and the place would be in uproar! 2,000 people screaming and laughing. Norman would traipse back off with everyone bawling for him to come back! It was amazing. He would do his routine, part of which was a question and answer thing. His sidekick would go out around the audience with a microphone and ask people for their memories of childhood etc, what were their favourite films, songs, to see if there was anything Norman could relate to. At the De Montfort the guy was asking a lady for her memories and she started crying. Taken aback, Norman went down to her, concerned, he was a very genuine fella, and she started telling him about how hard a life she'd had, her father had abused her, he used to beat her mother up, treated them like crap, starved them... she was sobbing. And Norman started crying! And the audience! It was heartbreaking. Her story reduced everyone to tears, we were all crying on stage! It really was emotional. Norman Wisdom was a really lovely guy, and a brilliant comedian.

Clem:

Norman Wisdom and Max Wall, both comedians who I had the pleasure to work with were real nice people. Genuine stars. They had no air of stardom about them. There are many with half the talent of Norman and Max who are so far up their rear end it's unbelievable. They're the ones who want to be but never make it to the top. Believe their own hype.

Alan:

Working with P.J. Proby was great, I got on like a house on fire with him, a lot of people didn't. We recorded some songs Proby wrote for Roy Orbison's wife Barbara. She had managed Roy's career during the 1980s and was a record producer for A&M Music and executive producer of Roy's acclaimed television special *A Black and White Night*. Barbara sadly passed away from pancreatic cancer in 2011. Getting back to P.J., he wrote the songs and I arranged them, basically. He was a great songwriter. The Searchers' *'Ain't Gonna Kiss Ya'* and Billy Fury's *'I Will'* were just two he wrote, under his real name of James Marcus Smith. We recorded four songs for Barbara, but unfortunately Proby's temperament with A&M didn't go down very well. They paid him off and shelved the songs. He was a great singer, some of the live gigs we did with him were fantastic. We had a twenty-piece band.

Alan Lovell played in local bands around his home town of Newton, Powys before moving to live in the Dingle, Liverpool.

I played in The Cavern with a few bands from 1968 onwards, first of all with Woodfall, supporting Stealers Wheel who included Gerry Rafferty and Joe Egan. This was just before they were about to break. Woodfall became Iron Horse, and we started writing our own songs and got a deal with Dick James Music – and it all went belly up. We were too young, just kids, but it was good at the time. We also played The Cavern with a band called Good Habit who later became The Racing Cars and had a huge hit with 'They Shoot Horses Don't They?' Fantastic band. Around 1969 our manager Dave Hall, who was from Shrewsbury, got us signed with the Wolverhampton Astra International Agency, whose clients included Slade. It went straight to our heads! We were touring with Mott the Hoople, Van Der Graaf Generator and The Faces with Rod Stewart. The tours those days were a week of six dates! But they were BIG dates. Chesford Grange Kenilworth, Birmingham Town Hall. It was magnificent. We recorded for Noone Music, made some records but never heard anything. They were just put on the pile of all the other recordings and forgot about. I went to Dubai around 1973, playing gigs with bands whenever I could, then came to London, just bumming around basically before I moved there permanently in 1976.

One thing I found strange and disappointing was the respect, or lack of it, the Blue Jeans received when we played at Liverpool Town Hall. It was a big gig, a lot of the old bands were playing, but talking to some of the people who were there, a younger generation they may have been... but they didn't have a clue about the groups, their heritage. 'Who are you?' we were asked. They didn't know the Jeans were from Liverpool, one of the original bands from those great days in the Sixties who played at The Cavern. Billy J. Kramer was sitting by us; 'Who's he?' I was asked. To me it just seemed so disrespectful, for what the Jeans, never mind Billy J. and the others had done, and for Liverpool, down the years. Apart from Gerry Marsden that is, everyone knows Gerry. But there you go... typical Scousers!

One of the biggest thrills I had was being invited to The Shadows' Bruce Welch's house. Bruce told me, 'Come on over, let's get the guitars out and have some fun.' When I went in, the first thing I saw was about 200 Gold Discs adorning the walls of his house. Unbelievable. Bruce had loads of guitars as well. He took one off the wall to show me, the one he played in the film *Expresso Bongo* back in 1959. It was awful! Another guitar was given to him by soul legend Al Greene. Then he gave me another one to play... the Fender Strat, THE Fender Strat! The one that Cliff bought Hank Marvin back in 1958 or whatever the year was. I couldn't believe it... this was like the Rolls Royce of guitars! This is the one! I picked it up and thought, 'Wow'. We played '*Apache*', and I only just got through to the end, I was so overwhelmed. I was on a high for days after that.

At the turn of the century Clem was still busy and still in demand.

I was working with Cliff Bennett on an album in a converted garage in Newham, East London. Also with Frankie Ford the guy who did '*Sea Cruise*' and Johnny Preston of '*Running Bear*' fame. The Cliff album was recorded with just me, a drum click and a bass player, and Cliff singing of course. The guitar part was put on afterwards. What irked me about that was later on, Cliff was selling CDs of the album at his gigs but hadn't included me on the band rota. It was just down as drums! Some recognition would have been nice, but there you go. As for the other tracks with Frank and Johnny, I never heard them at all after those sessions. The producer had a heart attack, and as far as I know they never got released.

12

Ridin' the Wind in the 2000s

If somebody had told Clem back in 1962 that he would still be playing '*Telstar*' at the turn of the century, the Millennium, he would probably have laughed. If it was time for reflection then Clem could look back on a remarkable career that started way back in 1956 when he and his friends walked out of the Trocadero cinema in South London. *Rock Around the Clock* had been the inspiration. Now, nigh on 50 years later, Clem was still rocking around the clock!

The year 2000 was greeted somewhat with trepidation as it was feared that computers would crash, sending the world into a whirlwind of panic. Aeroplanes would fall out of the sky, ships would crash into each other, shops wouldn't be able to operate their tills, hospitals wouldn't be able to cope, patients would die. There wasn't any reports of monks disappearing to the hills again, as there was in the '50s and '60s, but scaremongers had a field day. Of course it was all a load of rubbish; we all woke up on January 1st 2000 to surprisingly find that most of us were still here!

This is how many would recall one of those lifetime events that not every generation can witness.

For Clem, it's unlikely he was taken in with all this sort of nonsense. Always a realist, he would never have dreamt of taking to the hills with Anna and his daughters Giulia, Daniella, Victoria and their families to escape the possibility of a tsunami or something equally catastrophic. 2000 was a memorable year instead for being honoured with a well-deserved Gold Badge by the British Academy of Songwriters, Composers & Authors (BASCA) for his services to the music industry. Humble as ever, thrilled and delighted to be awarded with such a prestigious honour, you can imagine Clem's acceptance speech with the line, 'I was just doing a job.'

Rewards and recognition are delightful, but in the music business, financial reward is rather less forthcoming. In 2002, a report highlighted that 'royalties' for certain records and artists are 'coming of age' and due to expire, leaving many of the veteran artists from the '50s and '60s worrying about their retirement pensions.

'I hope I die before I get old' may once have been the mantra of rock and roll, but for those rock and rollers who managed to get old before they died, thoughts were turning to retirement. And the burning question was, as one journalist highlighted with more than a hint of irony:

> Who's going to pay the heating bills on that guitar-shaped swimming pool they built in the first flush of teen success?' Much was made of the 50th anniversary of rock and roll, but with the UK and Europe's copyright protection for sound recordings currently only extending to a period of 50 years, those original rock and rollers are waking up to the unpleasant fact that royalty payments are about to stop rolling in. Clem Cattini, 65-year-old drummer with The Pirates and The Tornados, complained: "Shakin' All Over' was released in 1960, so losing copyright is coming very close for me. It's like buying a house and then after 50 years it's suddenly not yours. Well, actually, it's like banging the hell out of a drum kit on a rebel rock anthem, then 50 years later worrying about how you're going to pay for a hip replacement.'
>
> The problem is that, when these records were being made, no one thought they would last longer than a chart rundown, let alone still be gaining airplay in the next century. Pop was supposed to be ephemeral – it was about youth and beauty and living in the moment. Musicians had a grasshopper approach to their careers. Who would have imagined in 1956 that there would still be an audience for the hits of the day, and that in many cases it would be the same audience, watching the same stars on a never-ending nostalgia circuit?

Clem's CV boasts work right across the spectrum, from the rock and roll days of Terry Kennedy, Terry Dene, Johnny Kidd, Billy Fury, The Tornados, sessions with every Tom, Dick and Harry, television, films, Musical Director, and into the millennium another venture with the opportunity to work in pantomime. Not as Buttons, Mother Goose, Widow Twanky or Jack in the Beanstalk, but as MD in the orchestra.

Clem:

It was a different road to go down, Cinderella, Hi Ho, what do you call it... Snow White. I enjoyed it most of the time but I did have a spat with one famous actress, Barbara Windsor, when we were performing Aladdin at The Swan in High Wycombe. I like Barbara, but she is not the chirpy cockney lady that is the public perception. She can be mean and throw a tantrum with the best of them when she is riled, as she was in rehearsal that day. Because I was in the band, I was down in the orchestra pit. I couldn't see what was happening on stage. My cue to play a note on a triangle – which was in turn Barbara's cue – was to come from a light coming on. Except there was no light that came on and Barbara was stomping round on stage in a right hissy fit and started to have a go at me. 'Where's my cue? Where's my cue?' she kept shouting. And I had enough. 'Firstly, I didn't see any light and secondly I am not being shouted at like that by you or anyone,' I said. 'See you!' and with that, I put my sticks in their case and walked off. Suddenly it was like Bedlam, with the producer saying 'The drummer's walked out! The drummer's walked out!' Eventually, Barbara came down and apologised. 'Any more and you can shove these drumsticks up your back end!' I said to her. It had the desired effect. That was another benefit of the way I chose to follow my career in music – I didn't kowtow to anyone. I think what really cheesed her off a bit was that, when everything was sorted out and the show went ahead, a couple of friends came down to see her afterwards. They had seen my name in the programme and were obviously Tornados fans. 'We didn't realise you had THE Clem Cattini in the show,' they said. Ironically, Barbara was given her Gold Merit award by the British Academy of Composers and Songwriters the same day as me in October 2001. And she gave me a lovely name-check after accepting her award. Nice touch, and it meant a lot to me. But moments like that recognition at the pantomime were rare over the years. I was just happy to be working and working regularly. After all – they will always need a drummer.

Clem played with a number of musicians, many of whom were still shakin' all over in short trousers when he was on the road with Johnny Kidd.

Classically-trained Roger Nicholas was a former County Youth level violinist who took up the bass guitar at age 14 and 'sold my soul to rock and roll'. Many years were spent working with local acts, backing cabaret artists, and being a member of '70s chart act First Class ('*Beach Baby*'). Roger also worked for '60s icons P.J. Proby and Billie Davis before taking up lead guitar when joining Gidea Park in 1992.

Roger teamed up with Clem following a Tornados booking at Sheppey Little Theatre, where he was Musical Director. Roger had formed a 'house' band to support '60s bands and artists who appeared, which included the Swinging Blue Jeans, Searchers, Tornados, Dave Berry, Billie Davis, P.J. Proby.

Roger (2017):

> Playing with Clem has and always is an absolute pleasure. He is amazing. An absolute metronomical drummer. Doesn't matter what you're playing or what kit Clem is using, he's always the same, solid. He's also the only drummer I've played with who chats all the way through when he's playing! In the middle of a song or an instrumental he will look over to you and ask some question that has nothing to do with the gig. 'What are we doing after the show?' he'll ask, or 'How's the wife?' Never misses a beat either! Incredible.

> It's well known that Clem played on over 40 number one singles in the '60s, but how many others did he play on? How many hit records that made the Top Ten or Twenty did he play on? He's too modest to talk about it – in truth he has no idea! Now and again though he'll hear a record or a song and recognise something. We were playing a '60s show with the Manfreds one time and I was sitting at a table chatting with Clem as Paul Jones went on stage for a sound check. He was going through '*I've Been A Bad Bad Boy*', his hit from 1967. In the middle of our conversation Clem turned

and shouted at Paul; 'Hey Jonesy!' Paul looked over. 'Hi Clem!' Clem shouted back, 'I hope you're paying your drummer more than what I got paid for playing that!' Then turned and carried on chatting to me as if nothing had happened! He'd heard a fill or something and recognised his drumming.

As Musical Director Roger has many stories to tell, often humorous:

I once had the idea of putting together a show with Mike Berry and Dave Berry to call it The Berry Brothers. When I called Dave to ask him if he was interested, he bellowed down the phone – 'Mike Berry? We're not brothers! I'm better looking than him – and I'm a better singer! Have you heard his wimpy *'Don't You Think It's Time'*? Yeah I'll do it, as long as my name is before his!'

'P.J. Proby was a strange fellow. A nightmare. One minute he'd talk to you as if he's your closest friend, then next time he sees you he'll blank you or be as ignorant as sin. He was always telling everyone he was a better singer than Elvis. He used to record demos for the King and said his version was always better. Elvis ruined them! He made demos for about a dozen Elvis films which, if to be honest, many were far from memorable. He did have a great talent for imitation though. He could mimic any singer, women as well.

Clem:

I remember working with P.J. Proby at EMI when he collapsed in the studio. Played a few gigs with him too. One in Bournemouth when I insisted on staying in the same hotel as Proby. I was asked with incredulation, 'Why do you think you should stay in the same hotel as the star?' My reply was blunt: 'I've travelled down from London to play for him. Left my wife and the comfort of my home to stay in a shit hole! Don't think so!' That's what it was like, unbelievable.

Edison Lighthouse drummer Simon Aldridge, a friend of Roger and Clem, recalls a gig he played with P.J. Proby:

We were playing one night when I had provided most of the gear, including the PA. Suddenly in the middle of a song he threw the mic, my mic, up in the air, and did a cartwheel! The mic went through the canopy above the stage and that was that! It was knackered! Proby retrieved it, went to sing again and you couldn't hear a thing. He stood there like a goldfish looking as if he was miming! He turned round to me behind the drums and mouthed something indiscernible off. Pissed me right off! 'That was my mic you've just broke!' I shouted back at him. He didn't give a toss...

Throughout the decades there's always been a yearn for nostalgia, rock and roll revivals as each generation puts their own stamp on the music scene. Tired, or bored, or both! Rock and Roll comes to the rescue for the Baby Boomers. During the 1990s the guitar bands had returned with Oasis, Blur and their contemporaries citing The Beatles, Kinks, Stones as their influences. It could have been on the back of this the 'Tribute' phenomenon came to be. Suddenly there were The Bootleg Beatles, Counterfeit Stones, Fleetwood Bac and countless others all joining the nostalgia bandwagon. Good as they are, they do little to impress Clem (2018):

> One thing I can't get my head round are tribute bands. You have to say they are obviously talented, but why don't they try to make it with their own material rather than riding on the back of the artists who made these massive hits? In some cases, long before they were even born! Doesn't seem right to me.

Clem may have been cheered when he heard one of his most famous records being played on the airwaves, *'Shakin' All Over'*. Not by Johnny Kidd and The Pirates, or indeed a cover version by a tribute band, but by an outfit that appeared in 2001 which wasn't so much a 'tribute' band, but a revivalist outfit of '60s veterans out to have a good time. The British Invasion All-Stars were much like Bill Wyman's Rhythm Kings, formed after Bill had grown bored with The Stones' 'stadium' gigs, admitting; 'I didn't get any pleasure at all playing to a sea of faces a 100,000 strong.' The bass player left The Stones after a 30-year stint and formed his Rhythm Kings with like-minded musicians Georgie Fame, Gary Brooker, Albert Lee, Terry Taylor and others.

The British Invasion All-Stars were hailed as 'a 21st century band with a '60s sound', which wasn't surprising as all of its members were veteran rockers who belonged to various '60s bands (some more prominent than others). In rock circles, the term British Invasion is used to describe the wave of British rock bands that made its presence felt in the early '60s. 'Rock and roll' may have originated in the United States, but when The Beatles and other British acts hit it big in the '60s, it was clear that Blighty had become a major player in the field.

The All-Stars boasted former Yardbird Jim McCarty on drums and lead vocals, ex-Procol Harum Matthew Fisher on Hammond organ and Eddie Phillips (formerly of The Creation) on lead guitar. The three other members were Ray Phillips of The Nashville Teens on lead vocals and two ex-members of the Downliners Sect: rhythm guitarist Don Craine and bassist Keith Grand, who also contributed backing vocals.

The British Invasion All-Stars released a self-titled debut album on the independent Mooreland Street label in 2002, showing no awareness of the alternative rock sounds of the early 2000s: 'The band was totally unaffected by any of the punk, new wave, post-punk, pop-metal, or alternative rock that came after the '60s.'

Unbelievably though, the liner notes for the CD would have had Clem shakin' his head in despair, displaying the ignorance or lack of research when describing '*Shakin' All Over*' by The Who!

> From covers of well-known songs by The Yardbirds ('*Shapes of Things*') and The Who ('*Shakin' All Over*'), to new material, everything on the British Invasion All-Stars' first album is unapologetically '60s-minded. The CD boasts several guest musicians who have strong '60s credentials, including bassist Noel Redding (who was one-third of the Jimi Hendrix Experience) and two ex-members of the Pretty Things: Dick Taylor and Phil May.

American star Bruce Springsteen was one of the biggest names on the planet in the early 2000s. Bruce had been inspired by the 1960s

British Invasion when he was a kid and was a huge fan of the Dave Clark Five. So it was that in 2003 Bruce and his E Street Band were appearing at the O2 in London and looking to hook up with some of their heroes.

Clem:

> I received a phone call from Max Weinberg, the E Street drummer, inviting me and Anna along for the show at the O2 and to meet for a discussion about some work. Max was due to work on a session with Mike Smith, The Dave Clark Five vocalist and piano player who was also going to be the producer. Turns out Max and Bruce were massive fans of The Dave Clark Five. I told him I'd give it some thought and later Max phoned me. During the conversation I happened to say, 'You know that The Dave Clark Five never played on their records?', which obviously went down like a lead balloon. He never phoned me again! Mike was a good guy though and a good rock and roll singer. It was terrible what happened to him. He died in 2008 from a bout of pneumonia which was connected to an accident he had at home when he fell off a ladder and injured his spine which left him paralysed.

Quite unexpectedly, Clem was back at number one in the charts in 2005 after playing on a session for comedian Peter Kay's Comic Relief re-release of Tony Christie's '(*Is This The Way To) Amarillo*'.

2006 saw Clem reunited with his old buddy from The Pirates, Brian Gregg, along with guitarist Joe Moretti's son, Joe Junior, to celebrate the life of Johnny Kidd, 40 years after his tragic death in a road accident. They were backing Johnny 'tribute' singer Kidd Kane, whose career began in 1976 in West London playing with various rock 'n' roll bands. In 1991 Kidd Kane went on tour to Portugal for six months before heading over to the United States for six years, working on the music circuit. His bio read:

> A dynamic and versatile entertainer, who once seen is never forgotten, with a truly original style, as he takes classic songs from the 1950s and early '60s and adapts them to his own unique style, this combined with his energetic performances of these songs will keep the audience on the edge of their seats right to the final

note. Kidd Kane has performed and appeared on TV and radio on an international basis from Scandinavia to Europe to the USA, as well as nationally and locally. Kidd Kane has also worked with the likes of Jerry Lee Lewis, Chubby Checker and James Burton and many other well known stars from this era. That groups like these are still popular today – even to those who weren't born first time round – are a testament to the enduring appeal of early British Rock 'n' Roll, and show that England was not quite the cultural waste land that many would have us believe.

An album to coincide with Johnny Kidd's tragic 40th anniversary was recorded at Western Star Studio in Bristol. *Cabin Down Below* by Kidd Kane & The Pirates on Castaway Records received great reviews:

> The release of this album is a great way of tributing one of the groundbreaking artists of British rock 'n' roll music. The musicians on this CD are none less than the original Pirates who recorded '*Shakin' All Over*' in 1960; Brian Gregg and Clem Cattini, plus Joe Moretti's son, also named Joe Moretti. Produced and engineered by Alan Wilson, quality is guaranteed. The record starts with Vince Taylor's '*Brand New Cadillac*', no surprise, because Joe Moretti Sr. also played guitar on the original recording by Vince Taylor in 1959. The sound is awesome, just as powerful, or maybe even a bit more, than the original recording. After just one song, I already have goosebumps on my arm. Kidd Kane has a fabulous voice and Brian Gregg's greasy thumping bass crawls under your skin.

> The track listing is a trip down memory lane, with Sanford Clark's '*The Fool*', Simon Scott's '*Move It Baby*', Johnny Kidd's original '*Please Don't Touch*' and '*Shakin' All Over*', Jack Scott's '*Baby She's Gone*', Willie Dixon's '*My Babe*' (Vince Taylor style), Jody Reynolds' '*Endless Sleep*' and a lot of songs played by The Pirates at one time or another.

> The title song, a cover of Tom Petty & The Heartbreakers' '*Cabin Down Below*', is absolutely top notch and surely my favourite track on this album. Joe Moretti Jr. is amazing on the lead guitar, also with additional Hammond organ by Alan Wilson. One of the best albums I've heard in a long time, five stars well deserved!

Clem:

> Kidd Kane lived in a caravan. I wasn't that impressed with him to
> be honest, he was a bloody awful singer, but I was asked to do the
> sessions for this album, which I have to say I thought was very
> good, but I couldn't make the start because I was busy. So I went
> down to Bristol two days later and spent four days there. When
> the sessions were finished Kidd Kane wanted to pay me less than
> what the other guys were getting! 'Hang on a minute,' I said, I've
> done the same amount of work as the others! He was funny about
> it, but he coughed up.

In 2008, Clem was probably surprised himself to find him back on
the silver screen in the movies. Forty-odd years after *Just for Fun* he
was cast as a chauffeur in *Telstar*, the story of the life and suicide of
Joe Meek, 'producer and composer behind the first British record to
go to number one in the American charts.'

Odd thing it must have been, Clem was portrayed as The Tornados'
drummer on the big screen by actor James Corden, who since became
a global star when his career lifted off as 'Smiffy' in the TV series
Gavin and Stacey. Rocketed to fame you might say. Clem is played
as 'a foul-mouthed bruiser, a working-class rock 'n' roller with little
time for Meek's avant-garde production techniques.'

Clem:

> That wasn't far from the truth. James came round to see me at my
> home to ask how he should play me and I told him to basically,
> just be bolshie! Though I didn't used to swear quite as much as
> James.

Reviews for the film were varied. The *Daily Mail*: 'A shambolic but
entertaining biopic. While enjoyable, not much good and definitely
not sophisticated.'

Scotland on Sunday was more generous, their critic Siobhan Synnot
praising the film: 'Because it didn't employ the usual cinematic gloss.
It begins with a humorous tone but transforms into a harrowing
film. *Telstar* knocks the wind out of the sails of *The Boat That*

Rocked [a film starring Bill Nighy about the story of 1960s' Pirate Radio], in that the performances are more substantial and engaged.' Synnot concluded; 'Like Meek's records, *Telstar* is raw, fatalistic and somewhat crudely put together, but it also boasts both-barrels, mega-watt energy.'

The Guardian: 'Corden contributes most of the film's more amusing gags, a one-man double act channelling both Sid James and Bernard Bresslaw. J.J. Feild as Meek's peroxide darling Heinz does a half-decent 'Alfie' impression. Justin Hawkins, formerly of The Darkness, pops up as Screaming Lord Sutch; Carl Barât of The Libertines is Gene Vincent and Jess Conrad plays impresario Larry Parnes. The stream of cameos and cartoonish characters lends the film something of the '60s folly, a low-budget, north London version of a star-filled, stage-to-screen caper like *It's a Mad Mad Mad Mad World*. Richard Lester's work with The Beatles is also referenced in occasional comedy montages and Keystone-like sequences. Director Nick Moran mainly avoids flashy visuals for a more static approach. However, he keeps it bubbling along with an acute feel for the clothes and vernacular. Seedy rather than Swinging Sixties, the film is like an ironic take on a Joe Orton farce, dressed in natty suits by Jeff Banks and full of memorable pop tunes you'd totally forgotten. Ultimately, inexperience both behind and in front of the camera takes its toll and the thinness of both script and budget test the patience. Meek is an unsympathetic lead character and O'Neill drags you into his descent without quite earning the necessary pity or understanding. But the production, like Meek's records themselves, has a certain catchy, lo-fi charm. Any film in which a lad jaunts in and says: 'Sorry I'm late, my mum was 'avin' her bad toe off' has to be worth a butcher's.'

An Oscar may have been a long shot, but on Monday 2nd April 2012 Clem was honoured with a Lifetime Achievement Award at the Buddy Rich 25th Anniversary Memorial Concert held at The London Palladium. The show was hosted by Buddy's daughter, Cathy Rich, and actor and accomplished jazz drummer John Thomson. The concert was taking place for the first time in the UK, celebrating the music of the late great Buddy Rich. Previous sellout shows had taken place in Los Angeles, Las Vegas and Boston.

The show was advertised as 'featuring heavy metal legend Bruce Dickinson of Iron Maiden who will be singing while fellow heavy rock legend Ian Paice of Deep Purple plays drums alongside the full Buddy Rich Orchestra. Dickinson has become one of the most acclaimed heavy metal vocalists regularly appearing at the top of lists of the greatest singers/front men of all time. Deep Purple's *In Rock* was the first album he ever bought, so hearing him sing with the drumming legend of the very band that influenced his unique style will be a treat indeed. Bruce joins singer Tony Christie and other drummers Dave Weckl, Gregg Bissonette, John Blackwell and Gregg Potter from the USA with Ginger Baker, Gavin Harrison, Clem Cattini and Elliott Henshaw from the UK. Tickets are priced from £25 to £60. There are a limited number of VIP tickets available, which represent the best seats in the house, an opportunity to meet the headline artists, admission to the after-show party and signed merchandise. This is one show not to be missed – the world's greatest musicians in the world's greatest theatre paying tribute to 'the world's greatest drummer'. Be there!'

Looking back on his career, spanning over 50 years, it must have been a surreal experience for Clem thinking back to when he spent many hours learning and practising from the *Buddy Rich Tutor Book*.

Clem was recognised for his substantial contribution not only to 'a burgeoning Sixties and Seventies UK music scene but to a world wide rock n' roll explosion that to this day still continues to resonate and evolve.'

The award was presented by Buddy's daughter Cathy Rich and John Thomson, who paid tribute:

> It feels long overdue that such an accolade should make its way to a musician who has had such an impressive, poignant career within the worldwide music industry, making his mark on so many hit records and continuing to this day to record and perform, keeping rock and roll alive.
>
> Clem, one of the best-loved figures from early British rock and roll, has achieved the amazing distinction among musicians of

featuring on over forty UK number one singles. Known for his full, straightforward, unpretentious style, he has proved the drummer of choice for sounds ranging from folk rock to hard rock. An original member of iconic group, The Tornados, he went on to work with many of the musical greats over the years, including The Kinks, Paul McCartney, The Bee Gees, Lulu, Dusty Springfield, Ike and Tina Turner, Joe Cocker; the list goes on and on. Clem was the drummer on UK number ones including Cliff Richard's *'Devil Woman'*, Tom Jones' *'Green, Green Grass of Home'*, Johnny Kidd's *'Shakin' All Over'*, Gene Pitney's *'Something's Gotten Hold of My Heart'* and many, many more. In fact, more recently he has been working with Paul Weller on his new album – still going strong at 74! He has also played on a number of albums by singer Tony Christie, and will be duetting with him in the concert.

Clem's humility is possibly one of the reasons he has been in such high demand for decades by the worlds best known stars from being the in-house drummer for Joe Meek and his various projects to performing with Roy Orbison, The Kinks, Gladys Knight, Lou Reed to name but a very few, this list goes on and its reading only gets better, it's a testament to Clem's character that he's been the first choice over and over again!

The audience erupted when Clem stepped up to make his emotional acceptance which choked the throats of the hardest tub-thumpers. After accepting the award, Clem took to the stage to perform a track with the Buddy Rich Big Band, a fine way to mark one of the most diverse and inspirational musical careers of all time.

Clem:

Great night and great honour it was, but one of my main memories of the night is of meeting up with Ginger Baker after so many years, and how rude he was! Ginger had made his name with the Graham Bond Organisation, Alexis Korner, Cream. Blues groups. He was always disdainful towards rock and roll. Didn't fit with his street cred. When he saw me he asked, ignorantly, 'You still playing that rock and roll crap?' Ginger liked to think he was above all that for some reason. A 'serious' player! I retorted, 'You're still playing that blues rubbish then!' Ginger could be rude and obnoxious. When introduced on stage by John Thomson –

'Ladies and gentlemen, it's a real honour to welcome one of the great British rock and roll drummers, Ginger Baker' – Ginger strode on and barked, 'I'm not a rock and roll drummer! I'm a jazz drummer!' It was embarrassing.

Clem was interviewed along with his friend Brian Bennett to talk about their careers by journalist Jerome Marcus at the London Drum Show in 2012:

I was seventeen when I started and, as I mentioned before, I wasn't taught. My music lesson at school was some old biddie coming in, putting on a classical LP and disappearing for a cup of tea. I was madly into big band before I actually started playing. I used to go to Ronnie Scott's when Ronnie Stephenson was the drummer in his Quartet to watch him play but I never thought of playing it because I started playing rock n roll.

When I was doing sessions, about three a day at that time, I had a call from Peter Grant, Led Zeppelin's manager. He rang me up and said 'I've got this project that I want to start and I'd like to take you to lunch to talk about it.' It was through Jimmy Page actually who mentioned that I should be the guy to have on drums. The long and short of it was I never went to that lunch. I didn't have a chance, I was so busy with sessions and it took over everything else I had planned. You were lucky to have a sandwich in them days. The next year when it all started happening for Zeppelin, I saw Peter and said, 'Was it that project?' and he said 'Yeah.'

Looking back, could I see myself with long hair and sticking stuff up my nose?

I also remember doing a session and Charlie Katz, the fixer, walked in and Jimmy Page was telling him that he was joining this band and he wouldn't be doing any more sessions. Charlie turned to him and said, 'You're not going to make much money doing that, you have a great career in front of you as a session man'. Now look at him, he's a multi-millionaire!

Brian:

For me personally, I didn't know anything about the business back then. I didn't know about publishing. If someone published your song, they were doing you a favour. What it really meant was they were going to take 50% for doing bugger all. The business side of things we didn't know because we were naive; all we wanted to do was play the instrument. We'd go out there, make a noise and if someone out there gave you a few bob, then that was great. Through my experience, you'd do a deal and work with people who were honourable and gave you a good to fair amount of money and if you were lucky enough and weren't greedy, then everyone was happy. But a lot of the time and even now, you have to watch people who are after something for nothing.

I've used this example before. If you put eight hours into your craft and you're good at it, then you want paying for it, it's your job! You'll never get someone round to fix your drain or electricity as a favour. They've studied their craft and they want paying for it. A lot people perceive it as, well you enjoy yourself and it's just making music. It's like copying records. You go into a studio where hundreds of thousands of pounds are spent to make an album and then someone comes along only to copy it. It's exactly the same as going to a supermarket and saying 'I'm not paying that for that piece of cheese' and then nicking it; it's stealing, it's exactly the same and there's absolutely no difference.

If you want a record then pay for it. If they've downloaded it for free then there will be nothing left in this business and no profession for musicians. That's one of the reasons the business today is in such a bad state, because it's being mismanaged by a lot of greedy people who want it but don't appreciate it.

Clem:

I rang up to put a band in and as soon as I mentioned the price they said, 'Christ, that's a lot of money.' I then said, you phone up three or four plumbers and ask them to work from six o'clock at night to one in the morning and see how much they charge you. Whatever they charge you, I'll charge you half.' They wouldn't do it. People don't expect it but with us, they expect music is for nothing. The problem is, and like, Brian says and rightly so, if music isn't paid for, there ain't going to be any music because it costs money to make music and record it. If people start downloading and taking stuff for nothing, there isn't going to be any music or any industry left.

During 2010 Clem was invited by singer Paul Weller to play on a track, '*No Tears to Cry*', for his album *Wake Up The Nation*, being recorded at his studio in Surrey. Weller was famed for being the frontman with punk rock/new wave band The Jam and later The Style Council before establishing himself as a solo artist in 1991. The *Daily Telegraph* described Paul Weller: 'Apart from David Bowie, it's hard to think of any British solo artist who's had as varied, long-lasting and determinedly forward-looking a career.'

The BBC concurred: 'One of the most revered music writers and performers of the past 30 years.'

Paul Weller received four Brit Awards, winning the award for Best British Male twice, and the 2006 Brit Award for Outstanding Contribution to Music.

In 2012 he was among the British cultural icons selected by artist Sir Peter Blake to appear in a new version of his most famous artwork, the Beatles' *Sgt. Pepper's Lonely Hearts Club Band* album cover, to celebrate the British cultural figures of his life. Sir Peter also designed the cover for Paul's 1995 album *Stanley Road*.

Clem, recalling his visit to Paul Weller's studio:

> I was as nervous doing that session as I was recording '*Shakin' All Over*', but Paul was lovely. He made me a nice cup of tea before we started. Mind you, I had to tell him to stop calling me sir. This megastar calling me sir! I couldn't believe it.

During an interview with the press, Paul explained that his respect for Clem goes back to his teenage years and his record collection. 'Clem played on so many of my favourite tunes, by people like Dusty Springfield and The Walker Brothers. The Love Affair's '*Everlasting Love*' and '*Jesamine*' by The Casuals.'

Clem may have carried a free bus pass for 12 years, but he quickly proved that he still had his 'chops' when he arrived at Weller's Black Barn studio. 'We ran through the song with him, then two takes and it was sorted. Yes, he's still got it,' says Weller.

The *New Musical Express* was impressed, commenting: 'Clem

provides a characteristically steady and economical backbeat for Paul Weller's new single, '*No Tears to Cry*'.

'It's a definite nod to The Walker Brothers and those epic ballads,' said Paul, 'I thought it would be fitting to get the man who played on a lot of those records to play on it. He's seventy-odd, but Clem came down and did it in literally two takes. He's that good.'

Internet music and pop culture magazine *The Quietus* gave this review:

> *Wake Up The Nation* sees Weller painting from a bigger palette and his constant striving to push himself has resulted in his most remarkable solo collection yet. It's still recognisably him but by drafting in guest musicians such as The Move/ELO tub-thumper Bev Bevan, session legend Clem Cattini, former Jam bassist Bruce Foxton and, most unexpectedly, My Bloody Valentine's Kevin Shields, Weller's tenth solo album is his most sonically adventurous yet. Perversely, rather than stretching himself out again, Weller has compressed the songs into bite-sized two to three minute chunks that create a wonderful sense of urgency.

As Clem approached his octogenarian age he was still finding himself in demand for cameo appearances and advice, including in 2013 a tribute to his friend Billy Fury being produced, advertised as 'The best Fury since Fury', featuring Michael King recreating the musical career of Britain's best-loved rock n roll legend.'

In 2016, just like Halley's Comet, '*Telstar*' returned again. The song that is probably associated with Clem more than any other of the vast catalogue that he has been involved in and has been a constant throughout his life once more entered his life. A Ska band from London wanted to record their version of it and wanted Clem to provide the distinctive backbeat.

Clem:

> A guy phoned me up, a sax player, asking if I would be interested. I put him off a number of times, but then in the end I relented and said I'd go along. The group was called The Skammers, well-known around the pub and club circuit of London. They were

a bunch of characters I have to say! The sax player had been a frequent guest of Her Majesty it turned out. An enthusiast of Jazz Woodbines, shall we say! We recorded a Ska version of '*Telstar*' which I thought was great. It was released on iTunes, which is the way nowadays. Was a lot of fun.

*

Clem Cattini, one of the most respected and revered musicians of the 20th century, an icon of the rock and roll years of the 1950s, '60s and '70s, a genuine legend, has seen it all. A remarkable career that to the present day still sees him in demand to play sessions by many 21st century 'stars'. If it wasn't for having a few replacements, like a new hip and a knee, Clem would be even more prominent.

In 2019 Clem and Anna celebrate their Diamond Anniversary, another remarkable story in a world of celebrity flimsy and mayhem. An Everlasting Love. Globetrotter Clem has been, When Will I See You Again? Anna may have asked many a time.

It's certainly been an amazing journey. Accolades and awards have deservedly been bestowed on Clem, the legendary drummer, one of the most self-deprecating people you could ever wish to meet. For all the success achieved in his remarkable life, at the end of the day though, all Clem will tell you, is...

'It was only a job.'

Postscript

Clive and I hope you have enjoyed reading about Clem's life, *Through the Eye of a Tornado*. However, there is quite a serious point to be made. How come Clem Cattini played on 43 number one hits?

Well, you could argue that being called in to play on '*Green Green Grass of Home*' to help give Tom Jones a massive hit record was quite legit, as Tom was a solo act having ditched his band The Senators many years previously.

But what about Steve Ellis walking into the studio to record '*Everlasting Love*', looking around him and seeing top session men Clem on drums, John Paul Jones on bass, and top brass players brought in to help produce an incredible number one hit for The Love Affair, when Steve was the only member of the band on the record?

Perhaps the biggest furore was caused when it was disclosed that none of the Bay City Rollers played on their records. So it was a bit of a farce for the young girls to have the band's pictures on their walls, when the band members didn't play on any of the tracks the girls would swoon over. Over in the States it was the same with The Monkees. Perhaps the most famous part of rock and roll history was when George Martin automatically booked the top session drummer Andy White for the '*Love Me Do*' Beatles session. It had nothing to do with Pete Best's drumming ability. It was just a well-known fact that most of the young drummers in these up and coming bands couldn't keep time for three minutes, so money would be wasted trying over and over to get it right in the studio. The Beatles' knee-jerk reaction took it as Pete wasn't up to the job, so Paul and John drove a couple of hundred miles to the Pwllheli holiday camp where

Ringo was playing with Rory Storm and the Hurricanes and signed him up. It was a good job Ringo was considered good enough by George Martin, or maybe he would have been sacked too.

Across the pond, you wouldn't ask Micky Dolenz to drum on a record. He couldn't even mime properly on the drums.

The crazy world of the music business. Ah well! It gave our mate Clem a great career, and if you listen to *'Everlasting Love'* with headphones on you will realise it's the session men's talent that helped produce incredible number 1 hits. It just, sometimes, goes a bit too far in misleading the public.

Cheers!
Bip and Clive

Clem's Number Ones

Clem Cattini has appeared on 42 number one hit singles:

1   *Shakin' All Over* – Johnny Kidd and the Pirates (HMV, June 1960)

2   *Well I Ask You* – Eden Kane (Decca, June 1961)

3   *Come Outside* – Mike Sarne (Parlophone, May 1962)

4   *Telstar* – The Tornados (Decca, August 1962)

5   *Diane* – The Bachelors (Decca, January 1964)

6   *Make It Easy On Yourself* – The Walker Brothers (Philips, August 1965)

7   *Tears* – Ken Dodd (Columbia, September 1965)

8   *The Sun Ain't Gonna Shine Anymore* – The Walker Brothers (Philips, March 1966)

9   *You Don't Have To Say You Love Me* – Dusty Springfield (Philips, March 1966)

10 *Out Of Time* – Chris Farlowe (Immediate, June 1966)

11 *Green Green Grass Of Home* – Tom Jones (Decca, November 1966)

12 *Release Me* – Engelbert Humperdinck (Decca, January 1967)

13 *The Last Waltz* – Engelbert Humperdinck (Decca, August 1967)

14 *Ballad of Bonnie and Clyde* – Georgie Fame (CBS, December 1967)

15 *Everlasting Love* – The Love Affair (CBS, January 1968)

16 *Cinderella Rockefella* – Esther & Abi Ofarim (Philips, February 1968)

17 *I Pretend* – Des O'Connor (Columbia, May 1968)

18 *Where Do You Go To My Lovely?* – Peter Sarstedt (United Artists, February 1969)

19 *Something In The Air* – Thunderclap Newman (Track, June 1969)

20 *Two Little Boys* – Rolf Harris (Columbia, November 1969)

21 *Love Grows* – Edison Lighthouse (Bell, January 1970)

22 *Yellow River* – Christie (CBS, May 1970)

23 *Hot Love* – T. Rex (Fly, February 1971)

24 *Grandad* – Clive Dunn (Columbia, November 1970)

25 *Chirpy Chirpy Cheep Cheep* – Middle Of The Road (RCA, June 1971)

26 *Get It On* – T. Rex (Fly, July 1971)

27 *Ernie* – Benny Hill (Columbia, November 1971)

28 *I'd Like To Teach The World To Sing* – New Seekers (Polydor, December 1971)

29 *Telegram Sam* – T. Rex (T Rex, January 1972)

30 *Son Of My Father* – Chicory Tip (CBS, January 1972)

31 *Welcome Home* – Peters & Lee (Philips, May 1973)

32 *Jealous Mind* – Alvin Stardust (Magnet, February 1974)

33 *When Will I See You Again?* – Three Degrees (Philadelphia International, July 1974)

34 *Bye, Bye, Baby (Baby Goodbye)* – Bay City Rollers (Bell, March 1975)

35 *Whispering Grass* – Windsor Davies & Don Estelle (EMI, May 1975)

36 *Give A Little Love* – Bay City Rollers (Bell, July 1975)

37 *Barbados* – Typically Tropical (Gull, July 1975)

38 *No Charge* – JJ Barrie (Power Exchange, April 1976)

39 *So You Win Again* – Hot Chocolate (RAK, June 1977)

40 *Angelo* – Brotherhood Of Man (Pye, July 1977)

41 *Figaro* – Brotherhood Of Man (Pye, January 1978)

42 *Save Your Love* – Renee & Renato (Hollywood, October 1982)

43 *(Is This The Way To) Amarillo* – Tony Christie ft Peter Kay. (CD, March 2005)

Tributes

Paul Wright (Broadcaster): 'I worked with Clem some years back and found him to be one of the most down-to-earth of guys, a real treat to be in the company of.'

Pete Day: 'Along with Ronnie Verrell, Ronnie Stephenson, Alf Bigden and Henry Fisher, Clem has to be one of the best session drummers I've had the pleasure of working with.'

Andrew Black: 'I worked with Clem Cattini in the '60s during my time as an A&R man and I have to say that he was the drummer for all occasions. I have worked with session drummers all over the world, and in my opinion he was, as an all-rounder, the best I have worked with.'

Jimmy Page (Led Zeppelin): 'Clem was a superb technician and all round good egg.'

Larry Page: 'I used Clem many times, as you would. Top man! Also worked on his *Impact* album with the Clem Cattini Orchestra.'

Les Reed: 'Clem was a great friend, and indeed played drums on quite a few of my sessions in the '60s and '70s. A very talented man, and always so lovely in the studio. A great pleasure to work with!'

Zoot Money: 'Clem was always good company, and one of the more proficient drummers in the rock world. He was wonderfully self-effacing and musically knowledgeable.'

Chas McDevitt: 'I first met Clem when he stepped in for Red Reece, the drummer of our resident group, who had left to join Georgie Fame and the Blue Flames. Clem was the best drummer around. He had this style what I called 'rockashake', I'm not sure what he called it but it was unique. Clem joined Shirley and I on tour for a few months before he teamed up with Colin Hicks and then later Johnny Kidd.'

Mick Avory (The Kinks): 'First time I met Clem was at the Pye Studios when I was there with The Kinks. The producer Shel Talmy was using Clem and Bobby Graham. I've had a lot of influences as I've gone along. In the rock world in the '60s Clem was an influence, as was Bobby Graham. I never took much off them though, you think well that's quite a nice thing and you try to emulate them.'

Vince Eager: 'Driving down from Scotland after a show all the way to the Isle of Wight! Long before the M1 and other motorways were built. We arrived with about an hour to spare, exhausted and starving. So much so that Clem bought a bag of chips and ate them off his Tom-Tom.'

Cliff Bennett (Rebel Rousers): 'I first saw Clem playing at Staines Town Hall with Vince Taylor and The Playboys. Then I saw Clem with Johnny Kidd. Clem was a big influence on me. Bill Williams, who did all that 'Jive Bunny' stuff, rang me around 2002 time to say he wanted to do an album with me. I said OK, and he asked me if I wanted to put a band together. I said 'Yeah' and the first name down was Clem. Bill asked me why Clem? I told him Clem was the best studio drummer there was. Just solid. I wanted somebody that anticipated the beat, not sat behind it. Clem's always on top of the beat, and I like the drummer to be right behind me... there was no question. We went into the studio, there was the bass player, a drum click and Clem, and me singing acoustically. That's how we did it. Then we added the guitar and other stuff on, keyboards, brass. The album was called *Loud and Clear*.

Kenny Lynch: 'Clem was on one of my first sessions. Forget what it was but he said to me, 'You're a West Ham fan aren't you?' 'I said 'Yeah, why?' 'Well I'm an Arsenal fan.' And from that day on we've always had arguments and banter about the football. He's been a season ticket holder for about a hundred years! Clem never went out after a gig, he always went home. Not like me, If I went into a pub I'd be the last person to leave. I did a few jingles with Clem, you never had any arguments with him, a very good musician.'

Pete York (Spencer Davis Group): 'Clem deserves recognition as one of the first big names in UK rock drumming.'

Con Cluskey (The Bachelors): 'Clem played on our number one hit '*Diane*'. His nickname was 'Thunderfoot' – as his kick drum was so loud!'

Gerry Conway (Fairport Convention): 'Clem's an A-Lister. A legend.'

Mike McGear McCartney (Scaffold): 'It was a LONG time ago and we worked with several top session drummers, but Clem strikes a chord... just can't remember which track or tracks. Seem to remember he was a nice bloke though!'

Acknowledgements

Simon Aldridge, Colin Allen, Mick Avory, Cliff Bennett, James Cave, Con Cluskey, Terry Dene, Mike Dolbear, Vince Eager, Bruce Eder, Ralph Ellis, Steve Ellis, Brian Gregg, Bill Harry, Eric Haydock, Keith Hubbard, Jack Lancaster, Frank Lea, Spencer Leigh, Alan Lovell, Kenny Lynch, Chas McDevitt, Zoot Money, Roger Nicholas, Simon Nicol, Larry Page, Tony Prince, Derek Quinn, Les Reed, Denny Seiwell, Ted 'Kingsize' Taylor, Bruce Welch, Mark Wirtz.

Select Bibliography

Books

Galactic Ramble (Foxcote Books, 2009)

Guinness British Hit Singles (Guinness Publishing, 1999)

Jazz: The Rough Guide (Rough Guides, 1995)

Leigh, Spencer, *Halfway To Paradise: Britpop 1955-62* (Finbarr International, 1996)

Leigh, Spencer, *Wondrous Face: The Billy Fury Story* (Finbarr International, 2005)

Marsh, Dave, *Before I Get Old: The Story of The Who* (Plexus, 1983)

McDevitt, Chas, *Skiffle* (Robson Books, 1997)

Nash, Graham, *Wild Tales: A Rock and Roll Life* (Crown Archetype, 2013)

Oldham, Andrew Loog, *Stoned* (Vintage, 2001)

Power, Martin, *Hot Wired Guitar: The Life of Jeff Beck* (Omnibus Press, 2014)

Power, Martin, *No Quarter: The Three Lives of Jimmy Page* (Omnibus Press, 2016)

Prince, Tony, *The Royal Ruler & The Railway DJ* (DMC Publishing, 2017)

Sharpe, Graham, *The Man Who Was Screaming Lord Sutch* (Gardners Books, 2005)

Wyman, Bill, *Stone Alone* (Penguin, 1991)

Let It Rock: Jack Lancaster Interview

Q Encyclopedia of Rock Stars (Dorling Kindersley, 1996)

Magazines

Melody Maker

Mojo

New Musical Express

Record Collector

Index

CPSIA information can be obtained
at www.ICGtesting.com
Printed in the USA
BVHW041353271020
591929BV00007B/173